Raking Light from Ashes

Relli Robinson

Raking Light from Ashes

Relli Robinson

TRANSLATED FROM THE HEBREW BY

Yardenne Greenspan

Raking Light from Ashes / Relli Robinson

Translated from the Hebrew by Yardenne Greenspan
Contact: robinson@research.haifa.ac.il

Library of Congress Control Number: 2017903393
CreateSpace Independent Publishing Platform, North Charleston, SC

ISBN: 9781690967835

To my beloveds,

My parents, Franka and Michał Głowinski, may they rest in peace;

My saviors and adoptive parents, Janina and Józef Abramowicz, may they rest in peace;

My children, Michalle and Nattiv;

And my grandchildren, Yarden, Shahak, Noor, Tchellet, Argaman, and Keshet.

Table of Contents

In Lieu of an Introduction   1

Chapter One: Lala   3

Chapter Two: The Journal   139

Chapter Three: Relli   199

Chapter Four: My Family in Words and Images   262

Light and Ashes and the Power of the Self:
an Epilogue by Ariel Hirschfeld   316

In Lieu of an Introduction

Grandma, how is that possible? Such a little girl, without a mother or a father? My granddaughter, Shahak, asked me when she was four years old.

She and her brother, Yarden, my eldest grandson, who was eleven at the time, were staying at my home in Haifa when Shahak suddenly turned to me and asked, *Grandma, where are your parents? I've never met them.*

They died a long time ago, Yarden answered quickly. *There was a war and an evil king named Hitler killed them*, he explained in his childish language.

Shahak looked at me, processing her brother's words, and then asked, *Grandma, how old were you when this happened? When he killed your mother and father?*

I looked at her and said softly, *I was your age, four years old.*

But Grandma, how could that happen? How is that possible? Such a little girl, without a mother or a father? Who took care of you?

I'll tell you about it one day, I whispered.

The years went by, thoughts came and went, memories rose and fell away, questions surfaced: should I? How do I? Halfhearted attempts were finally followed by a decision: I would write a book.

This book is my attempt to answer Shahak's question. As I weave my personal story into a patchwork of documented facts, painful memories of a deprived childhood, and the recounting of core shaking events, I too ask, *How is that possible? Such a little girl, without a mother or a father?*

Chapter One: Lala

A Glance at the Starting Point   5

Relli Meets Lala   7

Lala and the Children of Krochmalna Street   11

Daddy, Who Brings You Your Slippers Now?   15

A Dilemma   19

A First Friend   23

We Each Need to Know How to Stand on
  Our Own Two Feet   28

A Trip to the Basement   30

The Mind of a Merchant   34

The Visit   37

Wiśniówka—the Cherry Farm   40

Not so Innocent Child's Play   43

The Shock of Escape   47

Tovarish   51

A Village Cabin   54

An Encounter with a Horse   57

The Burn   60

The Surviving Treasure   62

Lala in the World of Letters and Words   68

Lala Says Goodbye to Relli   72

Sign of Life   76

The Show Must Go On	79
Large Half, Little Half	82
What Rewards are Given For	85
Road Signs	88
New Shoes	92
Not Like Everybody Else	95
Sick Child	98
Negotiation	102
Uncle Chaim	106
Who Was Jesus?	111
Doubly Orphaned	115
Goodbye Mommy Janina	119
At the Communist School	123
The Punishment	129
One-Hundred Dollars	134

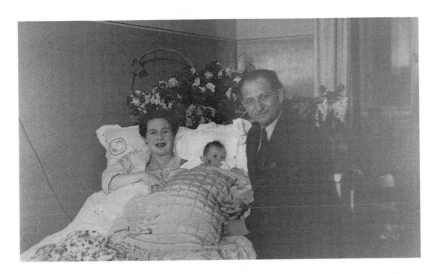

A Glance at the Starting Point

Today, at seventy years old, I can't take my eyes off my image at seven days old. Embraced in my parents' arms, peeking through big eyes into the seventh day of my life. Mommy and daddy look straight at the camera, and time becomes frozen and freezes all things: a reality dipping in blossoms, a life with the promise of love and color.

My parents' embracing arms imbue me with confidence. But the blossoms have wilted, life was murdered, the colors faded, and love was transformed into longing.

Only the confidence of the embrace lives on. My mother's hands—gentle, manicured; my father's hands—big, strong.

My parents have continued to embrace me through the seventy years that have gone by since the day the three of us were depicted, happy, among the blossoms…

On the back of the photo, Mommy wrote: "With our daughter, the one with the big, blue eyes."

These eyes have watched this hard world through the blue of logic and the depths of emotion for seventy years, forever containing love, blossoms, colors, the hope of seven days in the springtime of my life.

Relli Robinson (Głowinski), March 11th, 2009

Relli Meets Lala

Warsaw was awoken by a cold winter morning in January of 1943, illuminating it with sad, gray light.

Relli stirred in her sleep. She heard voices beyond the thick blanket that covered her up to the top of her head. Strange, she thought. It wasn't Mommy's voice, or Daddy's, or even Grandpa's… who could it be, so close to her?

She tried to peek out without revealing herself, but saw nothing. She tried to stretch beneath the blanket and realized she couldn't, because the bed was too narrow. Her left hand bumped into something hard. Where am I? she wondered. This isn't my bed. Whose voices are these? Then she heard a clear voice say, *Good morning.*

Relli sat up and answered the greeting. Mommy and Daddy had trained her to always answer grownups politely. She noticed she was wearing her pajamas, but that she in fact was not in her bed, but on a row of three chairs arranged against a dark, wooden closet. The back of first chair was protecting her head, the back of the last protecting her feet, and the back of the middle chair faced the room and protected the side of her body.

A man and woman were smiling at her. The man was taller, and his smile and mustache were familiar. She recalled having seen him several times before, when he came to visit the tiny apartment where she'd recently been living with her parents and grandfather. He would come occasionally to whisper with Mommy and Daddy in a corner while Relli played with Grandpa. The woman—short, very skinny, glasses—was unfamiliar. They smiled at her warmly and invitingly. Relli sat up. *Where are my parents? Where's Grandpa?* Her voice trembled. In spite of their smiles, she felt uneasy around these people.

Your mother and father asked us to watch you until they come to visit, the woman said softly.

Relli didn't like this answer one bit. *I don't want you to watch me, I want my mother and father and grandfather, they can watch me...* She swallowed her tears, her voice shaking. She remembered her parents repeating that she mustn't cry out loud even if she was very mad or very sad, and certainly mustn't raise her voice. It's all right to be upset, angry, even afraid, but do it quietly, don't let it be seen, don't let anybody—not *anybody*—know.

The man picked her up from her bed of chairs. The woman stroked her head. *We'll be your mother and father until your real mother and father can come pick you up.*

Why? Relli wondered. Why are grownups playing Mommy and Daddy? My mother is so pretty and my father is tall and strong. *I don't want to play Mommy and Daddy with you,* she answered sternly, trying to keep her voice steady, not to reveal the fear that had taken over her.

The man pulled the chairs away from the closet and set them around the round table by the door. The woman took Relli's hand and said, *Come, I'll show you what we've got here in the closet. You know it.* As she spoke, she opened the left door of the closet, and Relli spotted all of Mommy's fur coats—the short gray one that showed off her skirts, the brown knee-length one, and the long black one, reaching almost to the floor, shiny, with remarkably soft fur. Relli walked over to the furs, touched them with both her hands, feeling the softness imbued with Mommy's scent. She buried her face in the black fur, breathing her mother in. Looking up at the shelf above the furs, she recognized other items from her home—tall vases, deep bowls, platters. She remembered that these dishes, which her mother called "crystals," had been sitting in a box recently, in their tiny apartment, not on shelves and dressers, the way they used to in their older, bigger, beautiful apartment. That was so long ago that Relli could barely remember. When was it?

Her train of thought was interrupted by the woman. *My name is Janina, and my husband is Józef. You see? Your parents gave us all these beautiful things to keep safe for them, and we'll keep you safe, too.*

Relli began to cry silently, the tears rolling down her cheeks of their own volition. She swallowed them when they reached her lips. The woman kept stroking her head as she wiped the tears away with her handkerchief. In the meantime, the man set the table. Relli smelled fried egg and saw fresh bread and a cup of tea on the table. Thank God it wasn't milk. She hated milk. What was she supposed to do if they offered her some?

The woman led her to the table and Relli sat down to eat. She was very hungry. It had been a long, long time since she'd last had a fried egg. As she ate politely, using her knife and fork, just like her parents had taught her, the woman sat by her side and said, *Now you'll be our daughter a little bit too.*

Where is your own daughter? Asked Relli.

We don't have one.

Relli began to understand: that must be the reason these grownups wanted to play Mommy and Daddy with her. They didn't have a daughter of their own. *All right*, she said. *But only for a little bit, because I belong to my own mama and papa, and to Grandpa.*

Janina and Józef both smiled. *But,* Janina continued, ignoring Relli's remark, *now, like I said, you'll be our daughter a little bit, and you'll call us Mommy and Daddy and we'll call you Lala.*

But my name is Relli.

Of course, you're right, Janina smiled, *but we're playing a game. We don't want anyone to know our secret. We want other people to think it's all for real. So from this day on, you'll be Lala.*

Relli said nothing, repeating the new name to herself. *It's a pretty name,* she finally said. *But why do you want to call me Lala?*

Janina smiled again. Jòzef said, *You know that 'Lala' means doll, and you're so cute, with your blond curls and your blue eyes, you just remind us of a doll. And it goes well with the game we're going to play. From this day on we will be your mama and papa and you will be our girl—our doll—Lala.*

Now come, Lala, wash up and change your clothes, said Janina, using Relli's new name as if it were the most natural thing in the world. She must have realized that they were overwhelming the girl, not yet four years old, with information. So far she'd been more cooperative than Janina had expected. Here's hoping they could make it work. *Come, Lala, I'll read to you from the fairytale book. Your mommy gave it to us along with you and the other things.*

Lala smiled at the book she knew and loved so well, and a little bit at Janina, too.

This is the story of how Relli met Lala, and how her life was transformed forever.

Lala and the Children of Krochmalna Street

The house on 6 Krochmalna Street in Warsaw resembled all the other old houses in the city. The façade was narrow; at its center was a domed entrance with a metal gate opened and closed by the doorman who lived in an adjacent apartment. Inside, a large courtyard, partially tiled and partially dirt, and at its center a tree with a wide top. Around the courtyard were four wings positioned in a perfect square. At the corners were narrow doorways leading into each wing's stairwell. The Abramowicz family apartment was on the bottom floor of the central wing, on the right. The only window in the small one-room apartment overlooked the courtyard and front gate. The window was always shaded by a white, opaque curtain, and no one could see from the courtyard into the apartment. Standing close to the window and putting one's face against the curtain, which was glued on, one could see the courtyard and the gate.

The window was Lala's favorite lookout point. In the morning she stood there and watched enviously as the children who lived in the building left to go to school or kindergarten. Around noon she watched them come home, but the afternoon was her favorite time: she watched as the children played in the yard, running, jumping, climbing trees; the boys played soccer, the girls played catch or jump rope, and sometimes they all played hide-and-seek together.

From her spot by the window, concealed by the curtain, she could see all of their hiding spots, and sometimes felt the urge to open the window and shout them out. Mommy Janina turned down her repeated requests to go downstairs and play with the children in the yard, explaining that it was winter and snowing and that Lala could catch a cold. The explanation made sense but didn't quite convince Lala. The other children, down at the yard, building a snowman, could also catch a cold, she argued, trying her best to undo the permanent ban on outdoors time.

One afternoon the sun came out. Mommy Janina explained that she had to go out to the store to buy some groceries and that she would be right back. She reminded Lala that if anyone should knock on the door she must be completely silent and under no condition come near the door. Lala promised.

Janina locked the door behind her, and Lala went to the window to watch the children running around the yard, having an exceptionally good time on this sunny day. I want to play with them so badly, she thought. And today looks warm. I certainly wouldn't catch a cold today. The children don't know me, so I must seek out a way to get to know them.

Lala went to the closet, opened the drawer that contained yellow dust rags that she used to help Janina to wipe off dust, and took them all out. She tied two of them together to fashion a long, yellow rope, which she tied around her waist. She opened the closet to look at herself in the mirror on the inside of the door, watching the way the yellow belt stood out against her blue dress. She tied the ends of the rest of the rags to her makeshift belt, rotating the belt slowly until she finally created a billowing yellow skirt over her dress.

She walked over to the drawer where the previous night she'd placed the candy box given to her by Pan Aleksander. Pan Aleksander always brought her treats and toys. Last time he came, he brought her a pretty box filled with buttermilk candy, wrapped in papers decorated with a picture of a cow. They were called Krówka—Little Cow—and were delicious.

Lala carefully climbed on the chair by the window, candy box in hand, opened the window, reached out, and called out to the girls playing hopscotch below, offering candy. Since the girls couldn't reach the window, Lala threw some candy down to them. More children ran over, picking up the candy and inviting Lala to come downstairs and play.

Though Lala wanted nothing more than to receive such an invitation, she told the children that her mother wasn't home and that she was locked in.

The children quickly found an easy solution: they positioned a box beneath the window, and the two largest kids, a boy and a girl, climbed on top of it and pulled Lala out through the window.

The children all looked at her outfit with wonder. She looked strange in her dust rag skirt, but she was still a friendly girl who offered them all candy. They added her to their game of catch and then to hide-and-seek. The excited Lala ran around joyously with the other children, laughing along with them.

And then, without any warning, the iron gate opened and Mommy Janina walked in, carrying shopping baskets. A quick glance revealed the wide open window. Her heart raced, and as she tried to fathom the situation she noticed a familiar figure running toward her, glowing with happiness, her fair braids flailing and yellow dust rags blowing in the wind over her dress. Lala ran over and almost knocked the baskets out of her hands as she jumped into her arms. *Mommy, Mommy, I met the children, and now I have friends! And they loved the candy that Pan Aleksander gave me!*

Janina, who was resourceful under pressure, put down the baskets, took Lala in her arms, and said, *I'm glad you had a nice time, but now it's chilly and you aren't wearing a jacket like the other children. We'd better go back inside.* The disappointed Lala gave Janina her hand and they walked out, two of the older boys carrying Janina's baskets as she led Lala home.

After locking the door behind them, Janina also closed the window. Calmly but gravely, she explained that leaving through the window was incredibly dangerous. She could have fallen down and hurt herself!

Lala said the children were very careful as they pulled her out. When Janina asked why Lala had worn the dust rags, the girl answered, *I wore them so that the kids would notice me and want to play with me.*

Daddy, Who Brings You Your Slippers Now?

Lala, curled up into a ball as usual in her bed made out of chairs pushed together, her head completely covered by the blanket, breathing through a tiny opening between the blanket and the upholstery of the chairs, felt a hand rocking her gently yet ceaselessly. She sat up, her eyes open with surprise. She rubbed them with her little fists, rubbing the sleep away.

Janina stood beside her, persistent in her attempt to awaken the sleeping child. The room was illuminated by two oil lamps, painting the door and Janina and Joseph's bed, by the wall across the room, with a pale yellow light. Lala noticed that the bed was made, as if no one had slept in it. Strange, she thought as she tried to rouse herself.

Suddenly the door opened and three figures appeared—two men supporting a woman between them. The woman walked slowly, trembling with every step. Lala watched the three guests. *A surprise for your fourth birthday*, Jòzef said quietly yet cheerfully. Mesmerized, she opened her mouth wide, a fish out of water fighting for air, and almost cried with surprise before she pursed her lips tightly. The men were Jòzef and Daddy and they were supporting Mommy, who could barely stand up. Daddy looked at Lala with his kind, loving blue eyes. He put his finger to his lips, a sign she knew well. Lala wanted so badly to call out but obeyed.

Lala stood up from her chair bed and watched Daddy and Jòzef gently lead Mommy to the Abramowicz bed and sit her down. Daddy softly undid her head scarf, and Mommy's hair flowed down her shoulders. It wasn't done up, the way Lala remembered it, nor did it glisten as it had in the past. Mommy was still shaking as she sat on the bed. She must be very cold, thought Lala.

Janina picked up Lala and sat her on her mother's lap. Lala held her mother as tightly as a four-year-old can, then released her and brought her ear to her mother's mouth for their traditional game of secrets. Mommy didn't disappoint: she whispered into the child's warm, sleepy ear, *I love you very, very, very much.* With each reiteration she pressed a soft kiss onto the child's earlobe, her warm breath tickling Lala's ear. Lala turned to give her mother the other ear, and Mommy whispered again, *I love you, very, very, very, very much*, each "very" accompanied by a tender kiss. The girl clung to her mother, taking pleasure in their old game. She looked into Mommy's, big, dark, beautiful eyes. They seemed to have grown bigger and darker during their separation, sunk deep into Mommy's face, somewhat glazed over. As Lala watched them she saw round, glittering beads falling out. Lala stuck out her tongue to taste the salty, love laden tears of her mother.

Daddy, who'd removed his coat, came over. He reached down and gently picked up Lala. She curled in his arms, which to her were the strongest, safest arms in the world. She leaned against him, trying to physically convey how much she'd missed him and how glad she was to see him again. Here was tall, broad-shouldered Daddy, holding her high like she'd remembered. He sat her on one arm and with his free hand caressed her face and her hair. She put her head in the crook of his neck and breathed in his warm scent, enveloping her with safety and love.

But Daddy, who brings you your slippers now? She whispered. Daddy didn't answer. Perhaps he didn't hear her. *Daddy, who brings you your slippers now when you come home from work?* Lala repeated, this time louder. How could it be that Daddy, who always had an answer for everything, was now silent?

But Daddy, who? Who? Who brings you your slippers when you come home from work now that I'm not there? Lala tried again, her voice growing louder, so that everyone could hear. She was trying to explain to Daddy how essential her presence was back at home, that all she wanted was to go back with them, to them. She repeated the question a fourth time, persistently. She waited for an answer that never came.

Lala looked into Daddy's blue eyes, which were darkening, as if painted by an invisible brush. His eyes also glistened like Mommy's. Daddy said nothing. Her question remained hanging in midair. She caressed his face with her little hand. A transparent moisture clung to her fingers as she touched his closed eyes.

Afterward

Throughout the years of her childhood, Lala returned in her thoughts to that night in March, 1943. She always believed it was a dream, the dream of a child celebrating her fourth birthday and desperately missing her parents. As a teenager and adult, Relli convinced herself it was an illusion, a fata morgana coming to life in the imagination of a little girl, which, being a constant yearning, a persistent emotional thirst and hunger, continued to follow her, taking shape as a tangible vision in the folds of her memory.

It would be forty-one years before, on a 1984 visit to Poland, as a forty-five-year-old woman, Stefan Gilewski—her Polish uncle, husband of Aunt Hela, sister of Janina—would recount his meeting with her parents, Franka and Michał Głowinski.

You probably don't remember it, you were only four years old. Juzek—that's what we called Józef—was the one who acted on his and your father's crazy idea, to bring your parents for a visit around your fourth birthday and just before they left the Warsaw ghetto. They all knew they would be sent to the Trawniki camp near Lublin. Juzek recruited all the men of the family, as well as some close personal friends and fellow underground members. It was a highly complex operation that only Juzek, with his creative imagination and fearless resourcefulness, could have planned and executed. He managed to get your parents out of the ghetto one dark night and bring them to the apartment on 6 Krochmalna Street so that they could see you and say goodbye to you. Then he returned them to the ghetto, to your maternal grandfather, from whom your mother would not part.

All of us were on duty, guarding the apartment, the building, the street, and the neighborhood. I was lucky enough to be inside the apartment, to meet your parents and experience your meeting and parting. I'll never forget it. I've always consoled myself that you don't remember the occasion. I thought that was for the best. We were all crying silently, yet you were so pleased with Juzek's birthday gift: your parents.

Then, to Stefan's surprise, Relli would reply, *I've always remembered it, and always will. And yet, it is a memory of disappointment: why can't I remember the last words Daddy said to me? Instead, all I can recall is that question, that unanswered question echoing through my mind—Daddy, who brings you your slippers now?*

A Dilemma

A summer day in 1943, the warm sun bathing Warsaw. People rushing through the streets, unsmiling in spite of the bright and caressing sun illuminating all: buildings, store windows, trees, cars, and trams. In spite of it, they all appear as if frozen in time, their grave expressions fixed on the ground. The hot rays of sun cannot penetrate the gloom of war that pervades all.

A long line trails outside the tram station, beginning where the second tram car will stop. No one would dare leave the long line to try and enter the first car, though it would likely be almost empty, while the second would be crowded. The first car was meant only for Germans: soldiers, Gestapo, and gendarmes. Polish citizens of Warsaw would have to squeeze into the second car.

Janina is standing around the middle of the line, holding Lala's hand as the girl tightens her grip around her little doll, whom she never leaves home without. Janina remains steady in spite of the people pushing and shoving behind her, trying to get ahead in line. One of her hands is holding Lala's, and the other is placed protectively on her shoulder.

Suddenly, the crowd pushes forward, a wave of people shifting toward the second tram car that has just screeched to a halt at the station. Janina notices that the first car, the German car, has stopped right beside her. Its windows are all open. The people in uniform, so hated, spread out on the empty benches.

One of them, broad shouldered and thick faced, bends out of the window closest to Janina. *What a sweet little girl you've got*, he says to Janina in broken Polish, with an almost human smile. The blood runs out of Janina's face, possibly her body, too. She gets a hold of herself and thanks him with an awkward smile.

The German officer doesn't let off. *It's a shame you must stand in such a long line with a little girl, only to be left without a seat on the second car*, he says worriedly.

No matter, Janina answers curtly, feeling eyes on her, wondering at the casual conversation she was having with a German officer wearing shiny epaulets.

The German is persistent. *You know what?* He says with a smile. *Pass the child over to me through the window, I'll watch her until we get to your stop, and then I'll return her to you.*

Janina is frozen in place, bereft of all power. She must make an instant and fateful decision for her and Lala. If she turns down the officer's offer, who knows what his suspicion would lead him to do. But if she accepts it, who knows how Lala, only four years and four months of age, would react. She might burst into tears, or she might become chatty and innocently tell him that Janina isn't her real mother. Then what?

Janina's body is covered with cold sweat. The options run through her mind, and she knows she must make a quick decision. No more lingering. She glances at Lala, holding her hand confidently, and repeats the German officer's words with an encouraging smile. *Lala, you'll ride in the first car with this officer and I'll come pick you up when we reach our stop.* Her hand moves from the girl's shoulder to her head, caressing it, while using her other hand to squeeze Lala's. She hates the idea of hurting her, but Janina knows that this is the only way to convey the message to Lala, to imbue her with courage and tell her wordlessly that she trusts her. She hugs Lala, kisses her, picks her up and hands her to the officer.

The man lifts the little one through the air and places her on his lap. The girl can see Janina hurrying to find her place in the crowded line entering into the busy second car. Some of the people who saw what had happened make room for her and help her into the tram.

The tram begins to move, and with the last of her physical and emotional strength, Janina, squeezed among the other passengers, decides that she would get off at the next stop and redeem Lala from the hands of the German. Oh, please, let it all end well!

She gets off at the next stop, runs to the open window of the first car, and is astounded to find Lala chewing on chocolates and describing her doll's outfit to the German officer, teaching him Polish. Janina forces a smile and reaches her hands to receive the girl.

The German leans down to pick Lala up and return her, saying in broken Polish, *Thank you, you have a lovely daughter. She reminds me of my own daughter, whom I miss so much.*

Janina manages to nod, then watches happily as the tram moves out of the station, gaining speed as it rides along.

She hugs the girl, holding her to her chest, and letting herself cry, unloading the terrible tension that had been plaguing her. Lala wipes Janina's tears away with confusion. *I taught him Polish, she says. I taught him the names for all my doll's clothes, and told him my name is Lala, because he asked. He said I reminded him of a doll, like you and Daddy always say. I especially reminded him of the doll he left back home—his daughter. I didn't tell him anything but my name. Nothing. You squeezed my hand so hard.*

Janina looks at Lala. *I'm so proud of you and I love you so much!* She blurts through her tears.

Afterward

Lala and Janina would discuss this event many times in days to come: Janina's brave decision in the cruel dilemma and how she transmitted her message to Lala with a strong, steady squeeze of the hand. This squeeze would stay with Lala all her life, even as she becomes Relli, and then Grandma…

A First Friend

One morning, Janina informed Lala that new neighbors had moved into their building, on the second floor. *The new neighbors have two children. Their girl, Dorotka, is only two years older than you, Lala, and her brother, Adek, is almost nine years old. I've met them. They play together a lot in the apartment and never go out to the yard. You can play with them, Lala. I hope you and Dorotka will become friends.*

Lala's joy knew no bounds. She wanted to go meet Dorotka right away.

She and Janina went up to the second floor, sounded a series of rhythmic knocks on the door, and entered a dark apartment, the windows shut and covered with heavy blinds. The apartment looked bigger than the Abramowicz place. Lala noticed that Dorotka and Adek had their own room, as did their parents, and that additional doors opened out from the living room, into which they'd entered.

Dorotka's mother rose from her chair, smiling, to greet them. She was tall and pale with large, impressive, dark, and sunken eyes. She smiled widely at the guests and called Dorotka and Adek to come out of their room.

Two children, dark skinned, dark eyed, and dark haired, just like their mother, walked into the living room. Dorotka had two long, thick braids. Lala was charmed. Adek bowed politely, reached out his hand, introduced himself, and then returned to his book.

Dorotka gave her hand to Lala, her smile telling the girl that she too yearned for a friend to play with. Dorotka, who could already read, had lots of books, as well as dolls and other toys. The two girls played together happily, gulping down each other's company, quenching their shared thirst for companionship, which had formed under the circumstances. Their playtime went by quickly, and as they parted they promised to meet again and again, and to be each other's friend.

From that moment on, Lala would go up to the second floor regularly. Sometimes Janina allowed her to go up alone, watching her from the doorway. Sometimes Adek joined the girls' games, playing with building blocks and teaching them to construct card towers. Lala was happy. For the first time in her life she had a real friend!

One winter afternoon the two girls whispered together in Dorotka and Adek's room while Adek played checkers with his father and their mother was cooking. *I envy you, Lala, for your curly hair*, said Dorotka. *Your braids are short and thin and when you undo them you have golden locks.*

And I want long and thick braids like yours, Lala said. *When I grow up I hope my braids become longer and thicker too.*

I'm curious, said Dorotka, *if my hair were shorter, would it be curly like yours?*

Why don't you cut it and find out? Asked Lala.

Oh, my mother won't let me. She won't cut off my braids.

And you're sure you want to?

Of course!

Then let's do it, Lala said confidently.

What do you mean?

Simple, get me scissors, I'll cut off one braid and then your mother will certainly let you cut the other one off too.

What an idea! Dorotka gasped. *I never thought about that.*

As they examined their options, Dorotka found a pair of small, blunt scissors. The entrepreneurial Lala made up her mind that a small hitch like the wrong scissors wouldn't distract her from her goal.

Dorotka sat on a chair in front of the mirror in the closet door. Lala held onto one of the braids and attempted to cut through one of its strands. Persistently, she opened and closed the scissors, pressing until her fingers turned red and a few hairs submitted to the repeated attempts. About half of the braid fell to the floor, while the rest remained hanging down Dorotka's back. The two girls quickly undid the remainder of the braid and examined Dorotka's head, half of which was now cut into strands of different lengths. But to their disappointment, the hair did not curl up and wasn't even slightly wavy.

As they examined the results, Dorotka's mother walked into the room. She stood, stunned, before the mirror, watching her pretty daughter's reflection, with one long, thick braid, and uneven strands on the other side.

The two girls explained excitedly that they wanted to find out if Dorotka's hair was curly like Lala's.

Dorotka's mother was very angry with her daughter, who was older than Lala, for behaving so irresponsibly.

Lala wasn't startled. She explained it was her idea to help her friend find out what her hair really looked like.

Dorotka's mother ordered the girls to clean up the room and sent Lala home.

Lala took the stairs down to the ground floor and told Janina everything that had happened. To her surprise, Janina was also angry. She told Lala that little girls must not do things their mothers forbid, such as cutting off one braid while they both knew Dorotka's mother wouldn't give her daughter a haircut.

Lala was very upset. She couldn't understand why everybody was angry with her. She'd acted innocently, and could not understand the severity of her actions at such a young age. The adults were so angry, and Lala realized they saw things very differently than children. But who was to say they were always right?

A few days went by. Dorotka's mother had to cut off her daughter's hair to even it out. Dorotka's beautiful, straight, black hair was tied in a bow and fell like a wide fan over her shoulders.

You look just like a princess, Lala gasped when the two of them were allowed to meet again.

From that point on, Dorotka's mother made sure that the door to the children's room was always open. She poked her head in from time to time, and occasionally came in to read the girls stories.

Lala loved Dorotka, her first true friend. She never suspected their friendship would be short-lived.

One afternoon, Lala went upstairs as usual. Janina, watched her climb the stairs and then went back into her apartment when Lala reached the second floor. Lala knocked rhythmically, the way Janina had taught her, a special knock so that the family could identify their guest.

To her surprise, no one answered the door.

Lala knocked again, and when she was still not answered, she rose onto her tiptoes, pressed the doorknob and opened the unlocked door. She called out, *Hello, it's me, Lala, I've come to play with Dorotka.*

There was no answer. Lala walked into the familiar living room, her eyes widening as she saw Dorotka, Adek, and their parents lying on the floor, ignoring her. What were they doing sleeping in the middle of the day on the floor of the living room? Lala was mesmerized. The sight was strange and frightening. Why were they not responding to her voice? *Dorotka, Dorotka, it's me, Lala. I've come to play with you.* But Dorotka didn't move, and no one answered Lala's calls.

Lala ran out, striding down the stairs, her eyes torn open with panic, but her mouth silent. Only when Janina opened the door to her loud knocks did the little one burst into tears, describing what she'd seen upstairs.

Janina tried to calm Lala down. She wouldn't leave her alone to go upstairs. Instead she and Lala went to see Aunt Hela, Janina's sister. Lala saw Aunt Hela, her family, and later Janina and Józef too, whispering tensely about that day's events. No one shared anything with Lala. No one helped her solve the mystery.

Afterward

Lala would spend many days longing for her first good friend, Dorotka. Janina and Józef would never explain how and why Dorotka's family found their death. The last time she saw them, lying still on the living room floor, would burn into Lala's memory forever.

We Each Need to Know How to Stand on Our Own Two Feet

One day, Janina and Lala went to visit the Gilewski family—Janina's sister and brother-in-law. Aunt Hela and her husband, Uncle Stefan, lived on Cegielniana Street, which was walking distance from the Abramowicz home. Lala loved to visit them. They were warm people who always hugged her and fed her tasty foods. Uncle Stefan was a good artist. He drew flowers, trees, and animals which Lala solicited from him, and she colored them. Sometimes he helped her with the coloring, too. He told fascinating stories and talked to her about different things. Lala felt good in their home.

That day, Janina hurried off to run some errands and told Lala that she would be having dinner at Aunt Hela and Uncle Stefan's house. The girl was happy with this plan. The afternoon went by pleasantly, drawing, coloring, playing dominos and even hide-and-seek in the three-bedroom apartment. Evening came and Aunt Hela prepared dinner. It was wartime, and food was not plentiful, certainly not for the Gilewski family, who were of little means. Their younger and middle children, Tadek, who was fifteen, and beautiful Krysia, who was not yet twenty, lived at home. Their eldest, Marysia, was married and lived with her husband.

Aunt Hela made a special effort with dinner, wanting to feed their little guest well. Lala was such a skinny girl, as well as a picky eater. She tasted politely and turned down food kindly yet assertively. Even when she turned down a dish that was difficult to procure during wartime, her refusal never angered the adults. From the side, she always seemed to do her best to please.

Aunt Hela invited the family to the table, seating Lala on a higher chair than the others so that she would feel equal. She ate her potato and the red borscht with delight, enjoying her favorite dishes.

Suddenly, Aunt Hela stood up from the table, went to the kitchen, and returned with a pretty white cup with a painting of a bouquet of flowers. As she brought the cup to Lala, she blew into it gently to cool the liquid inside. There you go sweetheart, she told Lala. I was able to get milk today, and I warmed it up just for you. She placed the pretty cup before Lala. Lala glanced at the cup and noticed the skin that had already formed circles on top of the milk. The smell hit her nostrils, and, along with the sight of the skin, made nausea rise in her throat. Lala considered what to do, how not to insult Aunt Hela while still avoiding drinking that repulsive milk.

A moment later the child got a hold of herself, grabbed the handle of the cup, picked it up to bring it to her mouth, and then, bam! The cup fell to the floor, broke, and the milk spread its warm smell all over the room. Everyone around the table was stunned. They had all seen Lala letting go of the handle. *Why did you do that?* Asked Uncle Stefan softly but severely.

Lala looked at him and answered immediately: *Uncle Stefan, earlier, when you told me the story about the responsible dog, you said we each need to know how to stand on our own two feet. You said we were each responsible for ourselves, even little children. I thought, in that case, even objects need to take care of themselves. The cup should have known how to stand on its own two feet without my help.*

A Trip to the Basement

Knocking came at the door and a mélange of small voices filtered in from the stairwell. Janina opened the door to find five little girls waiting outside.

Zosia, a redhead, the eldest, maybe ten years old, stepped forward. *Lala's mother*, she said, *we want you to let Lala play in the yard with us.*

Janina hesitated. Danger was lurking at all hours. A single comment from one of the building's children or mothers, or a slipup from Lala herself, and who knew what could happen!

Her face turned grave and she opened her mouth to say no, but Lala clung to her pleadingly and begged to play with the girls just for a little bit. Janina decided she would keep an eye on the clock and would very soon go out to the yard to bring the girl back home. She put Lala's hand in Zosia's open one.

Meanwhile, in the yard, six boys had already arranged themselves in a row.

What's going on? Zosia asked Wodek, the leader of the group. *What's the game?*

We're taking a trip to the basement below the building. I heard that someone might be hiding there, Wodek whispered.

Isn't it dangerous?

Sure, if you're a scaredy-cat. You can stay here if you're too chicken, but you have to decide right now. If you're coming with us you have to join the row.

Zosia, who always did her best to mimic Wodek and gain his favor, swallowed her hesitation and instructed her younger friends to arrange in a row, dragging Lala behind her.

Wodek led the group to the stairwell of his building and began to descend the dark, narrow steps. He struggled with the rusty doorknob for a moment and finally pushed hard and kicked the door open.

As the door opened, the damp, musty stench of moss hit their nostrils. *Don't be afraid*, Wodek ordered his followers. *Hold each other's hands and don't let go.* The children walked ahead in the darkness, feeling their way, breathing in the nauseating, suffocating smell of rot. They took a right turn to discover a gray ray of light, also searching for its way through the dark, illuminating them with a beam of hope. The older ones knew that the basement was actually a deep, rectangular, underground tunnel that stretched below the entire building. Each wing of the building had an entrance to the basement, as well as narrow, barred, glassless windows. These little windows were visible from the outside, right against the ground of the yard.

A pale light filtered into the basement through these narrow windows, and they were now walking through this light, but, since the windows were few and far apart, within moments they were enveloped in thick darkness again.

Lala tightened her grip on Zosia's hand. What was this? Where were they going? This game was not as fun as she'd hoped. She was very scared of this place, but as usual was even more afraid to show her fear. She pursed her lips and tried to breathe only through her nose to avoid the taste of rot. She felt like she was suffocating. All around her she heard the footfalls of other children. Someone stumbled over a pile of coals, fell down, and cried that he was hurt. Another stepped on the tail of a mouse, causing it to squeak eerily. Zosia dragged Lala ahead, wanting to prove to Wodek that she could do it too, that she was no chicken.

When they reached another window Wodek looked at the group in the soft light and saw that most of the children were very afraid as a result of his plan—to walk through the basement under all four wings and find out if anyone was hiding there, as he'd heard his father tell his mother. To Wodek, who was a brave and curious child, the plan now seemed impossible. He had meant to leave through the same door they'd used to enter, which he'd purposefully left open. Now he wondered if they could walk a little deeper and find another door to leave through without having to go through the entire place. But what if that other door was locked? What then? Wodek was only twelve. He was the most mature in the group, the unannounced leader, but even he hadn't thought out all the details of this challenging undertaking.

As he tried to make up his mind, Janina's voice reached them as she ran around the yard, calling, *Lala, Lala, where are you?* She'd gone out as she'd planned, to find Lala and bring her home. Since she didn't see any of the children she assumed they were playing hide-and-seek. She hoped Lala would step out of her hiding place to answer her calls.

Lala heard Janina and without waiting for approval from Zosia or Wodek left the row, letting go of Zosia's hand, rushing over to one of the small windows, and shouting, *I'm here, I'm here with everybody!* She accidentally stepped on a sack of rotting potatoes and her feet sank into the repulsive mush.

In the meantime, out in the yard, Janina followed the voice and kneeled before the small window. She looked into the darkness of the basement and couldn't see a thing—it's impossible to see from light into darkness. To her growing anxiety, she heard Lala's voice again saying, *I'm here, I'm here with Zosia and everyone else.* Lala was crying now, unable to remove her feet from the mush.

Janina, stunned, called Zosia, who said, *We're here, taking a trip through the basement.* Using her authoritative voice, Janina ordered Zosia to turn back and bring Lala and the rest of the children back out to the yard.

Wodek was very upset about the interruption to his plan and muttered at Zosia, *I told you not to bring little kids on a grownup excursion!* But he knew they had no choice. The adventure was over. He ordered the children to turn around, reform the row, hold hands, and begin walking toward the exit.

Zosia picked up Lala, helping her out of the torn potato sack.

The darkness, the mold and the rot, the squeaking of mice as they scampered between their feet, these all made the children speed up. In spite of the darkness, they crossed the distance to the door very quickly.

Lala held Zosia's hand, shaking, silently swallowing her tears of fear as she tried to overcome her sense of suffocation and nausea from the sour stench now rising from her wet feet.

Janina was waiting for them by the basement door.

Afterward

For days, weeks, and months after the trip to the basement, Lala would continue to stand by the window, behind the white fabric, peeking out at the children as they played in the yard. A little girl safe in her hiding place. A little girl alone.

The Mind of a Merchant

It was a pleasant evening at Aunt Hela and Uncle Stefan's house. Lala liked sitting at the table with the entire family, who chatted amiably and always addressed her with express affection. She was especially fond of Uncle Stefan, who won her heart by drawing her pictures by solicitation.

I want to ask you something, Lala said to Uncle Stefan, who was sitting by her side.

Go ahead, go ahead, he said.

Does your house have a basement? She asked.

Of course, said Uncle Stefan, surprised. *But why are you so interested in our basement?*

Does every house have a basement? Lala continued.

Most do, said Stefan.

And why does every house need one?

A basement is an important part of every structure. You can hide things in it. It's like a large underground storage space. It can be used to keep coal for winter, for instance.

What else? Asked Lala.

Uncle Stefan was about to answer when Józef intervened. *Lala went on a trip to our basement and she's been very interested in basements ever since*, Józef explained, laughing.

Please don't laugh, said Lala. *I really want to know. Uncle Stefan*, she turned again to the one adult who always had patience for her. *Tell me, what else can you hide in a basement?*

You can store vegetables, the kind that keep for a long time, such as potatoes, cabbages, and beats.

Are you sure?

I think so.

And why are these vegetables kept in sacks?

Well, that's simple. It's an easy way to store a large amount of vegetables that would last all winter long, so that the entire family can be fed.

But why in the basement?

A basement is an underground space. It's dark and cool, and therefore it's a convenient place to keep food for winter, when it can no longer be bought, or during wartime, like now.

Lala fixed her eyes on Stefan and asked, *but what about a small family like ours, only Janina, Józef, and me. How would we finish an entire sack of potatoes?*

Very good, said Stefan. *Your question makes a lot of sense. In that case, the family members can sell some of the potatoes in their sack, and use the money to buy something else they need. What do you think about that?* He asked seriously.

Lala shook her head no.

You don't agree? Why not? Asked Uncle Stefan, surprised at her objection.

Because, because, because I really did take a trip to the basement with the children, like Józef said.

And? And? Stefan insisted.

And I stepped into a sack of rotten potatoes, Lala blurted. *It was like very soft, very smelly mud, and I couldn't pull my feet out, so Zosia, who's bigger, pulled me out. My feet, socks, and shoes were wet and smelled awful. I almost threw up! Janina couldn't even clean my shoes and socks and we had to throw them out.*

That sounds very unpleasant, said Uncle Stefan. *Perhaps it was an old sack that someone had forgotten down there?*

Perhaps, said Lala. *But no*, she said, changing her mind, *I have another idea.*

What kind of idea? Asked Jòzef. Janina and Aunt Hela departed for the kitchen to wash the dishes.

You said that people store coal in the basement, to use for heat in winter.

That's right, said Uncle Stefan.

So, Uncle Stefan, my idea is to buy lots of coal over the summer, store only coal in the basement, and then sell it to people in winter.

And what about potatoes and other vegetables for winter? Stefan and Jòzef asked.

Lala didn't falter. *With the money we get for the coal we can buy all the vegetables we need and we would never have to eat rotten potatoes.*

She's got the mind of a merchant, the men said, laughing.

Is that a good thing, what you just said about my mind?

It's a very good thing, they said, continuing to laugh.

The Visit

The stairwell of the central wing of 6 Krochmalna Street was almost entirely dark, illuminated only by one lamp on the second of three floors. The dark walls closed on Lala and even her own shadow was a little scary, hopping from one step to the next. Lala quickly descended from the third floor to the bottom floor apartment where she lived with Janina and Józef Abramowicz.

The third-floor neighbor, Mrs. Kwiatkowska, was friends with the Abramowicz family. Sometimes, when Janina and Józef were out, Lala went upstairs to her place. Mrs. Kwiatkowska, who was an old, lonely widow with no relatives, had formed a close relationship with the family and was especially warm and kind to their little girl, Lala. She liked having the little girl in her modest apartment, watching her when her parents were gone. This rare occasion was a cause for celebration for the two of them. Mrs. Kwiatkowska made sure to spoil Lala with any delicacy she was able to get her hands on during the sparse days of war.

She used to be a piano teacher, and the black piano was the central piece of furniture in her living room. It took up almost half the wall in the small room. The bench beside it was upholstered with faded dark burgundy. Sheet music was stored in a hidden drawer beneath the seat. Lala loved to open the lid of the bench and ask Mrs. Kwiatkowska to play something for her. The woman also liked to leave little surprises for her guest in the drawer.

Lala liked to let her fingers travel over the keys, collecting sounds, as if putting together a bouquet of notes from a magical black-and-white garden. However, her success was limited.

Mrs. Kwiatkowska made the diagnosis: Lala did not have a musical ear. But she still let the little one play and enjoy the piano in her childish way.

Now, in the early evening, already dark, Mrs. Kwiatkowska pressed the light switch by her door to turn on the only light in the stairwell. She asked Lala to go back home as planned and waited in the stairwell until she heard the door slamming downstairs and knew the girl had made it inside safely.

And Lala? She skipped quickly down the dark stairs as if fleeing from her own shadow as it chased her down the wall. When she got downstairs she was surprised to find the apartment door ajar. She walked in, and before she could even get her bearings, an invisible hand slammed the door behind her.

The surprised Lala looked at the round table that stood close to the doorway. Two strange men in uniform stood beside it. One of them was pointing a rifle underneath the table. Lala's eyes followed the rifle, and to her great distress she discovered Janina, her wrists and ankles bound, lying next to the leg of the table. The man with the gun muttered words Lala couldn't understand at Janina. The other man busied himself tossing dishes out of the closet by the sink.

A moment later Lala got down on her knees next to Janina and started to shout, *What are you doing to my mother? What do you want from her?* She caressed Janina's pale cheeks.

The two men in uniform ignored the girl's shouting, but the third, the one who'd slammed the door behind her, turned to look at her. *Who are you?* He asked. *What are you doing here?*

Lala sat up, turned toward the man, and said, *I'm Lala, and this is my mother.*

Really? The man asked. *We had no idea this woman had such a cute little girl.*

Lala stood up silently, watching him. With an indecipherable intuition she recognized him as the best of the three men. The fact that he wasn't in uniform soothed her. With his white hair and white mustache he looked older than the other two. Lala quickly scanned the room: the bed, stripped of its sheets, which were strewn on the floor; the open closet doors and her mother Franka's furs, also on the floor. Chaos prevailed. She looked back at the man and said, *Please help my mother get up. I'm too small to pull her from under the table.*

One of the two other men opened his mouth to speak, but at that very moment the older man, standing by the door, told the two in uniform, *We're finished here! That bitch has learned her lesson. We won't mess with little girls. Come on, let's get out of here.*

The other two tried to protest, but he urged them out.

He hadn't helped Janina stand up as Lala had asked, but he did respond with humanity toward the little girl. The three of them were gone in an instant. Lala kneeled again next to Janina, working hard to undo the towels tied around her wrists and ankles.

Afterward

Following this visit, Janina and Józef would decide that Janina and the child must leave Warsaw immediately. The identity of their visitors and the purpose of their surprise visit would never be revealed to Lala. Only the image of the upturned room and Janina bound under the table would remain engraved in Lala's memory.

Wiśniówka—the Cherry Farm

The ride from Warsaw to Wiśniówka took many hours. The passengers rocked up and down side roads, passing through small towns and godforsaken villages. They crossed forests, by the sides of rivers and streams. Lala gasped at the many shades of green and the richness of nature on this golden autumn day, as it conquered the eyes with its bold tones. She couldn't get enough of the beauty of the leafy world, strewn with shades of flowers and fruit orchards. The expanses hypnotized her, an urban child, leaving the city of Warsaw for the first time in her young life—a sad, gray city, even its pretty parks lamenting the cruel occupation and the ongoing agony of war along with its residents.

Lala was unaware of the circumstances and dangers of the trip. A little girl, only four-and-a-half years old, carefree, her eyes wide open toward the seemingly naïve, peaceful beauty outside the car window. She was stricken by the magical sight of animals crossing their path: cows in the meadow, horses pulling plows through the fields or wagons along country roads, barking dogs. It was as if the animals from her books were coming alive before her amazed eyes to greet her.

In the front seat of the car, Józef and Janina, their expressions tense, tried to convey business as usual. They whispered to each other, Janina practicing their cover story for bringing the child to the Wiśniówka farm near Lublin. The farm was owned by old friends of the Abramowicz family. It now housed the headquarters of the German occupation army. In spite of this unfortunate turn of events, Janina and Józef decided the place would fit Janina and Lala's needs. Lala had fair hair and blue eyes, and spoke perfect Polish from the time she still lived with her biological parents. In the months since she'd separated from her parents she'd adjusted well to her new environment, calling Janina and Józef Mommy and Daddy and practically becoming their daughter. Conditions in Warsaw worsened, and after the violent break-in at their apartment, the adults decided that Janina had to flee Warsaw with the child, while Józef went underground, so that the apartment on 6 Krochmalna Street would no longer serve as a target for surveillance, the end of which could not be foreseen. They decided on a cover story, according to which Janina would be presented as second cousin of her friend, the owner of the farm. Lala's health, pale and skinny for her age as she was, would serve as the reason for her convalescence in the village.

The presence of German headquarter officers in the farm seemed to Janina and Józef to guarantee the child's safety. The two of them prepared Lala over and over, telling her to stick to her Polish identity, repeating the names of their relatives to her, turning them into hers.

Lala knew the names perfectly and played the role of the Polish Abramowicz girl with natural grace. Józef trusted Janina's calm demeanor through this difficult time, believing it would save them. The two of them took a big risk choosing the lion's den as a safe haven, but who would suspect that a Jewish girl was living in the farm housing German headquarters?

They arrived at the farm in the evening, welcomed joyously by their friends—the owners—and their two children, ten-year-old Stefek and seven-year-old Magda. The family lived in the bottom floor, while the second floor had been expropriated by German officers. Janina and Lala were housed in a small room in the attic, accessible by an exterior stairwell. The bed prepared for them took up most of the small room, which also contained a narrow closet, a desk, and a chair. After a warm meal Józef said goodbye to his wife and adopted daughter, and went on his way back to Warsaw. Janina and Lala went up to the attic to rest after the long journey.

Wiśniówka would be their home until the Russian army invaded Eastern Poland in the spring of 1944.

Not so Innocent Child's Play

Lala was lying in the tangled grass, her fingertips stretched out to flutter over the blades. Her dress, spread beneath her, separated her naked body from the fragrant green bed. The grass wasn't prickly at all. Everything was soft to the touch, and the sun caressed her exposed body with pampering warmth.

She looked at the blue sky, so high and far away. The shades of blue were blinding in the light of the giant orange sun burning golden rays. Lala spotted torn clouds that appeared as if from nowhere, floating slowly, as if stretching invisible arms to join each other and form a large white mass. An enormous white comforter began covering the blazing sun. Strange, thought Lala. Could the sun be getting cold? But before she thought this through an invisible hand began removing the comforter from the sun, which was revealed to the child again, peeking out in its full size from under the cover to once more shine brightly. Its yellow light poured all over, and the warmth returned to caress Lala's naked body.

A fresh breeze brought with it a sour, nostril pinching smell, unfamiliar to Lala. She focused, trying to identify the pungent smell, when she heard the cows bellowing from the nearby shed. She recalled that on their way here she walked with Stefek and Magda by the cowshed. It was the first time she'd seen a real live cow from so close up, and not just one cow, but many cows! Standing there by the fence that blocked off the cows' yard, she watched wide eyed and wide mouthed as the gigantic creatures tread in the moist straw. One cow came over to the fence, and Lala, mesmerized, whispered to it, *I'm Lala.* The cow fixed her with round, wet, shiny eyes, and responded with a long mooooo.

Lala's train of thought was broken by Stefek's voice as he said, *Nurse Magda, the ear examination will be next.*

Magda bent down over Lala's head with a long, soft flower stem in her hand. Gently, she began to run the stem around Lala's earlobes, slowly invading the ears. *Her ears are clean and healthy*, Magda determined.

All right, said Stefek. *Now we have to give her a shot*, he added authoritatively.

Magda used a thin, brown, bent branch to poke Lala's left arm. The shot didn't hurt. Lala only felt a light scratch. *Good job, Lala*, said Magda. *You're a brave child and a model patient.*

Lala didn't know what the word patient meant, but decided to keep that to herself. Instead, she thanked Magda politely for the compliment she did understand.

In the meantime, Stefek released his grip on Lala's legs and sat up on his knees. *Now it's time for your physical*, he said gravely. He picked up two long blades of grass, one in each hand, and said, *Spread your legs, please, I need to examine you.* As he spoke he pushed Lala's knees apart and ran the blades of grass up her shins and thighs, up and up.

That tickles! Lala called.

Be quiet, Stefek muttered. *I have to concentrate.*

The tickle grew stronger, and then she felt a very sharp poke deep between her legs as the blades penetrated her. She quickly squeezed her legs together and sat up on her dress, the blades perpendicular between her thighs.

Startled by her sudden movement, Stefek looked up. *What's wrong with you? You're interrupting the examination!*

I don't want to play doctor anymore. I don't like it.

Stefek stood up, a tall, strong, country boy, ten years old, tan and formidable as he towered over the four-and-a-half-year-old girl, so skinny, her body pale as she sat, nude and trembling, at his feet.

The warmth of the sun really did disappear behind the clouds, Lala thought, trying to control the shivering that had taken over her body.

Magda got a hold of herself first. *No matter*, she said, *we're almost finished anyway. You're a healthy and very sweet girl*, she told Lala, gently pulling out the two blades of grass from between her legs. Magda helped Lala get up, put her underwear and dress back on. She smoothed the girl's hair and redid her braids, having undone them earlier to check the cleanliness of the girl's hair.

Stefek walked away quickly. He seemed angry, very angry. Magda did her best to try and appease the little girl, who was shaking all over. Lala had only arrived the previous night from Warsaw with her mother. Magda's mother explained that the guests had come to stay with them in their cherry farm because Warsaw had no food and the war was very bad there. Magda was glad to have a new friend to play with and promised both mothers she'd take care of little Lala, but Magda also respected the authority of her brother Stefek, and couldn't say no when he suggested they all go show Lala the cowshed and then play doctor.

He'd led them from the cowshed through an avenue of poplars leading to the cherry orchards. He chose a small mound of dirt covered in soft grass and hidden from view. He was the one who'd ordered Magda to undress Lala, lay her on top of her dress, and examine her as his nurse. Magda hesitated, but knowing her brother's wrath, she obeyed, and even enjoyed her role in the game. She too was surprised when the little girl suddenly protested and refused to continue with the game.

Secretly, Magda was glad that Lala had shown Stefek he couldn't get away with anything he wanted. Magda had never dared disobey her older brother.

Do you want to go pick cherries? She asked Lala now, trying to appease her.

Can we eat them, too? The city girl asked.

Of course! Magda said. She led Lala to the adjacent orchard, quickly climbing a tree, and tossing bright red cherries connected by thin stems down at Lala. The cherries mostly came as twins or triplets, but the biggest ones hung alone off their stems.

Lala hung cherry earrings around her ears, connected them to the buttons of her dress, and tied a few to the ribbons in her hair. Others she shoved into her mouth, the red juice dripping down her chin. She looked up at the sky and saw the sun becoming covered once again with an enormous comforter. The white cover slowly spread over the sun wheel that would soon become invisible. Could the sun already be going to bed?

Lala looked around, impressed and elated. The cherry farm captivated her with its magical sights, its delightful aromas, its blinding colors, and its mouthwatering flavors. Lala smiled with pleasure. She pushed away the bothersome memory of the doctor game, and the vision folded coyly into the folds of her mind.

Afterward

It would take an entire lifetime before the tickle of the grass and the pain of penetration would suddenly emerge from within the folds of memory as they slowly smoothed out by an invisible hand, revealing more and more repressed secrets.

The Shock of Escape

Janina spent most hours of the night standing before the dark attic window, concealed by a curtain, lest she be seen by the people in the yard. She watched the yard, which was illuminated by car headlights, noisy with ongoing traffic. Muffled voices came from inside the house as well, from the floor below the attic. Under the room she shared with Lala she kept hearing furniture being dragged around and doors being opened and slammed. Motors of jeeps and trucks rumbled in the yard, moving back and forth with low lights. The German soldiers carefully loaded different objects onto the vehicles, including lots of furniture that they'd taken from the main floor of the house. The floor below Janina and Lala's attic was used as officers' housing. Lala woke up several times in the middle of the night from the sound of never-ending activity, and when she found the bed empty, got up and joined her at the window, standing on tiptoes, trying to catch a glimpse of what affixed Janina to the window. Janina bent down toward Lala, picked her up, put her back in bed and soothed her back to sleep. Then she returned to the window, assuming her guard post, following the soldiers' preparations.

The sun began to come up, a gray light shone tentatively, as if attempting to invade the kingdom of darkness that still prevailed. The convoy left Wiśniówka with muffled hubbub, every other car shining its low lights, a thick, long, black snake twisting out of the gates.

Lala woke up early, brought a stool to the window, and climbed up to stand at Janina's side, watching the going-on outside. Her eyes wandered through the emptied yard and over to the strawberry beds beneath their bedroom window. The green bushes covered the reddening berries with rich foliage. Something strange caught her eye. *Look, Mommy,* she called. *There are fabrics in the strawberry bushes—sheets of pink, blue, yellow, and white fabric. What is that?*

Janina looked, marveling as well. She narrowed her eyes and could tell they were high quality sleeping gowns, probably taken by the soldiers as loot from a raid, and thrown out the windows tonight as they scrambled to retreat from the approaching Russians.

The sun came up and Janina opened the window to get a breath of fresh air, relieved to have the Germans gone. A sharp smell hit her, the smell of scorched meat, bitter and burning. She looked up, surprised to see plumes of black smoke climbing into the sky to cover the structures of the farm with a black canopy. As she focused on the smoke, high flames exploded into the sky, accompanied by whines, cries, moans, and growls. The noise grew louder, deafening.

Janina pulled Lala away from the window and closed it behind them, trying to escape from the smoke and keep the horrid, not-immediately-definable smell out. Most of all, she wanted to block out the dreadful sounds, which she still could not decipher. She picked Lala up and hurried down the exterior stairs into the yard. As they descended the stairs, which faced the farm, they were covered with the thick smoke and began suffocating from the smell, as the cries of panic continued to shake the world. Only then did Janina realize what was going on—the Germans, fleeing west from the Russian forces approaching from the east, had set the cowshed, the stables, and the chicken coop of Wiśniówka on fire, as well as all the cowsheds, stables, and coops in the nearby village. The flames and smoke reddened and blackened the skies alternatively. The burning animals cried with pain and agony from within the fire, and the pungent smell of their sizzling flesh prevailed—the smell of hundreds of animals nearing their cruel death.

Janina hugged Lala, trying to protect her from the horror all around them, but to no avail. When they walked into the owners' apartment on the bottom floor, their friends' grief over their possessions and life's work going up in flames joined the bellowing of animals. Janina sat Lala on her lap and explained what was going on in short, clear statements. The German soldiers had escaped, she told her, and they didn't want to leave behind any food, milk, meat, eggs, or horses, not for the Polish people of the farm, and certainly not for the Russian soldiers from whom they'd fled.

Lala listened, her eyes widening with fear and compassion. A five-year-old girl trying to fathom the inconceivable cruelty of people who set animals on fire, burning them alive.

Janina shared Lala's inability to comprehend such inhumane evil. Amongst herself she wondered how she'd gather the strength to one day tell Lala that her biological parents, Franka and Michał, had found their death several months earlier at the Trawniki camp outside of Lublin. They too had died in a fiery hell, inside an enormous mass grave that had been set on fire after the people standing around it were shot into it. Years later it would become known that some of the murderers had become so deranged by the sight of the horror that they'd jumped into the flames to burn along with their victims. The slaughter of Trawniki took place on November 3rd, 1943. Now, in the spring of 1944, Lala and Janina, also in the Lublin province, also witnessed hell, but they were safe. The Germans were gone.

Afterward

The shock of the Germans' escape would not lift for a very long time. For days, the embers would continue to burn, smoke pillars and the smell of fire would continue to rise; life burning out. The sounds of the horror would etch into Lala's ears, and the suffocating odors of sickening sweetness and choking singe would embed themselves in her memory forever.

Tovarish

Tovarish Grisha, Tovarish Sergey, Tovarish Kolya, Lala tried to repeat the names of the soldiers sitting around the fire, introducing themselves.

Janina, who could speak Russian, conversed freely with everyone.

The fire warmed them up, heating their cheeks, creating a pleasant sense of peace. Only that morning the enormous, heavy tanks approached with a deafening rumble, pulled up at the gates of Wiśniówka, maneuvered to the sides of the road and cleared the way for trucks and jeeps. Fair skinned soldiers hopped off quickly, yellow haired and blue, gray, or green eyed, all pastel colors, and met the dwellers of the farm with wide smiles. This was a happy occasion for both arrivals and greeters. Janina stepped forward and welcomed the soldiers with fluent Russian, immediately receiving hugs and applause.

The soldiers spread out through the yard and surrounding fields, erecting dozens of tents. In the evening, fires were lighted, and the tenants were invited to join the soldiers around the fires and share their battle rations. They handed out generous portions of military bread, sliced thinly and wrapped in oiled paper to preserve its soft, delicious texture. Tins of meat were opened, heated in the fire, and doled out. The children were offered chocolate and sweet biscuits. Lala, Magda, Stefek, and the others gobbled down the food, offering their hands to receive more surprises. The Russian soldiers enjoyed the excitement of the children, and asked them to memorize their names again and again—Tovarish Grisha, Tovarish Sergey, Tovarish Kolya, Tovarish Misha, Tovarish Alexey. Lala surprised them with her ability to remember all the names, earning her more and more chocolate. The singing, the camaraderie, and the warmth introduced by the Russian soldiers swept everyone away, children and grownups alike. The shock of the Germans' escape, the ruin and pillage they'd performed, drew away to the backs of memories as the embracing and enveloping presence of the Russian army took over their expanding hearts.

A few days later Janina told Lala that the soldiers were going to leave, continuing their journey west, toward Warsaw. Lala was saddened by the thought of saying goodbye to the new friends that had bestowed such generous gifts on her and the other children. Seeing the cloud of sadness over the little girl's face, Janina surprised her with some good news: *We're going with them*, she said.

Lala opened her blue, confused eyes.

I spoke to their commander, Janina explained. *My knowledge of Russian and Polish would help the soldiers and especially the commander communicate with the Polish citizens they'd meet in villages along the way. That would be my job—I'd translate from Polish into Russian and from Russian into Polish*, she explained to Lala. *In return, you and I will get to ride in the jeep with the soldiers, and hopefully we'll be back in Warsaw quickly, with Józef.*

Lala's face brightened. She'd caught the most important detail: she would get to ride in the jeep along with Tovarish Grisha, Tovarish Sergey, Tovarish Kolya, Tovarish Misha, Tovarish Alexey, and all the other Tovarish. They were all so nice to her, and the idea of riding with them and Janina on a long jeep journey excited her imagination.

The next day at dawn, without any further ado, they went on their way, both bundled up in thick, long military coats, only their eyes peeking out, taking in the sight of the tanks at the head of the convoy of trucks and jeeps, including the large commander's jeep, into which they'd squeezed. Like a long train, the convoy began to trail along the fields, gaining speed as it reached a paved road. Lala sat on Janina's lap, her eyes taking mental images of the sights, mental recordings of the sounds of the Russian liberation army as it moved west toward Warsaw, the capital city.

Afterward

The flavor of the battle rations, and especially the sweetness of the chocolate, would make a permanent mark on Lala's taste buds. The affection and cordiality the soldiers had bestowed upon them at the farm would remain in her private portfolio of memories, often standing the test of historical facts and images from documentary films about the invasion of Poland by the Russian army in the spring of 1944. In the face of these, Lala, later known as Relli, would always insist on her personal memory of the friendly meeting with the Tovarish at Wiśniówka.

A Village Cabin

The sky darkened, gray steam descending all around, enveloping the passengers in humidity. A cold wind gained speed, angrily blowing away the jeep's protective sheets. Heavy rain poured from all directions. Janina protected Lala as best she could, but it was for naught. The jeep driver had trouble keeping the vehicle stable, and often hit potholes in the country road, causing the passengers to become covered in mud. Their moist military coats grew wet and heavy over their bodies. The darkness, wetness and cold froze them, body and soul. Janina realized she wouldn't be able to go on much longer like this with a little girl. She was determined to stay with the Russians and get back to Warsaw as soon as possible, but what would come of Lala? She was grateful to the commander who agreed to take her along as a translator, but Lala was her responsibility, and she had no one else to help her. The child already had a fever; her health and safety were Janina's top priority. On the other hand was the golden opportunity of reaching Warsaw in relative safety within this storm of war. She didn't want to give up the chance of reuniting with her husband, her sister, and the rest of her family.

She was faced with a difficult dilemma, and eventually made a brave, uneasy, and possibly essential decision under the circumstances. She decided that the next time they stopped for the night at one of the villages she would find a peasant family suitable for taking care of the child and leave her there. Lala had a high fever and could not carry on in these conditions. They'd made significant progress with the liberating Russian army, and so the danger of the Germans, who had fled from the Russians, was no longer a threat. At any rate, Lala knew how to play her role perfectly: Lala Abramowicz, daughter of Józef and Janina. Janina knew she could trust her.

In the afternoon the rain let off, turning into a soft, bothersome trickle. The wind also seemed to have tired itself out. The convoy approached the village, and Janina shared her decision with the commander. He agreed to drive among the village cabins in search of an appropriate temporary home for her sick daughter while his soldiers settled in for the night.

When they entered the village the rain stopped completely, and soft rays of setting sun broke through the gray clouds, finding their way, thickening and enriching with color, bathing the rural landscape with an encouraging light. Janina saw this as a positive sign and hoped that her decision would prove itself. One larger cabin stood out among the others on the road that cut through the village, near the church. A fresh straw roof shone yellow and a thick smoke rose from the chimney. Janina asked the commander to pull over. She disembarked with Lala in her arms and knocked on the door. A large peasant opened the door, his gangly wife peeking from behind him, her face wide and kind. As she walked in, Janina noticed the long wooden table at the center of the cabin, along which was a bench that seated about ten boys and girls of varying ages. The eldest looked to be about fourteen, and the younger ones were about Lala's age, or a little older. Bowls of steaming borscht were set on the table and the children busied themselves with the soup. Many beds were arranged along all the cabin's walls, set close together. The stove was located by the door, covered with large pots, and the oven smelled of baking bread. Another small wood burning oven stood at the center of the cabin, adjacent to one of the beds, and its hot pipe rose up through the ceiling and into the chimney, spreading a pleasant heat.

Janina's well-trained eyes took in all these sights, and most of all the owners' amiable expressions. She walked inside, introduced herself by her true identity, and told them she was a refugee from Warsaw who'd escaped with her daughter several months ago to a farm near Lublin, and was now traveling with the Russian army as an interpreter in order to return to her family in Warsaw. Unfortunately, she explained, her little daughter was ill and would not be able to withstand the hardships of the road. She was looking for a family who, in exchange for payment, would be willing to take care of the girl, Lala Abramowicz.

The peasants looked at each other and invited Janina to sit with them at the table so they could discuss her idea in further detail. Janina invited the jeep driver and the commander to join them as well, and the three sat comfortably around the table and were served some of the delicious borscht and potatoes, while the burning Lala was laid on one of the beds.

Janina and the officer agreed that she would spend the night at the peasants' cabin. Since he had already decided the convoy would spend an additional day's rest in the village, Janina would have the following day free to hash out all the details of their transaction. She would also have time to inform Lala about the change that was about to take place in her life.

With the help of the peasant woman, Janina gently undressed the sleeping Lala and tucked her into the bed they would share that night and the next. Lala's fever burned in her sleep, but the warm cabin and the soft bed did her good. She woke up the next morning refreshed, alert, and happy, entirely unaware of the new chapter upon which she was about to embark.

An Encounter with a Horse

Janina said goodbye to Lala with a promise to return soon and take her back to Warsaw. In the meantime, she explained, the kind peasants would care for Lala and she would be able to play with their many children.

The separation from her biological parents was still very tangible in the child's memory. They too had promised to return for her, but it had been so long since she last saw them that she could barely remember their faces anymore. Nevertheless, deep down, she still waited and hoped they'd return. She didn't know why they hadn't come back as they'd promised. Neither Janina nor Józef had dared, at that point, tell her what had happened to Mommy Franka and Daddy Michał.

Lala knew very well that one must never reveal one's secrets to anyone. Even her old name, Relli, was a secret. She was another child now, Lala Abramowicz. She didn't dare tell Janina that she still secretly missed her parents and was so disappointed that they hadn't kept their promise. They were the ones who'd taught her that promises must be kept. She didn't know what to do with these feelings, other than do her best to ignore them.

Why hadn't her parents returned? The question remained unanswered.

And now Janina left too, in the jeep with the Tovarish, leaving Lala alone in a strange village among people she didn't even know. When would she return? Would she return at all? Lala asked herself these questions silently. The days went by and, having no other choice, Lala gradually adjusted to Janina's absence.

The peasants and their children treated her with affection. Everyone liked the little city girl, so different from them in her clothing, her diction, and her behavior. Her natural curiosity and the interest she took in all of their doings made them feel respected and important. They gladly answered her many questions, though their answers didn't always satisfy her.

One morning after breakfast, when the other children had already left for school, Lala went out to the yard. She followed the peasant, watching him work. The chickens roamed freely in the yard, and the peasants scattered seeds for them with wide gestures. At her request, he placed some seeds in her small hand and she scattered them as well. From there she followed him to the stable. The peasant brought the horse out to the yard, tied him near the feeding trough, and filled it with fresh hay. Lala watched with concentration as the horse bent his neck, dipped his head into the hay, raised it a bit as if looking at her with his big, shiny eyes, and chewed his food slowly and thoroughly.

The horse was beautiful, his brown coat glimmering in the morning sun. The round motions of chewing and swallowing and his rhythmic breaths hypnotized Lala. She sat on the ground near him, smiling at him and at herself, keeping him company as he ate. She liked him so much that she wanted to touch him, to express her affection and admiration. She stood up, walked over behind the horse, stood on tiptoes to reach the horse's behind, and caressed it softly. At that very moment the horse shivered with sudden panic, raised his back leg and kicked away the unexpected nuisance that was disrupting his mealtime.

The horse's hoof hit the girl's stomach with force and she flew through the air like a hot air balloon, landing terrified, aching, and confused, in the pile of hay. She was swallowed in the pile, the prickly hay invading her hair, her eyes, and her ears, and scratching her arms and legs.

Luckily, both the peasant woman, who was standing at the doorway, and the peasant man, who was working in the yard, had seen what had happened. The woman began to scream, *Jesus Maria! Jesus Maria!* while her resourceful husband brought the ladder near the pile of hay, climbed up quickly and fished the sinking child out. He carefully brought her down the ladder, curling her in his strong arms, and gave her to his stunned wife.

Lala was too shocked to speak. She shivered all over and held on to the woman's neck, searching for consolation from the kick and the panic of flying into the frightful hay, into the yellow, scratching darkness that had sucked her in.

In the meantime, the peasant decided to teach the horse a lesson. He naively thought he would be able to prevent similar behavior in the future. He led the horse away from the trough, tied him with a long rope to a metal peg in the ground, grabbed a long whip and began beating the horse wildly as the animal ran around in a circle, trying to evade the whip.

Lala watched the dreadful scene from the safety of the woman's arms as the woman explained that the horse was being punished for kicking her.

Lala watched the people and especially the horse, listening to his whinnies of fear and groans of pain and to the whistle of the whip as it tore through the air to wound him. Then she cried out, *Stop it! Stop beating him!*

The horror of her own trauma, along with her compassion for the horse, who was foaming at the lips, red trails forming through his skin, made her wail and weep uncontrollably. She kept crying, *Stop it! Please, stop it! Enough!*

The Burn

The child's scream shook the cabin and its dwellers. They all remained planted in place with the intensity of the vision before them: five-year-old Lala, naked and wet from bathing in the pail, lying on her stomach on the bed. One hand reaching for the towel that was tossed beyond her head, and the entire left side of her body clinging to the red-hot tin pipe. This was the pipe that emerged from the oven in the center of the cabin, rising up in a right angle to the ceiling, where it connected with the chimney. The pipe burned with the heat it spread through the cabin.

The peasant woman had just finished bathing Lala in a pail she'd set on a stool near the bed. She pulled the girl out of the water and sat her on the bed near the oven. She turned to get the towel from the other side of the bed, beyond the oven, but Lala beat her to it: the girl lay down across the bed, trying to crawl over to the towel, stretching her wet body to reach it. As she reached out her left hand, she unthinkingly placed her body flush against the red-hot pipe. The scream erupted from her mouth with the force of the sudden pain, and continued because she was unable to pull away from it. A sharp smell of burning skin and flesh spread through the cabin, and the girl's scream had everybody on their feet. For a moment, they all stared motionlessly: the ten children stood around her, speechless; the man of the house, who had just opened the door to come in, paused at the doorstep, crying, *Jesus Maria! Jesus Maria!* Only the woman miraculously got a hold of herself. In a tizzy, she hopped over the pail, climbed on the bed, lay between the child and the wall and pulled Lala to her, ripping her away from the pipe. Bits of skin and flesh from Lala's waist remained stuck to the pipe, continuing to smell. The children all burst into tears. The peasant rushed over to calm them as the woman wrapped the bleeding, aching Lala in a towel. Then she cleaned the open wound with a cloth dipped in vinegar.

Lala bit her lips so hard she drew blood. Her tears stained the woman's hands, and the burning would not relent. The woman spread lard over the wound, and the pain slowly eased up. She bandaged Lala with pieces of the linen sheet from the bed. Lala shivered and cried silently now.

The man boiled milk, sweetening it with honey and even adding some butter. He served Lala first, and then his children. Lala, who hated milk ever since she could remember, now took a big whiff of the sweet scent of butter and honey, and quickly gulped down the comforting beverage.

The next morning, the peasant bridled the horse. He and his wife took Lala to see a doctor in the nearby village. The doctor gently removed the bandage, his face paling when he saw the size and depth of the burn. He praised the woman for her first aid, smeared a pungent black ointment over the wound, and instructed them to apply it and change the bandages three times a day, and to come see him once a week. He promised the child that when the wound healed she would have nothing but a scar left. The scar would itch a little, he said, but he asked her to avoid scratching it, explaining that the itch was a sign of healing.

The peasant woman took dedicated, patient care of Lala and her wound, and within a few weeks the burn healed and, as the doctor promised, transformed into a long, dark, scabby scar.

Afterward

The scab of the scar would eventually fall off, leaving a kind of zipper etched across the skin, which would become Lala's, and then Relli's, distinctive mark.

The Surviving Treasure

Warsaw was liberated on January 17th, 1945. The snow piled on the city ruins. The wind whistled among the scorched skeletons of homes, swirling the white snowflakes around the extinguished inferno, whispering in the silence of nothing.

Janina walked down the demolished streets. Some still had pavements, and others were entirely in ruins. She'd already seen her house on 6 Krochmalna Street, witnessing with her own eyes what her husband had already told her: that nothing remained but the arch of the entry gate into the courtyard.

Now she decided to walk toward her sister Hela's place. Janina had last seen Hela and Stefan months ago, when, at the suggestion of her husband, she left Warsaw for the Lublin area with little Lala in the autumn of 1943.

Józef Abramowicz remained in Warsaw that entire time. He hid another Jew, Mr. Aleksander Malec, in his small metal workshop. In another hiding spot, he had Mrs. Halina Danziger and her teenaged twins. For this entire time, Józef worked hard to assist Jews in the ghetto. He made every effort to keep in contact with Franka and Michał Głowinski, Lala's parents, after they snuck the girl out of the ghetto in the beginning of 1943. The child had been put to sleep, tied inside a sack and transferred in the middle of the night beyond the wall and into the Abramowicz apartment on 6 Krochmalna Street, not far from the ghetto wall.

In the spring of 1943, shortly after the last time they saw their daughter at the Abramowicz apartment, the parents were taken from the Warsaw ghetto to the Trawniki camp near Lublin. At the beginning of 1943, before the Warsaw Ghetto rebellion broke, the Fritz Schultz factories were moved, along with their workers and the workers' families, from the Warsaw Ghetto to the Trawniki camp. Michał, Franka, and her father, Dawid Fersztendik, were among the workers. The Germans, who had planned to destroy the ghetto, made sure to first move the facilities they found necessary, including the tailoring workshop, the furriery and the brush factory. Józef told Janina that Lala's father trusted that in spite of the rough conditions and against all odds, they would survive. Michał continued to work at the tailoring workshop, holding on to every last shred of optimism.

With rare courage and limitless gumption, Józef managed to visit Franka and Michał at Trawniki several times. However, when he was planning his last visit, he learned that the prisoners, a total of about 10,000 people, had all been murdered between November 3rd and 5th of 1943, as part of the Harvest Project. They had been led, naked, to pits that had been dug in advance outside of the camp, where they were shot, their bodies falling into the pits, bleeding and choking among the bodies of those that preceded them, and finally buried alive under the bodies of those that followed. The pits and the dying people inside them were then set on fire.

Józef, who was an active member of the left-wing underground in Warsaw, fought in the Polish uprising of August 1944 as part of the Armia Ludowa, the "people's army," which had been established in January 1944 from the ranks of the Guardia Ludowa, the "people's guard," an underground army established in occupied Poland in January 1942. Józef survived in Warsaw until it was liberated, spending the roughest days with his friends on a wooden raft they'd built in the sewers, Warsaw's underground city.

Somehow, the resourceful Janina, a courageous, determined woman, managed to arrive in Warsaw as it was being liberated. Miraculously, she found her husband.

Józef had told her that immediately after the failed Polish rebellion, in August 1944, her sister Hela and her family were exiled, like many other people in Warsaw, to labor camps in Germany. Janina still didn't know what happened to them in Germany. Only when the war ended in May 1945, did she find out that not all of her family had survived their time in the camps. In the meantime she continued to make her stubborn and determined way toward Cegielniana Street, stumbling among loose stones in her impossible search of house number 10. The Gilewski family lived on the second floor of the right wing of the building. Like many other buildings in Warsaw at the time, this was a two-story building built as a square around a courtyard.

Janina located the former location of building number 10. Her husband had been right to warn her. It was all in ruins. Bits of furniture and broken dishes peeked out among the beams and bricks that had blackened with smoke. She began to climb over the ruins, making her way to the former location of her sister's apartment. Everything was gone. She stood there, tearful, in a moment of silence with the memory of her sister and her family. Suddenly her eyes caught a small piece of light brown paper. Janina bent down to touch it and could see now it was the edge of a brown envelope caught in a pile of rubble, broken ceramics, and bricks. Janina removed her gloves and began to clear the obstacles trapping and protecting the envelope. She couldn't believe her eyes. The envelope was made of brown, oily paper; fireproof. Could it be *the* envelope? Slowly, with unrelenting persistence, she continued to dig, her hands scratching and her fingers bleeding. The large, brown, well-packed envelope was plump and full, concealing a treasure.

Janina remembered the day when Lala's parents were brought by Józef in the middle of the night to say goodbye to their four-year-old daughter. That was shortly before they were sent from the Warsaw Ghetto to the Trawniki camp, where they were slaughtered on November 3rd, 1943. That night, Michał brought two brown envelopes with him. One of them contained all the family's certificates—a marriage certificate, birth certificates, and more. The other contained photographs of Lala from the day she was born, as well as other family photos. *Please,* he said, *try and keep these safe for Relli and for us. I know this is no easy task, because some of the people in these pictures are visibly Jewish. I trust you to find a way. It's very important to us that our daughter have a memento from her family and her first years in this world.*

Indeed, it was no easy task. Janina recalled discussing the matter with Józef. They knew they couldn't keep the certificates and pictures in their apartment, the same place where they hid the girl. They consulted with Hela and Stefan, who were in on the secret of the child's rescue, as were other family members and close friends. Her sister suggested they keep the certificates and pictures at her home.

In the central room of Hela's apartment there used to be a tall fireplace made of light brown ceramic tiles that covered the chimney. The fireplace rose almost to the ceiling. At its bottom was an opening for coal and wood. The brown envelopes were hidden in the narrow space between the ceiling and the top of the fireplace, carefully concealed by the dark brown tiles that adorned it from above.

Now, after long months, Janina stood there with one of the envelopes in her hand—the thicker, fuller of the two. She couldn't believe the pictures had survived. She sat down on a pile of rubble, opened the envelope and perused the pictures she'd never before looked at. She recognized baby Lala in her mother's arms, surrounded by colorful bouquets. There was another image, of Lala in her father's arms, and one with both parents, and there were her parents as children and teenagers, and Franka as a beautiful bride. Some of the photos were printed on hard brown cardboard. These were photos of older, well-dressed ladies, probably Lala's grandmothers. They seemed to have been taken in the beginning of the century. Some of them had Polish inscriptions on the back, and others, lines, circles, and semi-circles. *That must be Hebrew*, Janina thought. The tears ran down her face and fogged her glasses. She removed them from time to time, wiping the lenses before returning to the photos. All the people in these photographs, except for Lala, were no longer alive, she realized with a terrible bolt of logic.

Janina trembled, trying to understand how the treasure had survived, how all these dead people were meeting her here, in the ruins of liberated Warsaw? It was as if they were emerging from that frozen hell, demanding to live in the memory of their living, six-year-old daughter, who could no longer remember them clearly, or perhaps at all.

Janina gathered the pictures, returned them to the envelope, and stood up, paralyzed for a moment. She realized that, at some point, she would have to show these photos to their rightful owner. This would be a very difficult task, but she knew perfectly well that she would do it. She would rise to the challenge, she would search for the right way and the right time to show Lala the Relli she once was, and introduce to her again the people who loved her so much, her biological parents, Michał and Franka.

Afterward

About a year later, Janina would show Lala the envelope of pictures. Together, they would try to decipher the identities of the people in them so that, just as Michał had asked, Lala would get to know herself as a baby and a toddler, see who her parents were and guess at her grandmothers with their feathered hats. The envelope would be kept in a safe place, but always within reach. Just as she'd promised herself on the pile of rubble on Cegielniana Street, Janina would give the child the surviving treasure.

Lala in the World of Letters and Words

The peasants' children, from the seven-year-old twins Marianka and Zbyszek to fourteen-year-old Jurek, the eldest, all went to school in the village. The years of war disrupted the routine even in this small village, so that the children all ended up studying in the same classroom, most of them still learning how to read.

In the morning, after a breakfast of borscht or cabbage soup with potatoes, they all went to school. Then the peasant woman was free to devote herself to Lala. She liked dressing the girl in her city clothes, so different than her own children's, which she'd sewn herself, mostly from simple linen. She combed the girl's hair, braided it, and tied it with the colorful ribbons she found in the things Janina left behind. The peasant was very fond of their little guest. An alert child, curious, asking lots of questions, and telling stories from the fairytales and children's books at the bottom of her suitcase. Lala didn't know how to read yet, but she'd memorized her books and was happy to tell them to the peasant while the woman was cooking or washing clothes. Lala would sit on a stool by her side and tell her stories.

In the afternoon, when the children returned from school they all sat around the long table at the center of the cabin and had lunch, again borscht or cabbage soup with potatoes. The only change in the menu was the rotation of soups.

After lunch, the children remained sitting at the table, where they were instructed to do their homework. The majority of the homework was memorizing the Polish alphabet. Most of the children still didn't know the names of letters, and the secret of reading was a hard one to crack.

Lala, who loved being around the kids, sat on the floor beside them, playing with her doll and listening to the names of letters as they were read aloud again and again. Sometimes she climbed on the bench and sat between the twins, carefully following their fingers as they slowly traveled over the letters in their books in accordance with their reading. She often switched places and sat among the older children. She was surprised to find them also persistently repeating the names of letters each day anew. Both they and Lala were dismayed to find their success was minimal. Lala traveled, fascinated, around the long table, taking mental images of the shapes of letters, hearing their names, and gradually putting them together to recognize whole words in the children's textbooks. In the mornings, when the children were at school and she told the peasant her fairytales, she recognized the same letters in her storybooks.

She began reading whole words, surprised and hesitant at first, but with the wonderment and curiosity of an adventurer embarking upon an exciting journey of discovery. It wasn't long before Lala learned how to read—slowly at first, reading silently to herself, then whispering the words. With time she gained confidence and began reading out loud, to the peasant in the morning, then in the afternoon to the other children. She read from their own textbooks. Now she no longer had to ask for a place on the bench. They invited her to join them, occasionally even fighting over who would get to sit next to her and receive her help in learning how to read.

Thus not only did five-year-old Lala teach herself to read; she also served as a little teacher to the peasants' children. The parents, who themselves had trouble reading, were very impressed with this wonder in their home. They appreciated the little girl who, in spite of being alone in a strange place, navigated her way confidently and assertively, acquiring a position of power among the other children.

Many months later, when the war was over and Lala turned six, Józef and Janina came back for her. The first thing the peasant woman boasted about was Lala's ability to read from the local school's textbook. At her request, Lala read to them out loud from one of the twins' textbooks. Janina and Józef were doubtful. Familiar with Lala's strong memory, they were both convinced she'd memorized the story, making it seem like she was reading. With a cunning smile, Józef pulled the Warsaw daily paper from his pocket. He suggested that Lala read something from the paper. Józef assumed this test would prove that the girl couldn't read after all. Imagine their surprise, then, when Lala opened the paper and read its contents fluidly, though she didn't always know what the words she was reading meant. Janina and Józef could not contain their excitement about this accomplishment, and most of all about the fact that Lala was self-taught. She couldn't write yet, but she read smoothly, quickly. They realized that when they returned to Warsaw they would be faced with a problem—in Poland, children began school at age seven, and here Lala, their adopted daughter, was reading openly at age six. Even if the school accepted her early, she would still be ahead of the curve.

Afterward

This issue would be resolved when the elementary school principal met Lala and decided to let her into the second grade in spite of being two years younger than the other children. This acceptance would be conditional for the first trimester, assuming that if the child had any trouble she would be moved to first grade, where she would still be a year younger than the other pupils.

Upon entering school, Lala would choose the name Halinka, since Lala was a little girl's nickname. She would be enrolled as Halinka Abramowicz. This would be her name at school and on her report cards. At home and among her friends she would still be known as Lala.

Lala would continue to surprise everyone. She would do well in second grade, and the possibility of moving her to the first grade would never come up again. She would continue advancing along with her classmates until she finished fifth grade in the same school, at 10 Dworska Street.

Lala Says Goodbye to Relli

Janina walked quickly, her face expressionless, holding onto Lala's hand and hastening the girl's steps with an encouraging remark from time to time. *Remember*, she warned her, *this will probably take a while, and we're going to have to wait patiently.* They approached a large, gray building. People stood in groups outside, conversing fervently. Janina cleared a path through the crowd and began climbing up the steps, pulling Lala behind her. It was clear from the look in her eyes that this visit and the task ahead of her were ones she approached unwillingly.

Lala recreated bits of conversation she'd heard at home, when Janina and Józef discussed this visit with Lala to the office building. They didn't involve her in the conversation, but she sensed that they disagreed and that Józef had ended up enforcing his opinion. Janina finally gave in and accepted the mission. Rationally, Janina acknowledged the veracity of the arguments he used to persuade her, but her heart rejected them nonetheless. Eventually, logic won and she did what she had to do, determined as always to succeed.

They went up to the second floor. Before them opened a lengthy and fairly wide hallway. Along the walls were long wooden benches seating dozens of men and women of all ages. There were no children among them. Their clothes were ragged, faded gray and black ruling all. It was as if they were all wearing a school uniform, thought Lala, glancing at them curiously. Some looked at the little fair haired girl in a red dress and red ribbons with surprise as she was led by a confident woman toward the closed door with confidence, as if the door were meant to miraculously open for them.

As she approached the door, Janina turned to the people sitting closest to it and asked cordially yet assertively that they make room for the child. Lala found herself squeezed next to a wizened and hunched old man with a white beard and a very strange, very small, shiny and flat black hat with no brim that seemed to be glued to his head. Lala couldn't recall ever having seen such a funny hat before. The woman on her other side also looked very old to Lala. Her eyes were dark and sad and her long hair was thin and rested carelessly on her shoulders. Lala looked at the woman's smooth, flawless skin. She was like a young girl who'd dressed up as an old woman.

Lala, Janina broke her train of thoughts, *I'm going into this room now, right here, and you'll wait quietly on this bench and read the book I brought for you,* Uncle Tom's Cabin. *I'll call you in to join me as soon as I can.* She caressed the girl's hair and fluttered a kiss on her cheek, then knocked on the door, opened it confidently, and disappeared inside.

Lala remained alone, squeezed between the two strangers, feeling all eyes on her, with her red dress and her unusual looks within this gray-black, hunched, hollow-eyed crowd, whispering in a language she couldn't understand. She caught a few words of Polish here and there, but mostly the whistles of foreign and unknowable "zes" and "vi" sounds. The hallway reeked of sweat. People's clothes smelled of mold and old age. Lala glanced around, trying to figure out where she was, who were all these sad people whispering whistles and muttering "oy vey" and something that sounded like "vos" or "wos." She spotted that funny, black hat on some other heads.

To distract herself, she opened the book in her lap, but had trouble concentrating. Her eyes wandered, taking mental images of the gray and black figures filling the hallway. She wanted very badly for Janina to step out of that room and take her away from this bizarre place, and, more importantly, away from all these repulsive, even frightening people. As she watched, she noticed two men who had their feet amputated limping on crutches, a woman missing an arm, and a young boy leading a blind man in, searching for a seat for him.

Fortunately, the door opened and Janina pulled her into the room. A man sat behind a desk laden with files and folders, wearing dark rimmed glasses. He looked up at Lala with a smile and asked for her name.

Halinka Abramowicz, she answered proudly. *That is the name I registered with at school. But at home they call me Lala.*

Do you have another name? He asked softly. *Perhaps a name you no longer use but can still remember?*

Lala looked to Janina imploringly, and Janina patted her shoulder softly, reminding Lala of the name they'd repeated at home. *You can tell this man the name you used to have a long time ago.*

Lala looked at the smiling man behind the desk and said quietly, *I used to be called Relli Głowinski, but I'm no longer that girl. I've been Lala Abramowicz for a long time, Janina and Józef Abramowicz's daughter. And soon I'll go into second grade, because I can already read.*

Very good, said the clerk. He stood up to approach the girl, shook her hand, and wished her luck at school as she curtsied before him, as was the custom for Polish girls.

Janina thanked him and shook his hand as well, and the two walked swiftly out of his office and the building.

After they'd gained some distance from the building Janina stopped, bent down, hugged and kissed Lala, and said, *You did great. I'm very proud of you.*

But who were all those people there? Lala asked. *They looked very bad and they spoke a language I couldn't understand. And I didn't like the way they smelled, either.*

Janina looked at the child and said quietly, *Those people you saw today are Jews.*

I don't want to be like them, said Lala, starting to cry.

Janina held her close. *You used to be Jewish, but you're not anymore. Now you're my daughter and Józef's, like you told the clerk. You're a Polish girl.*

Then why did we have to go there?

The war is over and there's a food shortage. The people working in that building give food to those who don't have any, and especially to Jews. You saw the people who came there for help. And because you used to be Jewish you can get food parcels too, so that's why we wanted you to be registered there.

But I'm not Jewish anymore, Lala insisted.

Correct, said Janina confidently. *You're not Jewish anymore, you're Polish, forever.*

I never, ever want to be Jewish Relli again, like those people over there, Lala said, looking into Janina's loving eyes and trying to convince herself of her own childish declaration.

Sign of Life

Fall 1945, early October, a golden afternoon sun cast rays to caress the world with radiant red. The patrons of Café Atara on Allenby Street in Tel Aviv relaxed under the canopy of sunset stretching from the nearby beach as they spread out in their tables, taking over the sidewalk. The café was full. The tables were very small and surrounded by folding wooden chairs, as was customary at the time. People sat close together, drinking tea or coffee, some eating cake. At one table sat two men: one tan, broad-shouldered, wearing local "Ata" clothing, a resident whose Israeli identity was evident. The other was a pale, skinny man, wearing clothes from "back there," which told his story wordlessly. He was one of the first people to arrive in the Land of Israel through ungodly routes immediately after the war. He was lucky enough to track down a childhood friend who had immigrated years before him and was now almost a native. They spoke in fluent Polish, friends who have spent years apart, attempting to bridge the gaps of personal, social, and familial information.

Suddenly the newly arrived friend from Poland paused, placed a hand on his forehead, as if remembering something, and said, *Listen, I'm on a mission. I'm supposed to find a certain family here in Tel Aviv.*

What family are you looking for? What's your relationship to them? Relatives? Friends?

I'll tell you the truth, said the immigrant, *I don't even know them and I don't have their address. All I have is a first and last name. But I do know they live in Tel Aviv and that I simply must find them right away. I have to!*

All right, all right, his semi-native friend assured him. *What are the names? And why do you care so much about finding someone you don't even know?*

This is the story, the man answered excitedly. *I know a Polish couple back in Warsaw, Janina and Józef Abramowicz. They are a childless couple who rescued a little girl during the war. I know she has family here in Israel, her father's relatives. They left Poland years before the war. So I have to find the Głowinski family and let them know that this little girl, Relli, the only daughter of their brother and sister-in-law, is still alive. Now do you understand?*

As they spoke, a man sitting at the nearby table turned to face them. He tapped the shoulder of the man "from there" and said in Polish, *Forgive my impoliteness, but I couldn't help but overhear. The story of this little girl fascinates me. May I join your table and see what I might do to help? Can you repeat the name of the family you're looking for?*

The two friends, surprised by the man's intervention, invited him to their table.

The man who had listened to his friend's story furrowed his brow. *Yes, I understand now. I'm trying to think of a way to help with this mission. As you know, I'm a member of a kibbutz in the Galilee and don't know that many people in Tel Aviv. We need to figure out a way to do this.*

The man who joined the table said again, *Could you please repeat the name of the family you're looking for?*

The Polish immigrant said, *It's not so much that I'm looking for them, it's more like I have to find them. The last name is Głowinski, and the first name of the girl's uncle, her father's brother, is Chaim. I have to find Chaim Głowinski.*

The man turned red and pale alternately. *Chaim, you said? Chaim Głowinski? I have a friend by that name. If he's the one you're looking for then the problem is solved.*

A wide smile spread over the immigrant's face. *I can't believe this coincidence! What luck! It's unbelievable! I'm looking for Chaim Głowinski to let him know that the daughter of his brother Michał and his wife Franka, may they rest in peace, this little girl is alive in Warsaw. Her name used to be Relli Głowinski, but her rescuers, who adopted her, call her Lala Abramowicz. She's about six-and-a-half.*

The two men gobbled the story up, their eyes welling up with tears.

What a coincidence, said the man who joined them. *It's so lucky that I overheard you. Honestly, I was just curious before, but now I'm overwhelmed. Come with me, we'll go see Chaim Głowinski right now. This is a sign of life from the beyond!*

Afterward

The fateful, coincidental meeting at Café Atara in Tel Aviv would shake the life of Lala Abramowicz. It would be another five long, busy years before her life changed again and she returned to live as Relli Głowinski.

The Show Must Go On

The gym of the elementary school on 10 Dworska Street, Warsaw, bustled with joy and excitement. In celebration of the first Christmas since the end of World War II all chairs were brought down from the classrooms to be arranged in rows in the gym. The rows stretched from the elevated stage to the edge of the long, rectangular room. Streamers, posters, colorful holiday decorations, and student drawings were hung all over the walls and exercise ladders. The students chosen to participate in the holiday show waited, nervous, on stage.

Lala was at the center of the front row of participants, the youngest of the lot. Her fluent reading abilities and her memorizing skills led the teacher to choose her to recite a Julian Tuwim poem, *The Locomotive.*

The school principal stepped to the front of the stage. With a raise of a hand and a soothing smile she silenced the loud audience. She greeted everyone, mentioning the uniqueness of the celebration, the first after the war. The room erupted with applause. The students on stage began to sing, softly at first, but then louder, sweeping everyone along. When they finished, the second grade teacher, who was standing on the side, gestured for Lala to come over. Very excited, Lala could hear her heart pounding in her ears, the sweat making her glasses fog up. She stepped out of the row and walked confidently to the front of the stage. The lower class students sat in the rows right against the stage. Behind them were the guests. Lala spotted Janina and Józef and smiled at them. She placed her hands against her dark pleated skirt, gaining confidence from her posture. She opened her mouth and began to recite clearly:

A big locomotive has pulled into town,

Heavy, humungous, with sweat rolling down...

As she continued to recite, Lala felt something coming lose beneath her skirt. She focused her concentration on the poem, but the elastic of her woolen underwear had broken, the woolen underwear that Aunt Hela had knitted for her as a holiday gift, so that she didn't get cold in her skirt. The thick woolen underwear were worn over socks. They were a light brown, and now they were sliding down her legs. Since they were long, reaching almost down to her knees, they now began crawling down over the long blue socks. In the cold winter the children wore underwear, long socks, and often woolen underwear on top of it all.

Lala realized what was happening. She knew she couldn't disappoint her teacher who chose her for the opening act, and certainly not her adoptive parents, sitting proudly in the audience. Lala pawed at her skirt, but it didn't help. The brown underwear continued to ride down her legs. She noticed her classmates sitting in the first row beginning to giggle. The festive silence was broken. Her classmates and the other students, seeing the woolen underwear wrap around her ankles like cuffs, all laughed out loud.

Lala could feel tears of shame burning her eyes and impairing her vision, but she continued to recite, even louder than before:

She's fully exhausted and all out of breath,
Yet the coalman continues to stoke her to death...

As she continued to recite, her voice resonant, her pacing controlled, she saw that her classmates had piped down, serious and amazed as Lala pushed on, ignoring the underwear that had embarrassed her in her debut. The laughter had died down, and her voice rung out.

Lala finished the poem to loud applause. She took a bow before the teacher came over to help her pull the underwear off over her shoes so she could retreat backstage. The applause kept going. The teacher hugged Lala and kissed her warmly. *Good job, our brave Halinka, you proved today that you're a very brave, very responsible girl. It's thanks to you that the show could go on.*

Large Half, Little Half

The Abramowicz family and the Dolinski family were friends. The parents, who'd known each other since before the war, continued their relationship through the difficult years. When the war was over the Dolinski family returned to Warsaw and the get-togethers became more frequent. There were joint holiday celebrations, theatre outings, and out-of-town excursions. Mrs. Dolinski was a tall, pretty, warm, and kind woman. Her husband was restrained; a quiet and amiable man. The couple had one daughter, Mariola, two years older than Lala. Mr. and Mrs. Dolinski liked Lala. They often invited her over to their house so that the two girls could play together. Lala felt comfortable around Mrs. Dolinski. She was polite to Mr. Dolinski as he was to her and to everyone else.

But Mariola was a different story. She was a fat girl, very big for her age. She was neither pretty nor kind. She was nothing like her mother. Mariola had two long, thick braids, like Lala, and wore glasses like Lala, but hers were large and thick. It was as if everything about Mariola was big, like her. The way Mariola looked didn't really bother Lala, but she had a problem with her personality. Though she liked Mrs. Dolinski, Lala didn't like visiting the family home. She felt uncomfortable with the girl, who treated her with condescension.

Maybe it's because you're younger, Janina offered when Lala complained. *But you're a smart girl, Lala, and I trust you to know how to deal with her.*

But in spite of Janina's encouragement and Lala's pride at having her adoptive mother trust her, she did not enjoy playing with Mariola, most of all not at Mariola's house.

Mariola had a large, pretty bedroom filled with dolls, toys, books, and other interesting items that were not found in other homes. When the two girls played, Mariola always divided the toys and dolls between them, choosing the biggest and best ones for herself and leaving the lesser, older ones for Lala. She divided make-believe rolls the same way: she was the queen and Lala was the servant; she was the doctor and Lala was the nurse.

Everything was offered in abundance in Mariola's house. Even refreshments were served generously. Mariola's mother showered her spoiled only child and her little guest with delicacies. She had a habit: after the girls spent some time in Mariola's room, she called Mariola over and handed her a tray of delicious and beautiful food. Mariola loved to eat, especially cookies, sweets, and, most of all, chocolate. Mrs. Dolinski gave her the tray and said, *Mariola, sweetheart, split everything in half and share it with Lala.* Little Lala didn't know what "half" meant, but knew that Mariola was supposed to share the wealth. Indeed, Mariola placed the tray on the table with great pomp and divided the refreshments into two piles. The candy—into one large pile and one miniscule one. The cake she sliced into one thick slice and one sliver. The cookies received the same treatment. The worst was the chocolate. Mariola's mother placed a whole pack of fine, dark, raspberry filled chocolate made by the famous Wedel factory, which Lala loved. Mariola slowly and carefully removed the wrapper. When the many squares of chocolate were revealed, Mariola broke one row off the pack and left the rest whole. When everything was divided thusly on the tray, Mariola turned to Lala with perfect Polish manners and a toxic smile, and said, *Please help yourself.*

Lala, a well-educated, polite child, was forced to pick the smaller half. Choosing the bigger one would have been out of the question. This angered her. She knew very well that Mariola had her in a corner, forcing Lala to always choose the remnants of the abundant delicacies.

Once, Lala dared tell Mariola, *Your mother told you to divide everything equally. Why do you always divide it into one big portion and one small one?*

Mariola glared at Lala mockingly, smiled a small, malicious smile and said forgivingly, *You're still a little girl Lala. You might be in second grade, but you're only six, and you haven't learned fractions yet. I'm in third grade and I learn fractions. I learned in math that when dividing a number in two there is always a small half and a large half. Since I'm the older one, I deserve the bigger half. Besides, I'm the hostess and you're the guest, and I gave you first pick, and you picked the smaller half...*

Thus Lala learned her first lesson in fractions. When dividing a whole, there is always a small half and a large half.

What Rewards are Given For

Lala started school in September, 1945. She loved to learn and went happily. She had a good relationship with her homeroom teacher, Maria Janiszewska, an older, stout woman with light wavy, hair, bright eyes, and a warm smile. She was meticulous, but also patient and tolerant, and a fascinating teacher. Lala made friends in class and was very happy indeed.

One day toward the end of the last trimester, the teacher announced to the children that she had a habit of giving out a reward—a book—to the most outstanding student. She bought the book with her own money, since the school didn't have a budget for this kind of thing after the war. Lala listened carefully. From that day on she paid even more attention to her handwriting, decorated her notebooks, and spent lots of time doing homework and memorizing lessons. She secretly hoped to receive the reward: a personal gift from her beloved teacher! Lala already knew that her conditional acceptance into second grade was no longer an issue. Not only would she not be taken down to first grade, but she was one of the best in her class.

The special day approached. All the children worked hard and awaited the decision nervously. On the morning of the special day, Maria Janiszewska asked the children to arrange their chairs in a circle. The atmosphere was festive, yet alert. The teacher explained that the choice was very difficult, but because she could only give out one reward, she had to choose among several, very deserving candidates. Finally, the teacher said, *I decided to give this special reward to Halinka.*

Lala felt her heart pounding. Halinka was her official name at school, the name she chose herself. When the teacher spoke her name, Lala got up from her seat, forgetting that there was another girl named Halinka in their class—Halinka Kowalski, who also stood up at that moment. As they both stood, the other children all looked at the teacher, who completed the name of the winner—*Kowalski*.

Halinka Kowalski rushed over to the teacher to receive the reward along with a hug and a kiss. The children applauded. Halinka Kowalski's friends jumped up to congratulate her for this great honor.

Lala—officially, Halinka Abramowicz—sat down, ashamed. Tears filled her eyes. Her disappointment was three-fold. First, until just a moment ago she was convinced she was the winner—she'd heard the teacher say *Halinka*! Second, by getting up she embarrassed herself in front of the entire class. Finally, and most painfully, Lala knew she was the best student in class, recalling the many times she'd received higher marks than Halinka Kowalski. Then how? How could it be? Why did Maria, her beloved teacher, overlook her? Why did she not give her the reward?

The children began to leave the classroom, but Lala stayed seated, crying. Suddenly she felt a soft hand on her shoulder. She looked up and saw her teacher standing very close. Maria smiled kindly and said, *Let me explain to you, Halinka, why I didn't give you the reward. You are indeed the best student in class, but Halinka Kowalski is working very hard.*

I work very hard too, Lala said tearfully. *And you said yourself I'm the best. Then why didn't I get the reward?*

The answer is, the teacher said, *that you are a talented girl and your achievements come easily to you. Halinka Kowalski isn't as talented as you are. She must put a lot of time and effort into achieving her goals. Rewards are not given for talent, but for hard work. Remember that, Halinka Abramowicz.*

Afterward

Lala, Halinka Abramowicz, and later Relli Głowinski and Relli Robinson, would never forget the lesson she'd learned that day: that rewards are not given for talent but for the effort made in order to achieve greatness. More than sixty years would go by, but the event would continue to resonate in her memory.

Road Signs

The sign of life from Relli, delivered by the three men from Café Atara to the Głowinski family in Tel Aviv in the autumn of 1945, shook up the entire family. Michał, Relli's father, was the eldest of the five Głowinski children of Lodz. The children, born at the beginning of the twentieth century, lost their father, Hanoch, when Michał was seven years old and the youngest brother was one. The widowed mother, Cipora Głowinski, nee Lipszyc, never remarried, raising her five children on her own. The age differences between Michał, Rita, Chaim, Roma, and Paweł were between a year and eighteen months. They were a close-knit family, maintaining a warm relationship as they married and started families of their own. The mother and four of the children, Chaim, Paweł, Rita, and Roma, immigrated to Israel in the 1920s and '30s.

Michał, the eldest son, stayed back in Poland, where he founded and managed a commercial business, first in Danzig, and later in Berlin and Warsaw too. He visited the Land of Israel, supported his mother financially, and did his best to help his siblings, the Hebrew pioneers, too.

When World War II began, the family members in Palestine lost touch with Michał, Franka, and Relli, and for years no one knew what had come of them.

The mother, Cipora, died in the spring of 1944, never knowing what had become of her eldest, Michał, or her daughter-in-law and granddaughter, Franka and Relli, whom she'd never met. Chaim, her second son, was taken hostage by the Germans as a volunteer soldier in the British army.

Then, in the autumn of 1945, mere months after the war was over, the groundbreaking news reached Tel Aviv: little Relli had survived. This happy news was a ray of light in the dark grief of the Głowinski family over their beloved brother and sister-in-law, whom they now knew for certain were dead.

Chaim Głowinski spent five years in a German war prison with other soldiers from Palestine. They were taken hostage in Greece at the beginning of the war, and returned to the Land of Israel when the war was over. Chaim took over the search efforts for Relli. His brother and two sisters were active participants, as well.

At first they didn't know how to proceed after receiving the first sign of life. They had the name of the girl's rescuers, who lived in Warsaw, but no specific address. At that time, trying to locate someone in the ruined Warsaw, from Palestine, without an address, was an impossible mission. Relli's aunts and uncles tried to digest this unfathomable information that had reached them practically by miracle. A few more weeks went by before another miracle, just as unbelievable as the first, illuminated the mystery around the life of Relli.

The central post office of Tel Aviv received a letter from Poland. The letter was addressed to Chaim Głowinski and was sent by Józef Abramowicz. Here too, an invisible hand navigated the way, revealing footprints and leading to the destination. The clerk stared at the envelope that had no clear address. Suddenly, his face lit up with a smile: who didn't know Chaim Głowinski in little Tel Aviv? Chaim was the kind of guy who could actually end up receiving an unaddressed letter from abroad. The clerk made up his mind to hand the letter to Chaim in person later that day. At the end of his work day, the clerk delivered the letter to the home of Chaim Głowinski.

The letter of November 4th, 1945, signed by Janina and Józef, confirmed the story of the immigrant at Café Atara, shedding more light, and, most importantly, providing an address for six-year-old Relli, the only survivor of her small family.

This was the contents of the letter:

Dear Sir and Madam,

We are very sorry to inform you of the death of Michał Głowinski and his wife Franka, who both died in the Trawniki camp, near Lublin, on November 3rd, 1943. They were murdered along with all other prisoners. We won't describe their cruel death, though we were the only true Arian friends they had until their very last moments on earth.

Little Relli had been saved. She wasn't with them in the camp. Instead, she was left here, with us, and is here right now. She is healthy, a big girl, in the seventh year of her life. These days she lives with us in difficult conditions. Like the other residents of Warsaw, we have lost everything in the Polish uprising of 1944. She goes to school, though irregularly. When it's cold— and here, unfortunately, it's already getting very cold—she is forced to stay in bed, because we don't have enough warm clothes for her. Our apartment had been damaged in a fire, and has no doors or windows.

We won't go into the details of Relli's young and troubled life at the moment. If you care to learn more, our next letter will be longer. As for her future, we can come to a decision together, as was the wish of her late parents, Michał and Franka.

Awaiting your response,
Janina and Józef Abramowicz
47 Pszyokopowa Street, Warsaw
November 4th, 1945

The letter was accompanied by two lines in the girl's handwriting, in which she asked for candy. This request was directed to her grandmother and signed, *Your granddaughter.* The Abramowiczes knew that Michał had a mother, two brothers, and two sisters in Palestine.

New Shoes

January of 1946 was especially cold in Warsaw. It had only been six months since the end of World War II, and the city was still mostly in ruins. Piles of rubble from destroyed homes lined the streets, becoming covered in a white blanket of snow, granting them the appearance of fairytale castles.

Little Lala, six years and nine months old, walked to school. She walked especially carefully in order not to scuff her new shoes. Whenever snow sprayed on one of them, she bent down and used her glove to polish it off, smiling at herself and at her shoes, shining in beautiful bright brown. The sight of the gleaming color warmed her heart. That morning she woke up early, unable to wait any longer to wear her new shoes to school. She woke up several times the previous night to glance at them, waiting by the bed. One of those times she even brought them under the blanket, where she caressed them, promising to take good care of them and keep them as good as new. Now she thought how wonderful her feet felt inside these new, soft, beautiful shoes.

These special shoes arrived the previous day in a package from a faraway country. She was told they were sent especially from a country named Palestine, where her aunts and uncles lived. They were the ones who sent her these shoes to wear in winter. *How strange*, thought Lala. *They don't even know me, but they still care about me having winter shoes. If they chose such a beautiful pair they must have good taste.*

They were tall, brown boots made of soft light leather. The heel was extra special, not cut straight as in the black shoes the other children had, but in a round arch. The sole featured a picture of an elephant and said *Elephant* in letters she could read. Next to it was an etching of lines and circles that she could not decipher. The shoes fit her perfectly with the warm socks that came inside them. Lala was overcome with joy and pleasure. In her book bag, next to her textbooks and notebooks, was a cloth bag with a hanging lace in which to store the shoes at school.

Lala's school was one of the only buildings in the area to survive the bombings. The floors of the classrooms and hallways were made of parquet, and stepping on them with outdoor shoes was not allowed. At the entrance was a special hall, the walls of which were lined with wooden boards with pegs, one for each classroom. Each boy and girl hung their shoes in a bag from one of the nails, wearing slippers or specially knit thick woolen socks inside.

When Lala arrived at school that morning, wearing her new, special shoes, the girls in her class gathered around her, calling out with enthusiasm. Most of them had their older siblings' hand-me-downs. Any new shoes received were always black, made of the thick, coarse leather sold in Warsaw shops. The children had seen shoes like Lala's only in books and newspapers. With sorrow, Lala parted with her new shoes, carefully placed them in the bag, and hung the bag on a peg among those of her classmates before going inside.

Lala liked school, and she enjoyed this day as well, though her thoughts often wandered to the bag she'd left in the entry hall. She couldn't wait for the end of the day, when she could wear her new shoes again.

The bell rang, the children ran out of the classroom, and Lala, who was smaller than her friends, arrived to the entry hall with the last of the children. She was surprised by the strange silence in the room. The children stared at her, as if having awaited her arrival. She walked over to the peg on which she'd hung her bag in the morning. She touched the bag and was astounded to find it empty. She stared at it, confused. Where were her beautiful, soft, brown shoes? She'd put them in the bag that morning.

One of the girls came over and said, *Don't you get it? Your shoes were stolen!*

Lala was stunned. She broke into tears, besides herself with sorrow.

Another friend, a practical girl, said, *You can't walk home in socks, it's snowing outside. Don't worry, we'll carry you. It's lucky you're so little.*

And so, four of her classmates volunteered to accompany her on her way home, taking turns, two of them linking arms at a time to carry Lala on an imaginary throne. When those two got tired, the other two took their place.

Lala's tears slowly dried, but sadness choked her throat. When they arrived at her house, the girl who'd offered this arrangement said, *I'd be afraid to go in there if I were you!*

Why? Asked Lala.

My parents would kill me if I didn't take care of my shoes!

Lala wiped away the rest of her tears, glanced at the girl who was two years older, then got a hold of herself and said, *They won't kill me. They send me to school to learn, not to take care of shoes.*

Afterward

The stolen shoes were never found. The school principal, in an unusual decision for the time, donated money from the school's petty cash to buy Lala new, black shoes made of coarse, thick leather, just like the other kids had.

Not Like Everybody Else

But why not? Lala insisted. *You always say how important it is to read, and that we learn something from each and every book.*

That's true, Janina said, *but not this book. We don't want you learning from this book and we don't want it in our house.*

What's wrong with it? Asked Lala. *What's wrong with catechism?*

It all began the previous day, when Miss Maria Janiszewska introduced a new teacher, Miss Ludowska, the Holy Scriptures teacher. Miss Ludowska was a full bodied woman, limping in her right leg. She wore thick, black framed glasses. Her voice was soft and pleasant. She explained quietly what holy scriptures were. She said there were three major religions in the world: Christianity, Islam, and Judaism. She also mentioned the faiths of Southeast Asia. *All of us here,* she said, *are Catholics, and we're going to learn the prayers together. That way, when you join your family in church on Sundays, you'll know the prayers and understand them.* She showed the children a small book with a dark cover. *This is the catechism,* she explained— *our prayer book. I want you all to have one. You'll each ask your parents for twenty-five złoty, and next week when I come in here you'll give me the money and I'll give you the books.*

Lala came home filled with excitement about the new teacher and the new subject. Janina and Józef were not as pleased. They explained that they weren't Catholics and did not need this book, and that they were certainly not going to shell out twenty-five złoty for it.

But the teacher, Miss Ludowska, she said that all the children in class are Catholics, and that it's important we know the prayers.

Maybe the other children are, but you aren't, Jòzef said curtly.

Why not? Is it because I used to be Jewish?

No, that's not why. You were born Jewish, but you've been a Polish girl for a long time, our adopted daughter. You know we don't pray and don't go to church.

But I did go to church every Sunday, Lala insisted. *With the entire family, when I stayed with the peasants in the village. Doesn't that make me a little Catholic too?*

Listen, Lala, said Janina, picking up where Jòzef left off. *We're members of the Communist party. We don't believe in this God the Catholics talk about. That's why, like Jòzef said, we don't go to church and we don't pray. You're going to be like us. It's got nothing to do with the fact that you were born Jewish.*

And what should I tell the teacher? Asked Lala.

Tell her that your parents are Communists and they won't give you the money to buy this book.

Lala said nothing, disappointed and confused. *I'm not like everybody else,* she finally said quietly. *I used to be Jewish, and now I'm Polish, but not really Polish, because I'm not Catholic like the other children. I'm just not like everybody else.*

A week later, when Miss Ludowska collected money from the children, Lala asked to speak to her after class. *My parents are Communists,* she explained, *and they won't give me the money for the catechism.*

The surprised Miss Ludowska caressed the child's shoulders and asked quietly, *Do your parents ever give you pocket money, to by a lollipop, for instance?*

Yes, Lala said with a smile.

Well, I have an excellent idea, the teacher said, smiling too. *Each time you get pocket money you'll give it to me. I'll save it up for you, and when it's enough, I'll give you the catechism. But*, she added with a wink, *this has to be our little secret. You can't tell anybody.*

On her way home Lala considered the teacher's secret idea. She didn't like it. She decided she'd tell her parents and only keep it a secret from her classmates.

Janina and Józef were livid. They saw the teacher's suggestion as an attempt to incite the girl against her parents and drive her to lie to them. The next day Janina went to see the principal and complain about Miss Ludowska, who was reprimanded.

Afterward

Following this event, Lala would be exempt of Holy Scriptures class. Secretly, she would continue to think of herself as "not like everybody else."

Sick Child

Warsaw wore white. All night long the snow piled in the streets. The windows were covered with frost, beautiful, imaginative paintings created by a mysterious artist.

Lala woke up with a strange sensation. Her head was heavy and she had trouble lifting it off the pillow. She tried to sit up in bed and saw her room spinning around her.

She removed the blanket. Her pajama top lifted with it and Lala was surprised to find her belly covered with red spots. *Strange*, thought seven-year-old Lala. *What could this be?*

She lingered in bed. Janina peeked into her room, surprised by the girl's tardiness.

I feel weird, said Lala. *My belly has red stains on it.*

Janina approached the bed, looked at the child and saw red dots on her face. She touched her forehead. The girl had a fever. *You're sick*, she said. *It must be rubella. It's a very cold day, a good day to stay in bed, under the covers. You won't go to school today and you probably won't be going in the next few days, either. I'll put a pitcher of sweet, hot tea next to you, just the way you like it. Promise me you'll drink a lot and stay in bed. I'll try to come home early from work.*

What's rubella? Asked Lala.

Oh, it's just a childhood disease. It isn't dangerous. You'll see, in a few days you'll be as good as new.

And I'll be able to go back to school?

Of course, once you're healthy. Here, I brought you some books, too. I hope you sleep well. You'll see that after you get some sleep you'll feel much better. Like I said, I'll come home early.

The door closed, and Lala remained alone in the apartment. She was very sad that she couldn't go to school. She loved to learn. Why should she stay in bed all day? It was no fun. Her exhaustion got the best of her and she fell asleep for a short while. When she woke up she felt much better, just like Janina said.

She got up, and on the way to the bathroom glanced at her belly and saw that the spots hadn't disappeared. No matter, she thought. When they were covered with the pajamas no one could tell they were there. Lala decided she was very close to being better and should go to school after all. She had some sweet tea and felt encouraged. She went to the closet, took out warm underwear and clothing, and bundled up. She went out to school. Since it was late, she decided not to walk as she normally did, but to take the tram. She stepped onto a full car. Many other people must have decided to take the tram rather than walk on such a cold day. There were no free seats. To her surprise, a woman stood up and offered her a seat.

Lala thanked her politely, wondering why a grown woman would give her seat to a little girl. Manners required children to give their seats to adults. She couldn't figure it out, and meanwhile the tram approached the stop by the school.

Lala stood up, feeling unsteady. She got a hold of herself, grabbed her book bag, stepped off the tram, crossed the street, and quickly walked through the school gates. She walked into the entry hall to drop off her shoes and winter jacket. She still felt a little dizzy, but decided to ignore it. The important thing was, she'd made it to school. She went up to the second floor and opened the door to the classroom. All eyes were on her.

I'm sorry I'm late, she said quietly, noticing the teacher's surprised expression. Everyone was staring. *What's going on?* She wondered, repeating, louder this time, *I'm sorry I'm late.*

Lala began to walk into the classroom, approaching her regular seat, but the teacher walked over and said quietly yet assertively, *I want you to wait outside, by the door.*

Lala's eyes filled with tears. *But I've never been late before. Why are you punishing me?*

I'll explain in a minute, just wait outside.

The defeated Lala gave up and stepped outside the classroom, hearing her classmates laughing behind her. From beyond the door she heard the teacher instructing the children on what to read while she stepped outside.

Then the teacher came out and asked Lala to join her at the main office.

Lala was stunned and confused.

At the office, the teacher and the principal spoke to Lala, trying to find out why she'd been late. Lala didn't want to tell them that her mother asked her to stay in bed because of rubella, but gradually, as the tears ran down her face, the story unfolded. Lala repeated over and over that she felt fine and wanted to stay at school, but the teacher and the principal insisted that she had to go home until she got better. The teacher accompanied her to the entry hall, made sure she was bundled up, and sent her to the tram stop.

On the way home, once again someone offered her their seat. Again, she couldn't figure out why. *Probably because I'm crying, she thought. I wanted so badly to stay at school.*

When she got home, Lala immediately took off her clothes. The ugly red spots seemed to have multiplied and grown larger. She drank more of the tea that had grown cold and got under the covers. She cried herself to sleep, soaking the pillow with her disappointment.

When Janina came home and asked how her day had been, Lala told her what happened. Janina didn't raise her voice, but explained to Lala gravely that what she did was very dangerous. *Lala*, she said, *you risked your health, and you might have made it worse.*

I have to know, said Lala, how did everybody—*but I mean everybody, the people on the tram, the teacher, the kids in class, even the principal—how did they all know I was sick?*

Janina smiled and handed Lala a mirror. Lala saw that her face was blossoming like a red rose. Her eyes glowed with fever and her entire face, except for her eyes, was covered in red spots. She looked very strange indeed, a red child. Only then did Lala realize that the secret of rubella could not be concealed under pajamas. No winter clothes could hide it. The rubella glimmered in her blushed face, disclosing the very industrious, very naïve girl's secret.

Negotiation

Uncle Chaim Głowinski and the rest of the family hoped that the Zionist Coordination for the Affairs of Children and Youths in Poland, based in Lodz, would be able to represent them in a negotiation with the Abramowicz family to return Relli to her biological family. The Coordination located Jewish children who survived the war and handled their return to Judaism and their immigration to the Land of Israel. After receiving the Głowinski family's application, members of the Coordination tracked down the Abramowicz family in Warsaw and contacted them on the matter of Relli.

Janina and Józef did not appreciate being contacted through an official organization, as was apparent from the opening statement of their letter of January 31st, 1946:

We are the Arian family in charge of Relli Głowinski. You don't even have to look for us. We've never lived in Lodz. We've been Warsaw residents our entire lives.

They continued to write:

Little Relli, now called Lala, was adopted by us back in the days of German occupation. The adoption itself did not protect her or us from potential murder. Still, in spite of great danger and impossible circumstances, we've made it through. Today she's a big girl, almost seven years old. She's very polite and very smart. She knows the truth about her parents and can still remember them. Her family photos had survived, but her family documents were burned. Lala goes to school. She's in second grade, and a very good student. She's a healthy, physically developed child, who stands out in her level of maturity. Perhaps in the next letter we can attach a picture.

This letter was sent to Aunt Roma Ben Shaul, who was in charge of correspondence with the Abramowicz family.

Janina and Jòzef told Lala that her family in Palestine were aware of her existence and prepared to negotiate her return. They warned her not to talk to any strangers on the street or anywhere else and not to answer any questions. Lala was very sad and concerned. On the one hand, she was glad to receive clothing and gifts in regular packages from that distant, mysterious land, Palestine; but on the other hand, she didn't want to go back to being Relli, the Jewish girl she used to be, whose parents were murdered simply for being Jews. No one explained to her what it meant to be Jewish. With her childish insight, she knew it was very bad to be Jewish—Jews were killed just for being Jews. The sight of the people in the tattered clothing at that large office building was vivid in her memory. She thought that her family in Palestine must look a little like them; that all living Jews must look like that. She was a bit curious about her cousins in that faraway country, but those were transient thoughts. She only vaguely remembered her biological parents. Once in a while she looked at their photo, which Janina kept in that same old envelope, but Lala couldn't imagine ever having to say goodbye to Janina and Jòzef and stop being Lala—Halinka Abramowicz, the Polish girl she was now. She wrote a letter to her aunt Roma:

Dear Aunt, I received the dress you sent and I like it very much. Why don't cousins Nurit and Ruth write me? I want to have a letter to remember them by since I don't want to come over there. I don't want to come over there because I don't want to be apart from my mommy and daddy.

Hugs and kisses,

Halinka Abramowicz

Aunt Roma Ben Shaul continued to send clothes and to correspond with Relli-Lala and the Abramowicz family, while Chaim was in constant communication with the Coordination office.

Negotiations with the Abramowicz family were exhausting. The fact that Relli was their adopted daughter further complicated things.

Lala wasn't aware of the details of the negotiation revolving around her. Janina kept promising her there was nothing to worry about. They were not about to return her to her biological family or send her to Palestine.

Still, the girl was afraid. She tried to be obedient, polite, a good student, a pleaser. Deep inside, she believed that if she was always, always good and made Janina and Józef proud, they would keep their promise. Józef sometimes teased her jokingly, telling her he was the only one who knew her date of birth. Once, he claimed that the birthday they celebrated on March 11th wasn't her real birthday. He liked to tease her, insulting her a little, saying she had a "Jewish mind." Józef claimed it was a compliment, because the Jews were sharp, intelligent people. Lala hated those jokes. Sometimes she would cry, which led Józef and Janina to fight.

Finally, on July 7th, 1947, a letter was received in Tel Aviv from the Coordination offices in Lodz:

Mr. Głowinski,

As we continue to make every effort on the matter of your niece, Relli, we find ourselves facing great difficulties, which make it imperative that you come to Poland in person.

Perhaps your presence would tip the scales in your favor.

As matters appear now, we are likely going to lose the court hearing, unless we can pay the Abramowicz family two million złoty. The court has decided that an adopted child cannot be removed from a Polish family and sent to a relative abroad.

In an attempt to resolve this matter in the best way possible, we beseech you to come to Poland.

Afterward

The invisible hand of fate would continue to weave the threads of Relli's life story. About a month after receiving the letter, Chaim Głowinski, an active contributor to sports in the Land of Israel, would receive an offer to head the *HaPoel Eretz Israel* soccer team on their tour of New York. During his time in America, Chaim, a man of outstanding resourcefulness, would acquire a visa and a ticket to Poland.

Uncle Chaim

The gate opened and a black car rolled slowly along the avenue of thick trees, screeching to a halt near the door to the elegant villa. From the windows of the main hall, which served as a dining hall, dozens of eyes of councilors and children, attendants of the summer camp for the children of Communist Party members, followed the car's trajectory. The guides, convinced that the car was carrying a delegation paying them a surprise visit, ordered the kids to rise from their seats and arrange themselves in pairs in order to go out and play on the grass outside.

Lala comprehended the situation immediately and jumped up, forming a pair at the head of the row. Only she knew the reason for her swiftness. Every day at four o'clock, after their afternoon rest, the children all assembled in the dining hall to receive a glass of milk and a slice of bread with jam. This was a mandatory snack. Anyone who failed to finish their milk was not allowed to go outside and play. Lala often lingered at the dining hall for a long time, filtering the detested milk slowly through her teeth. Now, hearing the instruction to quickly get up and form pairs, she happily pounced off the bench, leaving an almost full glass of milk behind.

When all the children had formed a long straight row of pairs, the camp administrator opened the door and proudly led them to the grass. Everyone's eyes were on the black car, the doors of which were now open. To Lala's great surprise, the man who stepped out from the driver's side was her adoptive father, Jòzef. She let go of her partner and ran into his open arms. The administrator told the row of children to wait and walked to the car as well.

Jòzef smiled. *It's all right. I'm Lala's father and this is a private visit.*

The administrator mumbled a greeting and let the kids have a free hour to play on the grass and in the playground.

Two strangers came out from the back doors of the car. One was an officer in Polish uniform. The other, a tall, skinny man in a bright shirt, smiled widely at Lala. She curled deeper into Jòzef's arms.

Lala, Jòzef said clearly into her ear, speaking so that the other men could hear him too. *Lala,* he repeated, *you have a special visitor here today. This is Uncle Chaim, your Jewish uncle from Palestine who came to see you.*

The surprised Lala fixed Jòzef with appalled eyes. *My Jewish Uncle? Uncle Chaim from Palestine?* This shock of anxiety quickly replaced her joy and surprise at seeing Jòzef. She let go of his embrace and broke into a run down the avenue of trees leading to the gate and from there out to the forest.

The officer and the tall man were stunned by her speedy response. Jòzef got a hold of himself and ran after Lala. He caught up to her by the open gate, just before she disappeared into the forest. He grabbed her arm and tried to soothe her, wiping away the tears that were streaming uncontrollably.

I don't want to meet a Jewish uncle because I'm not a Jew anymore, the terrified girl begged.

Jòzef explained calmly that this was only an introduction, and that nothing bad would happen if she shook Mr. Głowinski's hand. *He's your biological father's brother,* he said, *and this uncle has come a long way just to visit you in Poland.*

Lala slowly calmed down and stopped crying. With Jòzef, she walked hesitantly back toward the two guests, clinging to his leg and never letting go of his hand.

The resourceful Józef utilized his sense of humor. He joked with the two guests that Lala simply wanted to demonstrate her running abilities. Now he introduced her officially—*Lala Abramowicz*—and she courteously offered her hand and curtsied to the two guests who introduced themselves: the tall one was Uncle Chaim Głowinski; the other one, the officer, was Olek Waiselfisz, Chaim's cousin from Poland who served in the Polish army. The four of them sat down on a bench at the edge of the grass, where Uncle Chaim opened his bag and began showering Lala with sweets. The men took an interest in the summer camp routine and asked what her favorite games were. Józef navigated the conversation lightly, as was his forte. Uncle Chaim searched for intimacy, but honored the distance Lala kept from him. The visit was shortly over and the men said goodbye, promising to come again.

Lala returned to her friends and shared the sweets with them. She was shaken up by the visit and could barely contain her turmoil. But she couldn't tell anyone her secret. That night she had trouble falling asleep, reliving in her mind the sudden visit that had broken her peace. In spite of Uncle Chaim's amicability, she was very frightened and very confused.

The next day, and for several days thereafter, Uncle Chaim returned for more visits with his officer cousin, whom Lala eventually realized was a distant cousin of hers, as well. They came with Józef or Janina, alternately. On one visit, Janina explained to Lala privately that since she refused to say goodbye to Lala and since Lala didn't want to be apart from her and Józef, the uncle would soon return to Palestine without her, and Lala would continue to live her life as usual, as Halinka Abramowicz.

The child was very happy to hear this news, and soon relaxed enough to get closer to Uncle Chaim. He brought her a big, pretty ball and invited her to play catch and soccer with him on the grass, and she had fun. He was a very friendly man, kind and sometimes even funny. He told her all about his family in Palestine: his wife Moni and their daughter Ruthy, two years older than Lala; his sister, Aunt Rita, her husband Abraham and their daughter Nurit, only six months younger than Lala; about Aunt Roma, who was the one that wrote her letters and sent her gifts from everyone, and her husband Zalman; and about his younger brother Paweł, his wife Anni and their little boy.

Lala imagined them all to resemble the sad people she saw back at that office building with Janina. She assumed Uncle Chaim only wore nice clothes on his visit to Poland. Over there in Palestine the Jews must all look like the ones she'd seen at that building; that much she was sure of.

After her conversation with Janina, Lala trusted that her future with the Abramowicz family was certain. Why not be nice then to the Jewish Uncle Chaim who wouldn't be her uncle for much longer? He would finish his visit and return to faraway Palestine.

Lala was surprised when, on their last meeting, he gave her a passport photo of himself as a memento, signing the back: *See you soon, your Uncle Chaim, summer 1947.*

He was just writing what was in his heart, Janina muttered when Lala showed her the picture.

Afterward

Chaim Głowinski would be forced to leave Poland without reaching any kind of agreement with the Abramowicz family.

Janina would reject any attempt to negotiate the girl's return, while Józef would pose impossible conditions which Chaim could never dream of meeting, such as an apartment in Tel Aviv and a very hefty sum of money to be paid immediately, in cash.

In spite of his determination and moral obligation to the memory of his older brother Michał, Chaim would not be able to see at the time any realistic possibility of getting back his niece, Relli.

Who Was Jesus?

Father Jan walked briskly down the hallway on his way to the fourth grade for his weekly religious studies class. This was the last class of the first trimester. Father Jan, a young priest and a tall and handsome man, loved teaching at the elementary school. He enjoyed the challenge of teaching the foundations of the Catholic faith to the children in this rapidly changing world. He did his best to keep them interested, retelling the stories of the New Testament as vividly and rivetingly as his imagination and the boundaries of religion allowed. He'd spent the trimester teaching them about the life of Jesus Christ, and today, for his last class, he planned on having a summarizing discussion of the life, strife, and accomplishments of the savior.

When he entered the classroom he found all students waiting quietly. He sensed the warm, reciprocal relationship he had with the ten-year-old children. At the back of the class he spotted a girl with blond braids and glasses, who was smaller than the others. He hadn't been informed of a new student. Then he recalled it was Halinka Abramowicz, daughter of Communist party members, who was exempt from religious studies at the request of her parents. She only rarely chose to stay in class, normally on rainy or snowy days. Then she sat at the back of the room and usually drew pictures or read books. Her presence did not bother him. On the contrary, she might pick up something interesting, which would serve as an indirect reward for all his hard work.

The class flowed well. The children answered his questions, and Father Jan was pleased. He decided to pose a challenging question, one that had no clear answer in the textbook. *Children,* he asked, *what do you think—was Jesus a man or the son of God?*

Many hands rose. Several children cried out, almost in unison, *Jesus was the son of God.*

The priest shook his head.

Others called out in response, *Jesus was a man.*

Father Jan shook his head again and asked the children to consider the question.

The room fell silent; the students were at a loss.

Then Father Jan noticed that Halinka Abramowicz had her hand raised. He addressed her gently. *Yes, would you like to say something?*

Yes, said the little one, standing up from her seat. She said confidently, *I know the answer to your question.*

Please go on, he encouraged her.

Jesus was both man and son of God, said Halinka.

That's an interesting answer. Can you elaborate?

Of course, said the girl. *He was born a baby, like any human, and grew up to be a man. He ate and drank and did all the things regular people do. But he didn't speak like the people around him. He said things people couldn't understand. He spoke of faith and spiritualism and delivered the word of God. I mean to say that in his body he was like us, but in his mind he was the son of God.*

As she spoke, Father Jan rose from his seat to approach Halinka at the back of the class. When she was finished a wide smile spread over his face. He applauded her, stroked her hair, and said enthusiastically, *Well done! That is the full and correct answer.*

The bell rang, the class was over, and the children ran outside to play.

A week went by, and the homeroom teacher invited the fourth graders to come in with their parents and receive their report cards. Halinka arrived with Janina. Being the first on the list, their conversation with the teacher was quickly over. As they received the report card and prepared to say goodbye, the teacher said, *The principal asked that you come see her in her office.*

Surprised, Janina and Lala headed for the office.

Unusually, the principal wasn't sitting inside her inner office, but in the main office, at the secretary's desk. *Please sit down*, she said amiably.

Halinka relaxed. The principal's kind tone of voice told her that nothing bad had happened.

The principal turned to Janina. *I gave my room to Father Jan today. He came here especially and asked to see you both. I told him I'd ask you. I know you're not a believer and that you asked to exempt your daughter from religious studies, but the priest said it was important that he speak to you and your daughter.*

Surprised by the request, Janina agreed. The two of them walked into the principal's office, where Father Jan was waiting.

Thank you for agreeing to meet me, he said. *I know you're a senior and active member of the Communist party, and that you do not share my faith. I'm a man of God, and just as you dedicate your life to Communism, I dedicate mine to religion. I disagree with your belief only in man and the party, but I respect your way, even if I can't identify with it. I came in especially today to meet you and tell you that, with all due respect, I believe you are depriving the child. She is not receiving a religious education. She does not attend church or religious studies, and in spite of this she demonstrates a deep insight and rare sensitivity toward the essence of Christianity and Catholic faith. I'm not about to try and convince you to change your educational ways. I'm only here to ask your permission to give Halinka a grade in religious studies, even though she is not an official student in my class. If you'll agree, it would be a great honor for me, as well as a means of expressing my appreciation of your wise daughter.*

Janina smiled awkwardly, considered the request, and finally agreed.

The priest asked Halinka to give him her report card. He opened it on the desk, dipped his pen in ink and wrote in the column *Religious Studies*, just over the line that had been drawn there to signify that this category was not applicable, the words *Very Good*. He smiled with satisfaction, dried the ink, and handed Halinka the report card.

To her great distress, the girl noticed that the new grade was marked with black ink, while the rest of the card was made out in blue ink, as was the homeroom teacher Maria Janiszewska's habit. Before she could say anything Father Jan bent down, stroked her hair, and said in his soothing voice, *No matter. This way you'll remember that this grade is unlike the others, and that you received it under special circumstances.*

He shook Janina's hand and said softly, *I thank you for this honor you've granted me and your daughter.*

Afterward

The report card of January 31st, 1948 would be kept among Halinka's personal effects. Even when Relli reached the eighth decade of her life, she would clearly remember the question about Jesus's identity, as well as Father Jan and their special meeting. The grade marked in black ink would always stand out among the others.

Doubly Orphaned

The train that had left Wrocław in the morning approached Warsaw in the afternoon. Two cars were designated for the Communist party members' children's summer camp and echoed with laughter and jubilant chatter. Only Lala sat quietly by the window, eating up the landscape painted in blue and green: the blue of rivers and lakes intertwining with the green of fields and forests. The blue sky above sparkled in the afternoon sun. She was hypnotized by the beauty. *My country of Poland is so beautiful*, she thought, planning a painting she would make of the colorful sights outside the train window. *I'm going to tell Mommy all about the beauty of our country and the wonderful summer camp*. It really was a special camp. They stayed in a large mansion that was owned by a rich German family before the war. The mansion, the orchards, the mysterious cemetery, which the children visited in secret... They even saw a mummified woman in a partially open grave. These all charmed Lala during the weeks she stayed there. Living in a small castle inspired her imagination. The apple orchard and manicured gardens were breathtaking. The apples had a special scent and flavor, a kind she'd never experienced before. The summer camp was burned into Lala's memory as a visit to a fairytale. She couldn't wait to get to Warsaw and share her experiences with her parents.

The train began to slow down. Its honking muffled the voices of the children, and the windows were covered with steam. The screeching of the brakes made the kids jump up from their seats. They each grabbed their suitcase and stormed the exit.

Lala decided not to push her way out. *I'll go out last and that way Mommy and Daddy will see me on the steps and I'll see them.* She finally walked over to the door and paused. She saw Jòzef walking over with a slow, somewhat heavy step. He wasn't smiling. He only looked at her sadly. Lala searched for Janina with her eyes, but she was nowhere to be seen. *How strange*, the child thought, skipping down the steps into Jòzef's open arms.

Where's Mommy? Why didn't she come? I miss her so much, she said.

Jòzef looked at her, even more serious than before. *Mommy's very sick*, he said in a tired voice, the words slow and measured, lingering before leaving his mouth.

Then let's hurry home and take care of her, Lala said, striding ahead in her thoughts and words.

We can't, he said decisively.

But why?

She's at the hospital, and children are not allowed.

Then what should we do? Lala asked with her usual practicality.

We'll go to Aunt Hela's and you'll stay there for the time being, said Jòzef.

Lala turned silent, as if sensing that nothing she would say would change the fact that she couldn't see her mommy.

As soon as they walked into Hela and Stefan's house, Lala noticed her aunt's puffy face and red eyes. She got up and walked over with her familiar limp, a sad memento of her days in a German labor camp during the war. Uncle Stefan sat at the table, his face as gray as his hair. Lala wondered at the unusual atmosphere. Her beloved aunt and uncle always used to be so glad to see her, and today, after being away for so long, she'd expected an especially joyful welcome.

As she wondered at the dark mood, Hela came over and held her close, tears running down her cheeks. *Oh, Lala, Lala,* she blubbered. *How could fate be so cruel to you? You've been orphaned again!*

Uncle Stefan opened his mouth as if to protest, while Józef rushed over to Aunt Hela's side, placing his hand on her shoulder in a desperate attempt to calm her nerves, but she wouldn't stop. *My little orphan, you're an orphan again!*

Lala stood in her aunt's arms, trying to breathe through the small opening in the crook of her elbow, confused. *But Aunt Hela, Daddy said Mommy's at the hospital and that I can't visit her. Why are you crying?*

That's what he told you? Her aunt cried.

At that moment Józef got a hold of himself and pulled Lala out of his sister-in-law's embrace. He sat her in his lap and said softly, pulling the words out slowly, *Lala, I couldn't tell you at the train station or on the way here, but now I'm telling you the truth. Aunt Hela's right. You've been orphaned again. Your mommy, Janina, who loved you so much and you loved her, has left us. She's gone. She was very sick and wasn't able to recover. She died.*

The words rolled onto Lala like heavy rocks from Józef's mouth, each one larger and weightier from the previous, pummeling her. Everything turned dark. First she shut her eyes tightly and opened them again, then she began to scream, *I don't want to hear this! It can't be! I don't want to hear you and I don't want to listen! I only want Mommy!*

Józef caressed her head and Aunt Hela came over again. Uncle Stefan joined and the three of them closed in on her, hugging and caressing, trying to soothe her. But Lala shrunk away from them, avoiding their touch. She stopped screaming and stared at them with tearful eyes. She tried, with the insight of a ten-year-old, to digest the painful words they'd said, trying to internalize the unfathomable notion that she no longer had a mother.

Aunt Hela continued to weep loudly and repeat, *You're an orphan for the second time in your life and you're only a child. You're an orphan again*, Aunt Hela kept repeating. She couldn't stop no matter how much her husband and brother-in-law tried to calm her down.

Lala gradually began to perceive her aunt's words. It was true. She'd been orphaned for the first time when she was four-and-a-half. That's when she lost her first mommy, the one who gave birth to her. Jewish Mommy Franka. She couldn't remember that mommy anymore. She only knew her from pictures.

Now she was over ten years old, and an orphan again, this time from her second mother, her adoptive mother, Janina, who raised her with love and devotion, the mommy who played with her, the mommy who gave her books to read, who drew with her, who always took pride in all of Lala's deeds.

I'm an orphan again, Lala repeated Aunt Hela's words. *I'm an orphan. An orphan. I have no mother. I'm motherless. I'm alone.*

Goodbye Mommy Janina

The ceremony was over. The lid of the coffin was closed and locked. Janina's face was gone forever. Lala was planted in place, unable to join the crowd of mourners that was moving toward the cemetery. Her blue gaping eyes had turned black like two wells filling with evil sights. The beads of her tears scattered over her moist face as she tried to etch into her memory the sight of her adoptive mother disappearing in the coffin. Janina, resting peacefully on the gleaming satin, her eyes closed and her face calm. Her short, dark hair was combed and pinned to the sides of her head. She wasn't wearing the glasses that were normally an inseparable part of her face. Lala knew that Janina couldn't see without her glasses. *There, in the darkness of the closed coffin, the glasses wouldn't do her any good anyway*, thought Lala.

Lala took comfort in the fact that Aunt Hela had accepted her request to bury Janina in the gray suit that was so becoming on her. Lala remembered vividly how they'd gone to the seamstress together and picked a soft, very light gray fabric. Mommy told the seamstress that her daughter had good taste and that she drew clothes for her dolls, whom she also drew by herself and cut out of hard cardboard. Janina showed the seamstress the cut Lala suggested for her new suit and the seamstress was impressed. Lala felt important and mature, a real part of the process. The product was a beautiful two-piece suit—a pleated skirt, its folds narrow by the waistline and growing wider toward the end, so that it fell like a bell down her hips, ending a little below the knee. The top part, which closed in the back, had a Chinese neckline and long sleeves, which also widened toward the end. Lala loved seeing her mother wear this suit and knew that Janina loved wearing it on special occasions. It was a comfort to have her buried in the suit that was so flattering both in life and death.

All the mourners had already left the prayer hall. Hela and Stefan gave their hands to Lala, trying to pull her away from the coffin and lead her toward the cemetery. The girl moved slowly and unwillingly, wishing to savor the final moments of proximity to her mommy, to Janina.

A thin, bothersome rain came down. The paths of the cemetery were covered with sticky mud. Lala saw that the new shoes Aunt Hela had bought her for the funeral were becoming wet and stained with mud, but she didn't even care.

The gray sky was crying softly over the sudden death of young, brave, socially active Janina; a special woman who devoted her life to others and never thought on herself. Fate closed its eyes and plugged its ears to all her human achievements and broke the burning wick of her life at once. She stumbled outside her house, hit her head, lost consciousness, and was dead within hours when blood submerged her brain. That's what Jòzef told Lala in response to her unending questions. The funeral and the burial were frightening, sad, painful, and inconceivable to the logic of a ten-year-old girl. Lala remembered well saying goodbye to Janina at the train station a few weeks earlier, when she left for summer camp. Neither of them knew it was forever. Now the girl stared at the gray, sticky mound of mud piled atop the coffin.

During the weeks of the camp, which she enjoyed, Lala missed her mommy as always. She wrote home regularly, describing in detail her life at the camp and adding illustrations. Janina's letters back were frequent. Jòzef occasionally added a few words. Her relationship with home was warm and continuous.

Ever since her return to Warsaw, Lala continued to miss Janina even more, attempting to grow accustomed to her absence. No caresses, no hugs, no kisses, no gazes filled with love and pride that had always been reserved for Lala. No secrets, no conversations, no smiles, or laughter. Now Lala was living a reality of "no". She'd known for a few days that she had no mother. She knew because she's been told. She knew that Mommy was simply gone, and this absence was what she went to sleep with and woke up with in the morning. Lala was always enveloped in this absence, its cold arms embracing and leading her. This absence was now her world. She was living in a bubble of absence.

You have no mother. You have no mother. The terrible words rung in her ears ceaselessly. *And you'll never have one!* What's never? What does this notion even mean to a little girl? She knew what yesterday and today were, but never? Forever? That sounded like a very dire future, a future stretching out to oblivion.

Lala couldn't figure out the meaning of all this until she saw the gray mound of mud over Janina's coffin with her own eyes. Not being able to hug or kiss her, to cuddle together in bed, to smell her, to see or hear her—these were the elements of her absence, all day and all night.

This absence would become a tangible thing, unfathomable and unimaginable, certainly not to a ten-year-old.

But, as inconceivable as it was, there was something very real, very certain about this nothing.

She had no mother.

Afterward

Janina Abramowicz died at the end of August, 1949. For ten years her grave would remain as nothing but a mound of dirt with no gravestone. Relli would learn about this from the letters of Aunt Hela and Uncle Stefan, who wrote to her that Józef did not erect a gravestone over his wife's grave and that they themselves could not afford one.

Only a decade later, when Relli was serving in the Israeli standing army, would she send her first paycheck to Hela and Stefan in Poland, for the funding of a gravestone.

It would be thirty-five years since Janina's death before, in 1984, upon her first visit back to Poland, Relli would go visit Janina's grave with Hela and Stefan. She would see a large headstone made of gray marble and engraved with Janina's information. The center of the grave, surrounded by marble, would be a blooming and colorful garden that Aunt Hela would lovingly tend to on her weekly visits.

What would come of the grave after Hela was gone, Relli would ask herself. It would be another eleven years before her next visit in 1995. Her aunt and uncle would no longer be alive, and Janina's blooming grave would become a marble rectangle of wild weeds and decrepitude threatening to take over the headstone.

Relli would leave some money for Małgosia, Hela's eldest granddaughter, to pay to fix up the grave. According to Relli's request, the grave would be covered with a marble plate matching the headstone and engraved with the words, *To Beloved Mother from Your Daughter Lala.*

At the Communist School

Halinka Abramowicz, the name was spoken beyond the partially open door. Lala stood up and walked hesitantly into the room. Behind a heavy desk laden with documents and books sat a tall, skinny woman, her face pale, her eyes small and dark behind round, dark-rimmed glasses. Her dark hair was carefully parted and done up in a bun. Everything was dark: the room, the furniture, and the teacher.

Are you Halinka Abramo-wicz? She asked drily, pulling on the last syllable of the name, as if having trouble pronouncing it. *You seem very small for a sixth grader. How old are you?*

I'm ten-and-a-half, said Lala.

Then there must be some kind of mistake.

No, there's no mistake, said Lala, gathering her confidence as she always did when she felt threatened. *I'm ten-and-a-half and I'm starting sixth grade because I skipped first grade and started second grade when I was six-and-a-half.*

The woman glared at Lala, narrowing her beady eyes. *I see,* she muttered. *I'm the sixth grade homeroom teacher, and since you are the only new student in my class this year I wanted us to get acquainted. Sit down,* she ordered harshly. *What does your father do?*

He works at a metal workshop.

What's his job at the workshop?

He's the owner, Lala said proudly.

The teacher looked up. *The owner? Then what are you doing at this school, Communist School No. 4? This school is for children whose parents are party members.*

But my mother is a party member and a party worker, or was, she isn't anymore, Lala said, lowering her voice.

Speak up, the teacher demanded, ignoring the girl's turmoil. *What do you mean she isn't anymore?*

My mother died, Lala said with a soft, shaking voice.

Really? When?

Ten days ago, said Lala.

I see, the teacher mumbled. Then it turned quiet.

After a short pause the teacher continued her practical conversation without addressing this new information. *In sixth grade we begin learning foreign languages. Students have a choice between Russian and English. Which shall you choose?*

I want to learn English, Lala said immediately.

Well, I regret the fact that you don't want to learn Russian, but with a name like Abramo-wicz I can't say I'm surprised. The teacher stood up. The classroom is on the third floor, second door to the right. Go up there now, class is about to begin. Today we start at nine, but on a regular day you must make sure to be here for morning line-up at eight o'clock sharp. I can see by your address that you have quite a long tram ride to get here, so remember to wake up early because you mustn't be late.

Lala left the meeting with a heavy heart. It wasn't enough that she didn't know anyone at the new school, now that she met her teacher she felt even more alone. She picked up her book bag and walked upstairs. She sat down in the empty seat she found in the classroom, third desk by the window. The teacher walked in right after her and Lala was glad she was already seated. The teacher turned to the classroom, greeted everyone back from summer break and welcomed them to the new school year. She didn't bother to mention that there was a new student in class, nor did she ask the students to help her settle in. She listed the strict rules of discipline and the different duties imposed on students. She mentioned the great privilege of studying at the Communist school and students' obligation to do well and excel. The most important task of the year would be to write a paper in honor of Joseph Stalin's birthday. This would require special effort, the teacher summed up.

Lala glanced around. The children all sat silently, looking at the teacher with unsmiling, extinguished eyes. Lala felt a yearning for her beloved elementary school, her old teacher, and the friends she'd never gotten a chance to say goodbye to. She felt lonely and lost. *No matter*, she consoled herself. *I'll study hard and show this teacher and these kids what I'm capable of.* The bell rang to mark the end of first period. The teacher reminded the students not to step outside because there was no break between this period and the next.

The geography teacher was already walking in, tall and quite fat, with dark straight hair that fell over his forehead and which he frequently pushed aside. He welcomed the students and took attendance with a wide smile. Lala's name, Halinka Abramowicz, was at the top of the list. *Oh*, he said, *we have a new student. Good luck to you and to us!*

Lala smiled at him and felt for the first time that morning a wave of warmth washing over her.

The teacher explained what geography was—a new subject for sixth graders. He said they would learn about faraway countries, beginning with an area called the Mediterranean. He hung up a large, colorful map, and pointed to the region with a long stick. With the help of the students, he listed the names of the countries surrounding the Mediterranean Sea and marked them on the blackboard.

He lingered over a small dot in the center of the map. *This is a very small and very young state, he said. It's only a little over a year old. Its name is written in the sea because it's too small to fit it inside. Who knows what it's called?*

The room was silent.

The teacher said, *even though I said it's a young state, the country is ancient and sacred to all major religions—to Christianity, Islam, and Judaism. What's the name of the country?*

Now several hands were raised. The children knew the country was called Palestine and that its central city was Jerusalem. They also mentioned Nazareth and Bethlehem.

Lala was paralyzed. She knew all the answers but was too embarrassed to participate. She knew the name Tel Aviv, the city from which she'd received letters and packages. She knew she mustn't mention this, and decided not to take part at all lest her voice or her knowledge disclose her secret, her connection to that tiny country at the center of the map.

The teacher went on to say that the first class would be dedicated to the fruit of the Land of Israel, now the State of Israel. He described the citrus—oranges, grapefruit, and lemons—as well as bananas, figs, and carobs. He accompanied his words with colorful, mouthwatering illustrations, which he pinned to the board one after the other.

The students were very interested and actively involved. They were curious about flavors, scents, and growing conditions. The exotic fruit sparked their imagination. Some said they were more appealing to them than the ones that grew in Poland.

The teacher might have felt that he'd raised too much excitement. He put an end to the discussion and said there was no room to compare the abundance of wonderful fruit that grew in Poland with the fruit of Israel, which, while appetizing, could never compare to the richness of flavor and scent of Polish fruit.

The change in his attitude was extreme. He seemed to have caught himself erring and quickly returned the students to a patriotic line of thinking. Lala was fascinated and moved by the teacher's descriptions. She felt no personal connection to that faraway land, and no special affinity to its fruit, but sensed a hidden pride for knowing more about the place than the other students. She imagined that one day she might visit and taste all the fruit the teacher had discussed.

Class was over. It had been interesting, and Lala felt she liked this teacher. He knew how to captivate students and sweep them off their feet, far away from the gray and dull classroom, even if he did pull the breaks by returning them to their own country. At the end of class he gave out textbooks and wrote the homework assignment on the board. Lala had enjoyed herself, forgetting her loneliness. The bell rang, and she awakened from her private journey to the fascinating Land of Israel on the map.

She went out with the other students to the long hallway and from there to the paved courtyard. She stood alone, watching the others running around. No one approached her and she approached no one. She felt distant and very alone, a new student in Communist School No. 4.

Had Janina imagined what a cold, estranged school this would be, she would never have enrolled me here, she thought sadly. *But what's done is done. Janina is gone and I'm the one who must work hard to succeed here.* She'd always loved to learn, but now for the first time she was at a school that was unpleasant. The homeroom teacher, the students, the building, and the yard—they all paralyzed her with fear. The geography teacher was a lone flower in a field of thorns.

Afterward

Ten years into the future, when Relli was accepted into the Hebrew University of Jerusalem, she would choose to major in geography, continuing with a master's degree in geography at UCLA. It would remain her favorite subject. Love at first sight or love at first class? The secrets of love cannot be explicitly deciphered.

The Punishment

I didn't do it, I didn't do it, she kept repeating, her eyes downcast. Tears ran down her face but her voice was steady as she continued to deny the accusations.

The severe school principal raised his voice again and slammed his hand onto the table. *Students from your class said they saw you throwing a stone at my office window.*

Lala looked up at the red faced principal who had been accusing her for a long time now. She glanced at the window frame, which was embedded with shards of shattered glass, forming sharp, uneven teeth surrounding a mouth that gaped in a scream. The floor beneath the window was also covered with shards of glass. Beyond her glasses, which were fogged up by tears, she looked right into the principal's eyes and repeated, *I didn't do it!*

I don't care what you say, he said. *I've got witnesses. You'll stay here after school. You'll stay all night for all I care, until you admit to it!* He shouted, turning his back on her and slamming the door behind him.

Lala looked around helplessly. Would he really leave her here all afternoon? All evening? All night, even? How could he? *But even if he does*, she thought, *I'll never admit to something I didn't do. I saw the boys in class doing it. They saw me seeing them, and then they probably conspired to tell the homeroom teacher that I was the one who threw the stone. I won't tell on them, because they might take revenge on me, but I won't admit to something I didn't do, either*, she thought, encouraging herself, wiping her wet face with the sleeve of her school uniform. Her handkerchief was in her book bag, which she'd left back in the classroom when the principal called her out in the middle of class and led her to his office, shouting all the while. *I'll show you!* He kept yelling over her head, before even explaining what he was talking about.

The door opened with a screech. The homeroom teacher walked in, carrying Lala's book bag. She tossed it angrily onto the principal's desk and walked swiftly over to Lala. *Enough with your stubbornness, Halinka Abramo-wicz,* she said, pulling on the last syllable unpleasantly as usual. *I can see that you people really are stubborn,* she mumbled to herself.

What people does she mean? Lala wondered to herself.

It's time you own up to what you did, and tomorrow you'll bring your father in and he'll pay to fix the window.

I didn't do it. My father won't come here and won't be paying for damage I didn't cause.

You have a choice, said the teacher. *You'll either tell the truth, or you'll stay here for hours, just like the principal said.*

But I am telling the truth! Lala insisted.

I'm very sorry to see you behave like this and lie about it, too, the teacher said sharply, then turned to leave.

Lala looked out the shattered window. She didn't know what time it was. She didn't have a watch. The light outside was fading fast, the sky darkening and heavy rain drops falling. Lala had no idea where the light switch was. Beyond the broken window she heard the students as they left the yard. She was being abandoned in the dark building that was quickly emptying of teachers and students. The darkness and quiet instilled fear in her. An imaginary voice kept whispering in her ears, *You have to confess, you have to confess.*

Time wore on, dripping slowly down the frightening glass of reality, a puddle of fear pooling at her feet as anxiety gradually took over.

Suddenly a weak ray of light filtered in from under the door. She heard footsteps and then the door slowly opened. Lala saw a tall man casting a shadow over the wall. He walked in slowly, flipped the light switch, and illuminated the room. *You're still here?* The janitor asked kindly. *I brought you some tea. It's so late. Why don't you drink this and then I'll walk you to the station.*

Lala wanted to hug and kiss this kind man, to thank him for his soothing voice, but she was too embarrassed.

After she finished her tea, the janitor offered his hand and she put her cold hand in his, feeling the warmth passing from his bony, work-worn palm. He turned off the light, and together they walked down the dark stairwell to the heavy front door. He locked it behind them and walked her to the tram stop.

During her long tram ride she relived the events of the day. She promised herself that she'd never own up to a crime she didn't commit, no matter what the teacher or the principal said. She knew the truth, but this knowledge didn't provide much comfort. No one would believe her, and she'd been punished anyway. *I'll show them,* she thought. *They won't break me, forcing me to confess to a lie. I must be brave and believe in myself.*

The next day at school the girls all gathered around her, asking about her punishment. Lala told them everything and praised the kind janitor. She finished by repeating that she did not confess to something she hadn't done.

But people saw you, the most popular girl in the class teased.

Anyone who says they saw me knows I didn't do it, Lala said quietly.

The popular girl turned away to a group of admiring boys, and together they walked to the janitor's room, perhaps to verify Lala's story.

When the bell rang, the homeroom teacher walked into the classroom and began to recount the previous day's events. She announced that the principal would be writing a letter to Halinka Abramo-wicz's father, charging him for the damages.

A whisper passed through the class. The popular girl raised her hand, stood up boisterously, and shook her head, fanning her fair curls from side to side. *Miss*, she said, *we the students want to ask you not to send a letter to Halinka's father.*

Really? Asked the teacher. *And what is the reason for your request?*

We think she's already been punished enough by being left alone in a dark room for hours after school. Many of us saw her throwing the stone, and if she's decided to lie about it, that's her problem. But we, as a society, think that her punishment has already been served. It's enough. There's no need to punish her father as well.

The teacher paused with surprise, narrowed her eyes, as she often did when she was listening to somebody speak, and finally said, *That's very interesting. I'll discuss your suggestion with the principal.*

After recess the principal came into the classroom, beaming. He told the students he was proud of the education and social values the school had managed to instill in its students. He felt as if he were living a pedagogical poem—a severe event in which a student vandalized public property and then lied and denied it led surprisingly to social cohesiveness and positive thinking among her peers: the students were now asking him not to punish her father as well!

The principal complimented the popular girl and her friends, first for exposing the criminal, and then for demonstrating advanced social thinking as to the severity of her punishment.

Filled with sweet talk and self-importance for his own educational work, the principal generously accepted the students' suggestion.

The whole while, Lala sat in her place, closed off, shrinking into herself, disappearing inside her embarrassment, her shame, and her fury. She was shaken up with emotion and was trying to put order in her thoughts. She felt as if she were watching a theatre of the absurd. How could it be that the people who had committed the crime accused her of it and then recruited other fake witnesses, and were now receiving praise for their actions? The ten-year-old Lala could not comprehend these events.

Her loneliness at school and at home was exacerbating. Her world seemed very unjust, threatening, and gloomy. The teacher and the principal ignored her completely and the children saw themselves as her saviors. As far as they were concerned, she was indebted to them—she owed them one. Lala felt tiny yet robust seeds of hatred sewed into the flowerbed of her heart, ones that would give rise to the durable plant of hatred toward the Communist school, the teacher, the principal, and most of all, her classmates.

I love to learn, she thought, consoling herself and trying to settle the contradiction that plagued her heart and mind.

One-Hundred Dollars

October of 1949 was very rainy. *This weather makes everything sad*, Lala thought as she walked quickly down the dark street, trying to escape the raindrops that began to soak her. She made sure to bypass the puddles on the sidewalk, careful not to get her shoes wet. She did her best to hide the book bag under her coat to keep it dry, all the while quickening her footsteps, trying to cross the distance from her aunt and uncle's house to her own, or the one that used to be her own until a few weeks ago, as quickly as she could.

As she climbed the steps to the third floor she thought sadly of the bed awaiting her, now set in the corner of the hallway, in the apartment that was until recently her warm and loving home. It had only been two months since the death of her adoptive mother, and so much has changed in Lala's life. Sometimes she wondered if she was even the same girl. Perhaps all these awful things were happening to somebody else?

Józef rented out the apartment that used to be their own to strangers, Mr. and Mrs. Pulaski and their sixteen-year-old daughter. Lala's bedroom was given to the daughter, while the parents took over the rest of the apartment. Lala's bed was taken out of her former room and placed in the hallway, next to the bathroom. A small cabinet was placed next to it, storing the child's few books and articles of clothing.

Józef had moved in with his girlfriend, Wanda, in the remote district of Praga, on the other side of the Wisła River. Lala remained a burden, an unwanted tenant in the apartment that was until recently her home.

Only a few months ago she still had a father and a mother and was a happy child. Now she was only allowed to use her home for sleep.

The Communist School, which was still strange, cold, and new to her, enforced a long school day. This was the school Janina had enrolled her in during the summer between fifth and sixth grade, wanting her daughter to attend a school for the children of party members. She couldn't know then that by the time Lala started school Janina would no longer be around to support and help her through this transition.

After school Lala wandered the streets, walking the long way to Aunt Hela and Uncle Stefan's house, where she did her homework and ate dinner. Aunt Hela made her a sandwich for the following day's lunch. Late in the evening, Lala would return to her old house, which was now the Pulaski home, for the night.

Lost in her glum thoughts, Lala unlocked the door and walked into the hallway on tiptoes. Her stunned eyes fell on the bed, which had been moved from the wall and was now placed in the hallway, the contents of the cabinet piled on top of it. Shocked, Lala looked at her socks and underwear, which were tangled up in her inside-out sweater, the shirts that had been folded so neatly strewn about all over. The empty cabinet stood there with its door open wide, and Lala's beloved books were all over the floor. She was overcome with insult and panic, her heart beating wildly.

From beyond the closed kitchen door she heard Mr. Pulaski's voice. *I'll show that thieving Jew*, he said. *I'll show her.* His wife tried to hush him, and Lala wondered who he was talking about, his words slicing through the silence of the chilly night.

Suddenly the kitchen door opened. Mr. Pulaski, a short and skinny man, his narrow, always pursed lips pursed even further, was striding over toward Lala, as if about to hit her. Lala retreated into the bathroom while Mrs. Pulaski got a hold of her husband. With her squeaky voice, the woman whispered, *Jurek, calm down, you have to talk to her. We need to get to the bottom of this and we can't do that when you're so angry.*

The furious Mr. Pulaski struggled against his wife, but her words, *Get to the bottom of this*, penetrated his infuriated consciousness. He stood in the center of the hallway, furrowed his brow, opened his mouth, took a deep breath, and said severely, *Get out of the bathroom and come into our room at once. We have to talk.*

Lala removed her wet coat, hung it up, and followed Mr. and Mrs. Pulaski into their room, the room that until recently was the center of her own home, where she used to play and talk with her adoptive parents in the rare hours when they were all home at once. The room contained so many sweet, distant memories.

As she walked into the room, she quickly realized that the storm had passed through it as well. The doors of the closet were open, the contents of the shelves, the drawers, and part of the bookcase strewn about the floor. Mr. Pulaski picked his way through the mayhem, sat down on the sofa, straightening his back as if to gain some height. *You stay standing*, he ordered Lala. *You won't sit until you tell us where you hid them!*

Hid who? Lala asked, her voice shaking.

Not who, what! My one-hundred dollars, he muttered.

Lala stared at him, her mouth closing and opening, like a fish out of water.

Where did you hide my one-hundred dollars? Mr. Pulaski muttered again.

Lala watched him, stunned. *What's one-hundred dollars?* She asked.

What do you mean? It's American money. A green bill with the number one-hundred on it.

But what are dollars? Lala insisted.

Dollars are the American currency, Mr. Pulaski roared. *It's money from America*, he said, raising his voice again.

I didn't know that, said Lala.

But Mr. Pulaski was striding ahead, his face red, screaming, *You're a thief! You stole that money and I demand that you give it back!*

Standing before this out-of-control man, Lala felt a calm take over her. *How could I steal something when I don't even know what it is?* She asked quietly.

Don't get smart, the aspiring interrogator yelled. *If you don't give back the one-hundred dollars, I'll take you to the police station and tell the cops that not only are you a thief, but that you're in possession of foreign currency, which is illegal for Polish citizens to do, and you'll be doubly punished!*

Mrs. Pulaski turned pale, trying to disappear into the corner of the sofa.

Lala listened carefully to the words that spat fire out of Mr. Pulaski's mouth. He seemed much more scared than she was. She wasn't afraid of the police. She hadn't stolen anything. But she realized now that Mr. Pulaski was the one who might have reason to be afraid. *I'll go with you to the police station*, she said. *But I'll tell the cops that you were the one committing a crime. You were the one in possession of foreign currency. What did you say that American money was called, dollars?* She asked with partially disingenuous innocence, as if reciting the lines of a character in a play.

Mr. Pulaski jumped off the sofa and stood against her. His wife jumped up after him to grab his hands. Lala ran to the hallway. *Can't you see the girl doesn't even know what you're talking about?* His wife said, trying to calm him.

In the hallway, Lala put on her wet coat, grabbed her book bag, and went out to the stairwell. Out on the dark and wet street she ran through the pouring rain back to her aunt and uncle's house. *One-hundred dollars, one-hundred dollars*, she repeated out loud, wanting to remember exact details so she could recount them to her family.

Afterward

Mr. Pulaski would eventually find the missing bill. He would apologize to Józef, to the Gilewski family, and even to Lala. The adults would all agree not to reveal his crime to the police.

And Lala? She was forced to continue to sleep in her bed in the hallway in spite of this difficult event. She had nowhere else to go.

Chapter Two: The Journal

Introduction

Tzipora Neshem of Haifa moved to Warsaw in January 1950 to work at the Israeli Embassy on behalf of the Ministry of Foreign Affairs. Tzipora was an old friend of the Głowinski family in Israel, and had undertaken a second, private mission: to locate Relli, redeem her from the hands of Józef Abramowicz, handle the matter of her return to Judaism, and bring her back to Israel. Tzipora's journal documents her journey to rescue Relli Głowinski.

Haifa, December 6th, 1949

Earlier this week I went from Haifa to Tel Aviv for four days in order to take care of different errands before I leave for Poland. As I walked down Dizengoff Street in Tel Aviv I saw the two Głowinski sisters—Rita Robinson, who lives in Pardess Hannah, and Roma Ben-Shaul, who lives in Tel Aviv—approaching me. The chance meeting lifted all of our spirits. We hadn't seen each other in so long. We caught up on stories of family and mutual friends. When they asked what was new with me, I told them about my approaching trip to Warsaw. They both froze, incredulous.

Tzipora! Tzipora! They both burst out, hugging me with excitement. *It's so lucky we ran into you! It's like the hand of fate! We have a mission for you.* They were talking over each other, cutting each other off.

We walked into a nearby café, where the two of them told me about their little niece who lives in Warsaw, ten-and-a-half years old. She is the daughter of their eldest brother, Michał, and their sister-in-law, Franka, who were murdered in the Holocaust. Relli had survived under a false identity, as the adopted daughter of Janina and Józef Abramowicz, who nicknamed her Lala. Mrs. Abramowicz had died suddenly last summer, and ever since correspondence with Mr. Abramowicz has dwindled and Relli's fate is unclear. Rita and Roma and their two brothers, Chaim and Paweł, whom I also know well, are all determined to bring the girl back to Israel. My time in Warsaw would allow me to have direct contact with Mr. Abramowicz and negotiate the child's release and immigration.

I empathized immediately, recalling my own family that had been murdered in the Holocaust. The only survivors were my two sisters, who are in Russia, and with whom I haven't been able to make contact yet. Rita and Roma's request touched my heart. I knew I had to say yes. I knew I had to take on this humane mission.

We agreed to meet again two days later. When we did, they gave me all the information they had. It was indeed a very complex mission. They hoped that now that he'd lost his wife, Mr. Abramowicz might be more flexible. There will be plenty of difficulties, but I wholeheartedly hope I can succeed.

Warsaw, January 10th, 1950

I've only arrived a week ago and have already done so much that it seems like I've been here forever. Work at the embassy is busy and riveting. Working with survivors wishing to come to Israel exposes me to human encounters and unbelievably heartfelt stories. We work long hours, trying to answer all applications and do our best to help. I've received a studio apartment with a kitchenette and small bathroom. It's small but pretty and tastefully furnished. It's on the second floor of the villa where the ambassador, Israel Barzilai, nicknamed Julek, lives with his wife Chava, whom everybody calls Eva. Julek and Eva are both members of Kibbutz Negba. They are here with their two children, ten-year-old Adda and five-year-old Avner. The villa also contains another apartment, where Azriel and Rivka (Gurffain) Uchmani, members of Kibbutz Ein Shemer, live with their fifteen-year-old daughter Rachel. The villa is located on Aldony Street in the Saska Kępa suburb. It's a quiet side street shaded by beautiful trees. The villa is surrounded by a blooming garden, and it's all so friendly and inviting.

In my very first conversation with the ambassador I shared my private mission with him. The ambassador listened carefully, stood up, walked over, put his hand on my shoulder and said, Tzipora, you'll receive any kind of help you need from me. I wish you the best of luck! His warm words encouraged me to no end.

Warsaw, January 18th, 1950

Today I finally located and met Relli. People here don't have phones in their homes, and so making plans in advance is almost impossible unless done in writing. I wrote to Mr. Abramowicz immediately upon my arrival and he called the embassy. When we spoke on the phone I explained my purpose. Though he was hesitant, he promised to meet me and hear me out. The fact that he didn't turn me down immediately was encouraging. In the meantime, he gave me the address where I could find the child.

My first meeting with her was tense. I realized I was facing a very difficult, twofold challenge: first I had to acquire the child's trust, and then I had to succeed in my negotiation to release her from her adoptive father. This double challenge would require lots of mental prowess, resourcefulness, and patience.

Acting on the ambassador's advice, I went to the address given to me along with an embassy security guard. On 6 Wolska Street, in a tiny two-room apartment on the second floor, I met the Gilewski family. Stefan Gilewski and his wife, Helena, the late Janina Abramowicz's sister, were practically the girl's aunt and uncle.

They informed me that after his wife died, about five months ago, Józef Abramowicz moved in with his girlfriend, whom he seemed to have been involved with for a while before Janina's death. They lived in the Praga suburb beyond the Wisła River, but the girlfriend didn't want the Jewish girl in her home. He therefore rented out the apartment on the corner of 47 Pszyokopowa and 90 Grzybowska Street, where the Abramowicz family used to live with their adoptive daughter before Janina's death.

The apartment was rented out to a couple who had one daughter. The daughter received Relli's old bedroom and, according to the lease, Relli's bed was placed in the entry hallway. The late Janina Abramowicz had enrolled the child in the Communist party school before her death, and Relli was now a sixth grade student. The school was far from home and she had to take the tram. It featured a long school day and included lunch, therefore she spent most hours of the day there. Upon her return from school she wandered the streets and went to see her aunt and uncle in the late afternoon. She did her homework and had dinner at their place, before going back to the apartment that used to be her home, but was now only a place where she was allowed to spend the night in the hallway.

When I arrived at the Gilewski home along with the embassy guard I received a warm welcome, even though I'd arrived unannounced. They seemed to love the girl very much, but they were living in poverty and were limited in their ability to care for her. The day of my visit was wintry and stormy, and I found Relli in the couple's bed with a fierce cold, burning with fever.

Mrs. Gilewski was concerned about the fact that later that night the sick child had to go sleep elsewhere. There was no suitable place for her to spend the night in their apartment. My attempt to speak to Relli all failed. When she heard I'd come from Israel bearing greetings from her family, she turned to face the wall, covered her head with the blanket, and wouldn't even look at me. Stefan and Helena's pleading was no help. Relli refused to communicate with me.

Disappointed, I said goodbye to Mr. and Mrs. Gilewski, promising to return within two days to check on Relli, but also to attempt once again to get to know her. As I said, this is not going to be easy. I have to meet with Mr. Abramowicz and figure out his plan of action. I have a feeling that he foresaw Relli's response, which is why he allowed me so generously to meet her without any preparation. The truth is, right now I'm completely helpless, but I know I cannot let go until I complete the mission I'd undertaken.

Warsaw, January 20th, 1950

I returned to a second visit at the Gilewski home today. We'd agreed I'd come early this time, before Relli returned from school. And hoped she'd get better by the time I came. This plan was designed to give me the opportunity to speak to them in private.

When I arrived I was glad to hear that Relli had recovered and returned to school. They called her Lala, and I concluded I'd best use that name too, the name she is accustomed to. They are modest, warm, and amiable people. Mr. Gilewski is an autodidact. He works in electronics, mostly fixing radios. His workshop is located in the main room of their apartment. The other tiny room is mainly taken up by a bed and a closet. Mrs. Gilewski is a homemaker. Their quality of life seems rather low.

I listened to their personal story, becoming familiar, for the first time, with non-Jewish Holocaust survivors. I learned that they were part of the network that saved Relli's life during the war. They hid her family photos, left by her parents as a keepsake, above the fireplace in their home. The photos miraculously survived the destruction of the city and were found again upon the liberation of Warsaw among the ruins of their old home, by Janina.

They were exiled to labor camps in Germany immediately after the Warsaw Rebellion of August 1944 and were separated there: Stefan spent time in labor camps and was finally released from Buchenwald, while Helena was in different camps. On the day of liberation she was accidentally shot, and her right triceps were torn clean off. She still limps and suffers pain to this day. Their son-in-law, husband of their eldest daughter, Marysia, was exiled along with them. Marysia, who was pregnant, Krysia, and Tadek, their three children, all stayed behind in Warsaw. Janina and Helena had another brother, who had also been sent to Germany. He and Marysia's husband died in captivity, probably at Dachau. And so their eldest daughter gave birth to Małgosia in the beginning of summer 1945 without a father, and has been raising her alone with her parents' modest help.

I'd always known that the Polish people had also suffered under German occupation, but this was the first time I met a Polish family that had actually undergone physical and emotional suffering and grief, just like our people.

Helena and Stefan commended my intention of removing Relli from Mr. Abramowicz's care and handling her immigration to Israel, where she could be with her biological family. They love her and admire her talents and the grace with which she'd dealt with being orphaned twice. Most of all, they are sad to see her adoptive father neglect the child. They continue to marvel at her strength. They both would have wanted to see Relli, or Lala, as they call her, grow up to be a Polish woman and remain in their family, as the late Janina would have wanted it, but they know they cannot take responsibility for her. Therefore, as much as it pains them, they think it would be best if the child returns to her roots. They promised to help me as much as they can.

As they warned me against Relli's decisive objection to let go of her new identity, a knock came at the door—Relli arriving from school. She seemed surprised to see me and said assertively that she had plenty of homework and no interest in speaking to me. She still agreed to sit down and have tea and some of the cake I'd brought. While we were having tea we talked about the books she was reading. I must admit, I was impressed by the number and quality, as well as with her knowledge of Polish literature. She's only ten-and-a-half, and she'd already read Sienkiewicz's The Teutonic Knight, as well as his trilogy, With Fire and Sword, The Deluge, and Sir Michael. She read his novel Quo Vadis, and of course In Desert and Wilderness. She also read Prus's Pharaoh and The Doll, and even Mickiewicz's Pan Tadeusz. Truly amazing!

She's a very skinny girl, poorly dressed, her fair braids tied with ribbons that had seen better days. She wears round thick framed glasses that are missing the right lens. When she saw my inquiring look she explained that her right eye worked fine. The lens had broken accidentally, but she really didn't need it, because it was only her left eye that was problematic. She gave me this entire explanation before I could even ask about the missing lens. I figured out on my own that no one was able to pay to have her glasses fixed, which is why Relli came up with this explanation, which she found convincing.

I invited her to walk me out to the tram stop, but she turned me down politely yet firmly. I said goodbye to all three of them and promised to come back again a week later. I suggested that maybe on my next visit Relli would accompany me somewhere where we could have some fun. She didn't make any promises, but neither did she say no. Maybe I've cracked my way in… I sighed with relief and left.

I feel encouraged by Mr. and Mrs. Gilewski's positive attitude and by their promise to assist me, most of all in convincing the child. She's a hard nut to crack and I'm going to have to work hard to gain her trust.

Tomorrow is my first meeting with Mr. Abramowicz. I know it won't be easy.

Warsaw, February 3rd, 1950

My meeting with Mr. Abramowicz has been postponed. He lives in Praga, a suburb close to Saska Kępa, not far from my home. I will probably meet him tomorrow at a nearby restaurant.

In the meantime, with his approval and Hela (Helena) and Stefan's encouragement, Relli agreed to spend a few hours with me.

This afternoon I picked her up from the Gilewski home and we took a taxi straight to the Bristol Hotel. It's the fanciest hotel in Warsaw, and used to be famous in its elegance even before the war. Two families of embassy employees live there. The entry hall is attached to a very nice café which serves delicacies even to patrons who aren't hotel guests. As we walked in, I glanced at Relli and could tell she was charmed by the beauty and splendor of the place.

Relli was wearing her school uniform, which girls here wear over their regular clothing. In Polish, this uniform is called a fartuszek—a shiny satin apron reminiscent of a robe in black or navy, knee-length and buttoned in front. Relli's is navy blue with a white collar, which unfortunately looks quite gray and must not have been washed in a while. The collar is tied by two grayish white laces. I realized she preferred to keep wearing her school uniform because she had nothing nicer to wear. I made no remark on the matter.

She kept rubbing the laces between her fingers, out of embarrassment, or perhaps nervousness, which was entirely understandable, though she tried to disguise her emotions as much as a ten-year-old can. At any rate, one of the laces eventually broke, which made her very sad. This was going to be a problem, she explained, Because Aunt Hela won't have time to sew it today and tomorrow I won't be able to wear this shirt for gym class. She seemed truly concerned.

Did you have gym class today? I asked.

No, Relli said, explaining, the shirt I'm wearing today is actually a pajama top from my aunts in Palestine. It's bright turquoise with a white collar. It's made of a soft wrinkle-free fabric. I sleep with it inside-out and then in the morning turn it right-side-in so that I can use the white collar over my navy blue apron at school. Since it's so soft, I wear it in gym class too.

A truly multi-purpose shirt, I said with a smile, and complimented her efficient and varied use of a pajama top. I was impressed by Relli's resourcefulness: having nothing, she'd managed to find solutions to her need, pretending everything was fine. She truly was a mature girl with admirable mental resources.

As we spoke, a waitress came by with a dessert cart. This is a Polish custom: the cart is loaded with the café's entire dessert menu, and the customer chooses one right from the cart.

Relli's eyes widened. I guessed she'd never seen such a variety of cakes in her life. She was thrilled.

You can choose whatever you like, and as much as you like, I said, trying to win her heart and show her a good time.

Relli consulted with the waitress, looked over all the cakes, and finally chose a Napoleon cake, the largest of three available sizes. The cake had two layers of thin and crispy puff pastry on both sides of a thick layer of yellowish vanilla cream. Above the top layer of pastry was a gleaming white dusting of confectioner's sugar, sprinkled generously. Relli also chose a tall chocolate torte with dark chocolate cream and layers of dark dough and light milk chocolate, and a cherry torte made of light flaky dough studded with large, dark, wine-colored cherries. The top layer of the torte was covered with shiny glazed cherries that made it look especially appetizing. The desserts were very large and smelled wonderful. We also ordered a pot of tea. I watched, mesmerized, as Relli bit into each cake, devouring them one by one. I noted how politely she ate, using a knife and fork and chewing with her mouth closed. Even when a cherry pit found its way into her mouth, she covered her mouth with her hand and spat it out daintily before placing it in her plate. The desserts were gone. After two cups of tea, she seemed to have had enough.

We chatted about this and that and I felt we were both having a nice time. I was about to ask for the check when I saw Relli's eyes wandering over to the next table. I saw her staring at an enormous glass goblet filled with strawberries and cream. I didn't know they serve fruit here, she said. That's too bad, I would have ordered that.

It was important to me that Relli leave our meeting in high spirits. You think you'd be able to finish that? I asked.

Of course! Said Relli. I love strawberries and cream, and they must taste especially good in such a nice, big goblet.

Without further ado I asked the waitress to get us the exact same dish. It's for two, the waitress commented politely.

Relli sensed my hesitation and said, That's fine, I can finish it myself!

An enormous goblet filled with fresh strawberries and hills of whipped cream was brought to the table. Relli began to eat, first with fervor, then slower, but she wasn't one to admit that she had trouble finishing. She ate with quiet concentration, taking pleasure in every spoonful. To my growing amazement, she emptied the entire goblet. I couldn't believe the appetite on such a skinny child.

We left the hotel and got into a taxi. A few moments into our ride, Relli complained that she wasn't feeling well. Before she even finished speaking, she began throwing up uncontrollably. Strawberries, cream, and cherries that had not yet been digested smeared over her school uniform, my jacket, but mostly over the taxi's seats and floor. The vomit came in waves that the child seemed unable to control. The driver pulled up in a rage and demanded that we get out. His loud screaming about how we'd destroyed his taxi stayed with me for a long time as I stood in the street with the girl, who never stopped throwing up. Her face turned very pale, and I was truly worried.

Finally she stopped vomiting and got some color back in her cheeks. She felt relieved but very embarrassed, and said, I'm sorry for making such a mess. I guess the fruit wasn't fresh, otherwise why would I get so sick all of a sudden?

You're probably right, I said, avoiding an argument.

Had it never occurred to Relli that she'd eaten too much? Perhaps it did occur to her but she didn't want to say it. Either way, we both learned a lesson. She would keep her lesson to herself, while I can share mine here: I must find a way to the girl's heart that is not so corrupted. This is yet another challenge for me, since I have no experience in childcare. This special child truly is a challenge. On the one hand, she's mature and serious for her age, and yet still a child, only a little over ten years old, living in poverty. She's smart, but very sensitive; she's opinionated and stubborn. I have a lot to learn!

Warsaw, March 1st, 1950

My weekly meetings with Relli continue. She's slowly opening up to me, sharing her world with me. Thus, for instance, she told me about a school assignment—to prepare a special notebook about the life of Josef Stalin. Each child has to buy special pictures to glue inside the notebook, and of course to read and write about Stalin's life. Stores were already selling designated kits, which included a notebook, pictures, and decorations for this assignment. The teacher explained to the students that on May 1st a large gift exhibition would open at the National

Museum in Warsaw in celebration of the leader's birthday. The gifts would be prepared by factory workers and craftsmen from all over Poland. The projects prepared by students from schools the country over would also be shown in the exhibition, and later, after all Polish citizens had a chance to see them, would be delivered to Russia on a special train. Relli explained that the kits came in different versions and prices; the most expensive ones contained lots of pictures of Stalin. I realized that this project meant a lot to her, and surprised myself by suggesting that we go together and purchase a kit for her. We strolled down the main street, walking into several stationery stores. Relli looked at some kits and when I encouraged her to pick the prettiest one she responded with untypical spontaneity, almost knocking me down with a hug and a kiss. It was the first time I felt her letting herself get close to me.

After I bought the kit she chose, I told her I wanted to buy her a gift for her birthday that was coming up on March 11th. She was stunned. You know, Tzipora, she said, I've never had a birthday party. Maybe my real parents, Franka and Michał, maybe they threw me a party when I was little? I don't remember them at all, and even if they did, I can't remember it because I was too little. Janina told me that Józef smuggled me out of the ghetto in a sack in the middle of the night and that I woke up at their home. I remember waking up there, and I remember everything ever since. I've been Lala since then. I just stopped being Relli, the Jewish girl I once was. But I can't remember anything that happened before age four, when I was a Jewish girl in the ghetto with my real parents, right?

The question remained hanging in air. Choked with tears, I couldn't answer.

Relli looked at me and continued calmly. That was back when I was Jewish, but you know I'm Polish now, right? I'm so glad I met you, Tzipora, because now I know that Jews aren't scary. They're even nice. For example, you want to get me a birthday gift! I can't believe it! She added that she would love a sweater, but it had to be red, with lapels and buttons in front. Warsaw stores didn't sell machine made knits, but only handmade sweaters. The selection and sizes were extremely limited. We walked into many shops until we found one she liked and that suited her. I already said she's opinionated, didn't I? Very much so. Another hurdle passed.

Warsaw, March 15th, 1950

Along with my weekly meetings with Relli I've also been meeting with Józef Abramowicz. The ambassador has been a big help in my negotiation with Mr. Abramowicz, and so has my friend Towa Klaiff-Rubinsztein. Two long conversations with Mr. Abramowicz later, and it turned out that for a hefty, but reasonable sum of money, he would be prepared to enter the special legal proceedings of annulling an adoption. He agreed to give his approval for Relli to leave Poland for Israel. He's now living with his girlfriend, whom he plans to marry, and this woman does not wish to take Lala in, he explained. Even though I love my daughter, I have no real way to continue to raise her as Janina and I had planned. Life strides on and we each have to adjust to changes. Lala will have to do so too. I know her well; she has no intention of leaving Poland or abandoning her Polish identity. But she'll have no choice. She's a minor and cannot decide her own fate.

As you know, Miss Neshem, I was personally acquainted with her parents. They were special people of noble spirits. They kept their dignity even in the worst of times, through travails one cannot understand or describe in words. Michał, the father, was a very practical man, organized, sociable, sensitive, broadminded, and a fascinating conversationalist. The war, the occupation, and the persecution undermined the world he knew. He lived in Danzig for a few years and was fluent in German language and culture. He couldn't comprehend what was going on around him, and was constantly disoriented in the new reality. Franka, his wife, was a beautiful woman, very sensitive. Her beauty and her tenderness were naturally preserved even through those dark days. She was an educated woman, knowledgeable in literature and art. Unfortunately, her nerves were shot during those years in the ghetto, and especially in the last months of her life in the Trawniki Camp. We offered to take her in as well, not together with Relli, that was impossible. Hiding her, just like hiding her daughter, was a gamble and involved many risks, but we were willing to do it. However, she decided to share her fate with her husband and father to the bitter end. She wouldn't leave them, not even for Relli. Both of them loved that girl, their only child, so much. In a brave, unusual, almost superhuman act, they decided to part with her, giving her a chance to survive. None of us knew if it would work. It was a huge gamble. They felt that their own fate had been sealed, and decided, in spite of the terrible pain involved, to save their little girl.

When we brought her home from the ghetto my wife and I were astounded by how those parents had managed to bring her up to be so polite, confident, wise, and adaptable in the hostile world of the ghetto, with its insufferable conditions. I still don't understand it. Janina and I were impressed to learn how formative those first years of childhood are. We withstood great danger while hiding Lala. Our friends and family were all part of it, supporting us. And we succeeded.

But now fate is knocking on her door once again. You, Miss Neshem, have come here, and she might go live with her father's family and return to being Jewish. Perhaps that is what's meant to be?

I know that when she learns I've agreed to give her up she would hate me for it, but in my new familial situation she no longer has a place in my life. She would always remain in my memory as my only daughter. I do not have, nor will I have, biological children of my own.

I trust you, Miss Neshem, to understand that giving her up requires compensation for all the years my wife and I raised her. I'm not asking for a thing in return for the risk we put ourselves in; we did that for her and for her parents, who were our friends, though our acquaintance was short-lived. We did the same thing for other Jews. We never asked for anything in return for our rescue missions. I've helped many Jews and supported the Jewish underground in the ghetto. I even risked my life, visiting Lala's parents at Trawniki before they were murdered. But enough, I didn't come here to boast. Janina and I did these things because we still had a heart and a conscience, even in the darkest years of Poland's existence. An outsider would never be able to understand what the Jews had been through, and what we've been through. I'm sorry, I can see I've said too much. Let's return to the business at hand.

I sat across from him and listened, taking in every word and sentence of his long, humane, and moving monologue. I tried— am still trying—to figure out this man. Jòzef Abramowicz is an exceptional person. A handsome man, a good conversationalist, and a friendly sort. Very intelligent and sharp, he also has a sense of humor. I'm beginning to understand, or come closer to understanding, his courage and his late wife's. How much will power, bravery, and resourcefulness were required of them to take in a Jewish girl in 1943, at the heart of Warsaw, walking distance from the walls of the ghetto, which cut through their street, dividing it into an Aryan side and a Jewish side.

Can we, who have not been there to experience the horrors, ever understand their valor? Not only the valor of the victims, but that of the few who attempted to rescue them, putting their own lives, their families' lives, even their friends' lives, at risk, as Józef had said.

I admit there is something captivating about him; or perhaps misleading. I'm becoming more and more convinced that people who risked their own lives to save Jews are unusual people in the average human landscape. Józef Abramowicz is indeed a multi-faceted man. I know his actions do not need my scholarly interpretations; Relli is living proof of what he's accomplished, and there are other Jews that are alive today thanks to him.

Now, sitting here to write and recounting my conversation with him, I too, like him, wonder about the hidden agenda of fate, which has summoned me here at the right time, when Józef is prepared to give up Relli. He demands compensation, but the starting point is his willingness to let go of her completely. Fate had put me in the path of her aunts on Dizengoff Street in Tel Aviv the day before my departure to Poland. Fate had also given me the Ambassador, Julek, who volunteered to support me through this journey. He opened his heart and offered his wisdom and connections.

Relli doesn't know any of this yet, and it's too soon to tell her. I continue to make efforts to get closer to her, as much as she lets me. I do my best to win her heart and her trust. She sees me as a friend of her family's from Israel, which I am, but to her the connection ends there. She is unaware of my activity here. According to my request, the Gilewski family hasn't revealed a thing to her yet. Jòzef barely sees her anymore, and anyway, there's no chance of him telling her.

I continue to wonder through sleepless nights: how will this all transpire? How would I be able to help this girl cross the bridge from Polish to Jewish? I have no idea. With the intuition of a child, she tries to preserve her independence, taking one step closer to me and two steps back. I am constantly concerned.

In the meantime, an application has already been submitted to the court to annul the adoption. Let's hope the process doesn't take too long. Later on I'll need to receive an official approval to take her out of Poland, since she's a minor traveling without a family member. None of this can be done against her will. The road is long. The conquering of Relli may last a long time yet and will probably be very, very difficult. It's already a bumpy ride. But I mustn't despair. I promised her family, and more important, myself. I must succeed.

Warsaw, April 10th, 1950

I've been trying for a long time now to invite Relli to spend the weekend with me. She always turns me down politely, but her excuses reflect her unwillingness to get closer to me. She's gracious, yet stubborn. She always makes clear without explicitly saying so, that she wants nothing to do with me and everything I represent—Israel, Judaism, her biological family, and her old identity, the one she's fighting not to return to. She insists that her name is Lala, and explains to me repeatedly in her very mature way that she'd been raised Polish and wants to continue to live that way. She refuses to see the reality, in which she doesn't have a real home, only a place where she's allowed to sleep. Her adoptive father no longer cares for her and is no longer attentive to her needs. Her Polish aunt and uncle shower her with love and devotion, but their means are very limited. I feel that the child does indeed understand reality, but tries to push it away. I wonder at how she's coping with this, having nobody to share her fears, her dilemmas, and her most hidden thoughts with. She truly is a little girl alone, simple as that.

On the one hand, she enjoys her relationship with me, the gifts and the fun, but on the other hand she doesn't want the relationship to become any closer and is anxious about what it represents: her return to her previous identity, to Judaism, with everything that goes along with it. She's anxious about detaching herself from everything she knows, for better or worse. Ultimately, moving from Poland to Israel, that unknown world, must seem impossible.

As a child she'd experienced enough disasters and crises for a lifetime. The horrors of war, life in the ghetto, being apart from her parents and grandfather, and finally losing them at age four. Getting used to a new identity, a new name, new relatives, and a strange environment, living in hiding under a false identity. She became orphaned once again at age ten, and has since lived a life of loneliness, emotional want, and social and economic strife. Then, on top of all that, the estranged environment of the Communist school. I keep repeating these things to myself; and that's only part of what she's been through.

To this day, her childhood had been overflowing with sorrow and pain; the life of two girls, Relli and Lala. I sometimes still can't understand how she'd become strong enough and wise enough to take the bit of good in all the bad that her young life had to offer. She has a strong personality and impressive will power. She's assertive, yet polite and graceful. She's intelligent; books are her best friends. She never had a good friend with whom she shared all her secrets. Her entire life was a secret that she was not allowed to reveal.

I'm putting all of this in writing because these thoughts are on my mind all the time. Her skinny figure follows me everywhere. I admit I find her company compelling, but I'm well aware of the challenge in acquiring her trust and her affections. I'm always put to the test with her.

I already like her a lot. She's managed to weave tender, yet strong webs around my heart and mind. She's entrapped me. Nevertheless, I always remember my mission. How can I convince her to pass the threshold, to cross the lines, to go back to being Relli… She does not want that at all. It's so hard. She's happy to receive all my gifts and was touched when I paid to have her glasses fixed. And yet, none of these gestures is enough to convince her to visit my home and perhaps spend the weekend. She's consciously resisting getting closer, emotionally, and, just to be on the safe side, geographically.

Spring is here and it's almost time for Passover. I promised myself this time I wouldn't give up. I have to find a way to get Relli to celebrate the Passover Seder at the embassy. I've recruited Stefan and Helena to this cause, and made sure to receive approval from Józef in advance. Stefan and Helena already had a long conversation on the subject with Lala. They told her it was nothing more than an invitation to spend the weekend in a pleasant environment. They couldn't really explain what the Seder would involve, but I'd told them there would be a festive dinner with singing and merriment.

Finally, to my great joy, Relli accepted. Nevertheless, I knew that even though I'd crossed the first hurdle by receiving a positive response, I would now face the true test: the event had to impress her, awaken her curiosity, and make her eager for further visits. It's so important that she get to know the Jewish faith out of her own will and perhaps want to become a part of our people and culture. This is crucial in order to make her want to be Relli again.

I'm lost in a storm of thoughts, drowning in the challenges at hand. How will this all be done? I tell myself I must hope for the best. I'm not a religious woman, but I hope this time my silent prayers are heard.

Warsaw, Passover, 1950

It's late at night. Relli finally fell asleep, excited and filled with impressions, and I'm trying to recount our experience of the wonderful Seder dinner and the following day.

Relli arrived in the afternoon as scheduled. She came alone by tram, wearing the white shirt and red sweater we bought for her together, which were both very flattering. Her two braids were carefully tied with new white ribbons that Helena had bought for her especially. We had tea together and some strawberry jam I'd made, and all the while Relli commented on the beautiful china and silverware. She has a sharp eye and a taste for beauty. I took the time to recap the meaning of Passover in general and the Seder dinner in particular. She asked some questions, took an interest in my explanation, and I think I managed to arouse her curiosity.

In the evening we went downstairs to the embassy reception hall. Tables had been set up to form a long rectangle, so that all the guests could see each other's faces. Julek sat at the head of the table, surrounded by his wife Eva and their two children, Adda and Avner. Embassy workers and their families, most of them Israeli delegates, and some local employees—Warsaw Jews—were all seated around the table. There were also some community leaders along with their families. There were plenty of children. The tables were covered with white cloths, blooming flowers and branches, delicate china and wine glasses, and colorful Haggadas. All was illuminated softly by two large chandeliers hanging from the high ceiling. The festive atmosphere was completed by candles. It was breathtaking.

Relli paused at the entrance, gaping at the beauty of the hall and all the cheerful guests greeting each other with those words she couldn't understand: Chag Sameach. What she could clearly detect was the joy in people's faces, as well as the many children, all dressed formally, their faces beaming. We sat in our assigned seats, close to the Barzilai family. Lala stared with wonder at Adda, a pretty, tan girl, her dark braids also tied with white ribbons, giggling with her little brother Avner.

Julek welcomed the guests in Polish and Hebrew. He explained the essence of the holiday and the special significance of celebrating it in Warsaw, in 1950, at the Israeli embassy, in the presence of both Jewish Holocaust survivors and Jewish citizens of the independent State of Israel. He read the Haggada and invited some of the guests to read portions and the children to sing. Adda and Avner and some other children sang the "Four Questions" together, as well as other songs, while Julek accompanied them on the black grand piano. Lala sat beside me, hypnotized, insatiable before all this beauty, riveted with awe.

When we finished reading and reached mealtime, she glanced suspiciously at the unfamiliar dishes: matzo, hardboiled eggs in salt water, stuffed fish balls, chicken soup with matzo balls, and other typical Jewish dishes. She tasted everything and especially liked the matzo balls. After dinner we read and sang some more. The Seder was tasteful, festive, and filled with the honest excitement of all participants.

At the end of the ceremony, the guests mingled around the hall, chatting. The children gathered around the piano. To my surprise, Adda approached Relli, offered her hand, and introduced herself in slow, hesitant, yet clear Polish. Relli also offered a hand and introduced herself as "Relli." I trembled to hear her using that name and realized a change might have occurred. Adda pulled Relli into the circle of children. Later, as the guests began to leave, I introduced Relli to Julek and Eva. In spite of the burden of hosting they both took the time to get to know her. Familiar with the difficult and complicated legal proceedings and budding relationship between us, Julek took the time to chat with the girl, ask how she liked the Seder, and repeat his explanation of the longstanding tradition of this holiday, reminding us each year of the exodus. He expressed his hope that soon she, Relli, would come to live in my apartment at the embassy house and be friends with Adda. Relli shook his hand and curtsied, as is the habit of Polish girls when interacting with grownups.

As we left the hall and turned to climb up to my apartment, Relli paused, turned to me, and asked, Tzipora, it's as if I was liberated from Egypt tonight too, right?

I hugged her and said, Yes, Relli, it is.

Warsaw, April 28th, 1950

After Passover things progressed smoothly, most hurdles removed. I realized Relli had crossed over. I could now divide time into Before the Seder and After the Seder.

As I'd hoped, the night had made an impression on her, opening her mind. She began to see where this invisible train was taking her. Aunt Hela informed me that Relli was charmed upon her return from the visit. She couldn't stop talking about it. Most of all, she talked about the children she'd met. She liked them all, and especially Adda. She told her aunt and uncle that now she had a new friend.

Writing this now, I realize what a large role Adda played in introducing Relli to Judaism and to Israelis. Children have a language of their own. Seemingly, these two girls have nothing in common. Relli doesn't speak a word of Hebrew and Adda only knows a few words of Polish, but the day after the Seder they played together for hours, staying close together even as we had a second holiday dinner at the Barzilai home. The two of them had formed a deep, meaningful bond.

I keep seeing the image of Adda approaching Relli at the Seder and offering her hand, pulling her into the circle. Little Adda is like Moses, offering his hand to help Relli cross an imaginary Red Sea onto the other bank, where she belongs.

The legal proceedings are progressing well. I hope to see the adoption annulled within a few days. Relli's birth certificate had been reconstructed, since without it she has no official identity. Józef agreed to testify in court, giving Relli's parents' names and stating her date of birth as March 13th, 1939. I thought that was a little odd, seeing as how the family in Israel said that her birth announcement had her birthday on March 11th. I didn't want to argue with Józef. This seems like a minor detail. The important thing is, we're moving forward.

When all procedures are completed, I plan to take Relli in to live in my apartment. The ambassador has already agreed, even hinting at the matter on Passover. Luckily, the sofa in my apartment opens into a bed and is very comfortable. We can have breakfast together before I leave for work and dinner when I return. For lunch, I've located a pleasant and homey restaurant walking distance from the house, called Słodka Dziurka; A sweet little nook where two sisters prepare homemade food. When I'm at work, Relli can still have a homemade lunch. She can spend the morning and the afternoon with Adda, who is homeschooled. I would, of course, have to convince her to leave school before the end of the academic year. I'd also have to buy her some clothes and begin to prepare her for the journey. There is much to be done, a long road ahead, but ever since the Seder I feel that the train has left the station where it had been previously stalled.

I hope to find a family or a female immigrant traveling alone among the many I handle at the embassy—someone who would agree to accompany the child on the way to Israel, taking responsibility for her. The journey begins with a train ride through Poland, Czechoslovakia, Austria and Italy, all the way to Venice; from Venice the journey continues on ship to Haifa. The entire voyage lasts ten days. I hope to receive approval to join the train ride so that I can escort my own private immigrant to Venice.

There I go, getting ahead of myself. All procedures are slow-moving. It's the end of April and the process could still take several more months. I hope that by October things will finally be ready for Relli's immigration to Israel.

In the meantime, Relli has asked to stay in school at least until the beginning of May. They are preparing for the May 1st parade and it's important to her to participate. Her attitude toward school is complicated. On the one hand, she does not like the Communist school, to say the least; on the other hand her love of learning is practically an obsession and she never agrees to miss a school day. She's a very hardworking, ambitious child.

Warsaw, May 5th, 1950

I met with Relli yesterday, hearing her impressions of the May 1st parade. She couldn't figure out why I hadn't taken part in it, but was glad to have me listen to her experiences.

First, she described the entire school's visit to the National Museum. They visited the exhibition of gifts to be sent to Stalin from the Polish people in celebration of his birthday. She was especially impressed by a giant chocolate statue of Stalin made in the famous Wedel factory in Warsaw. The statue was placed in front of the museum and mesmerized her and her friends with its size. Relli was sorry they couldn't linger for longer in front of it. How did the artist manage to make each hair on Stalin's mustache and each feature of his face with chocolate? It was incredible!

Later, they walked through the museum, seeing lots of different items made in factories around Poland. An especially large hall was designated for hundreds of assignments prepared by Communist school students. I remembered how much time Relli had dedicated to preparing her assignment, and how we'd bought the kit together. Her teacher explained that all assignments from all schools were sent to the party headquarters, where the most outstanding ones were chosen—a few hundred—to be shown at the museum. Relli was doubtful that her assignment had won this honor. I didn't want to spoil her enthusiasm by telling her I didn't think it made much of a difference.

The parade was a thrilling experience for her. She walked down the streets of Warsaw with the Scouts that were active in her school. On top of a giant truck bed was an enormous globe painted with all continents and oceans. The globe was opaque but hollow, and contained dozens of white doves. It had a lid on top, where the North Pole would be, which the marchers could not see. The lid was tied with long red ribbons, and the scouts, among whom she marched, all walked around the truck, each holding the end of a red ribbon. When the truck rode slowly by the main state, a sign was given and the children pulled the ribbons. The lid opened and the doves all flew out at once into the heavens.

You see, Tzipora, she explained, the dove is a symbol of peace, and red is the color of Communism, and so we demonstrated that Communism would bring peace to all countries of the world. Isn't it a nice idea? The young Communist asked.

I nodded silently. I preferred to avoid the topic of world peace that Communist Russia would allegedly deliver.

Writing this now, I'm convinced that when Relli moves to Israel she would absorb some of our values and would one day become an enthusiastic patriot just as she is now a loyal Polish Communist.

I must remember that in spite of her difficulties at school, it is a major part of her life, and she internalizes everything she learns there. She also grew up in a Communist home and has been exposed to the ideology for years. I'd best not address the topic. I have enough challenges as it is.

My plan to have her move in with me in my single room makes most sense, but also poses another, more personal challenge. It means giving up my privacy and adapting to daily life with a stubborn child with a dark past. I'm an independent woman. I live alone according to my own habits. I've never raised a child. I love children and know how to spoil them. I'm very close with my friends' children back in Israel, and yet, living with one would mean gathering my strength each day anew.

No matter, Feigaleh, as my family and dearest friends call me. It'll be all right! It has to be! I've already overcome difficulty in my life. I'm sure I can do this, too.

Warsaw, May 18th, 1950

This afternoon, Stefan and Helena Gilewski visited my apartment. They asked to come and see for themselves where Lala would live after separating from them and her old life. I happily obliged. I like this couple and empathize with them. They've been the ones taking care of Lala ever since Janina died. Their love for her is apparent in everything they say and do.

Stefan, the man of action among the two, told me that last Sunday they took Lala on a morning walk in the most beautiful park in Warsaw—Łazienki Park. It's a large park with a beautiful statue of Chopin at the entrance, surrounded by red roses. Inside is a gorgeous castle that is open for tours, spacious expanses, lakes, and green trees shading the paths stretching all across the park. The name Łazienki comes from the public baths that used to serve the Polish nobles that lived in the castle.

The Gilewski couple and Lala walked for a short while, since Hela cannot walk too much, due to her limp. They then sat down in a pleasant spot and began talking to the child about her future.

At first, Lala was resistant, but finally she opened up, realizing that these two people were the closest people to her in the world. Stefan reminded her that they'd known her almost from the first day of her arrival from the ghetto, and how close they'd been all those years, spending many a happy and sad day together. They both told her how proud they were of her, and how they would have loved to see her staying in Warsaw and growing into a young Polish woman, an active member of Polish society, which Lala was so proud to be a part of.

Nevertheless, they reminded her, a person is not in control of his or her own destiny, and the hand of fate leads each of us down our own path, beyond what we can foretell. Unfortunately, they explained, they cannot assume responsibility for her upbringing and future education. They are doing everything they can under the circumstances, but seeing how her adoptive father had effectively abandoned her, they are unable to do more.

And now, fate has opened a window to a new life destined for her with her father's family. The new life would be taking place very far away, in a land that is warm and beautiful, with a large and loving family waiting for her. Tzipora was that family's representative, they explained.

Lala listened and began to cry, explaining her unwillingness to say goodbye to Poland, to Warsaw, to all her favorite spots, to the language, and most of all to them, her beloved aunt and uncle. What will I do when I feel homesick? She asked. Who will I speak to in Polish? How will I get Polish books? Where will my home be? Where will I live?

They explained that they didn't have answers to all her questions, but that they were hopeful and believed this was the right choice, to return to her birthright, to go back to being Relli.

We told her that you said all her aunts and uncles speak Polish and that they must have Polish books, too, they said. We also promised to send her books once in a while, and that we'd write to her, of course, and she'd write to us. Finally we told her we'd go see your apartment ourselves, so that we could see where she would spend her remaining months in Warsaw. We suggested that we keep seeing her while she lives here. We hope you have no objections. She'd already told us you live in a beautiful villa in Saska Kępa, surrounded by a garden, in a street shaded by trees. Still, we wanted to see it ourselves, and we promised Lala we'd do so.

Helena began to cry. It's going to be very hard to say goodbye to Lala, she said. She's my sister's only child and I feel as if I'm betraying my sister's memory by giving her up. I know there's no choice, and that's what hurts so much. Neither we nor Lala have any other choice.

I saw their honest sorrow and promised them that I would do everything in my power to ensure that Relli has a good future, certainly in the short term with me, but more important, in the long term with her family in Israel, whom I knew well and to whose kindness I could attest.

Miss Neshem, I want to tell you, said Stefan, that Lala admitted that holiday she celebrated with you, what's it called? Passover? That it moved her very much, and since then she keeps thinking she'd like to try to be Relli again. We agreed that it would be a trial run, though of course we know it's irreversible. Believe me, this is very difficult for us, but we're thinking about her future.

I was shaken up by their sincerity, their rationale, and their love for Relli. I'm grateful for their help in transferring her to my custody, and most of all for their emotional support.

Warsaw, June 3rd, 1950

The deed is done! Relli has moved in with me at the embassy home on 22 Aldony Street in Saska Kępa. I can't believe we've come this far. It's been almost six months since I moved to Warsaw, and the child is already living with me. She calls herself Relli and knows we are handling her upcoming immigration to Israel. The change is astounding. She's adjusting very well to living together. She's a very clean and tidy child, so our routine is harmonious. Of course we argue from time to time, but in general I am pleasantly surprised and most of my fear is gone. What a relief.

While I'm at work in town she preoccupies herself very well, cleaning up the room, washing the breakfast dishes, reading, and playing with Adda at the ambassador's home or in my apartment. Sometimes they go out to the nearby park. Their friendship enriches both their lives. Through Adda, Relli is becoming more and more familiar with Israel, and now she is curious about it. One day, I listened in on their conversation and heard Adda attempting to explain to Relli what a kibbutz is. Adda can only speak a little Polish and Relli speaks no Hebrew and certainly isn't familiar with the word or the concept of the kibbutz, which do not exist in Polish. Adda, who was born in Kibbutz Negba, tried to describe her home in Israel. It was quite a challenge. I held back my laughter, watching the girls communicate with lots of hand gestures and grave expressions. Relli seemed to have eventually comprehended the uniqueness of the place, since she later asked me if her family lives in a kibbutz and if she would live in one too, like Adda.

I told her she had three families in the city of Tel Aviv and one in the village of Pardess Hannah, so she wouldn't be living in a kibbutz in the near future. I myself have no idea which of her family members she is slated to live with.

Now I must take care of some matters concerning her health. I took her to see a dermatologist to look at the blisters on her right hand. There is one big and ugly one near her thumb, and other, smaller ones surrounding it. They are strange, dry, do not itch, but make her hand very unappealing. I've noticed others growing on the back of her hand. The doctor explained that the only cure is burning the blisters off with nitrogen, a painful procedure with a long recovery process. I discussed the idea with Relli. She's a brave child and agreed to undergo the treatment. She's ashamed of her blistered hand. It really did hurt, but now her hand is healing. Let's hope that's the end of it. The doctor warned us to be patient.

Warsaw, June 29th, 2015

It's been a week since the event that frightened me so much. Only now that I'm calm can I write about what happened on the night between June 21st and 22nd, the shortest night of the year. About a week before that night, Relli began to badger me about visiting Stefan and Hela that night and celebrating Wianki, which takes place on Noc Kupały, the Night of the Saints. She described the holiday in detail, as is her habit. It is an ancient holiday in Polish tradition and is also referred to as the Holiday of Love. In rural areas it has been a longstanding tradition to light bonfires near lakes or rivers, burn herbs, dance around the fires, and ask the saints for love and happiness. Young women like to make wreaths of wild flowers and stud them with candles. They throw the wreaths into the water as the boys attempt to fish them out. A boy who succeeds in pulling out a wreath returns to the group of girls and is introduced to the girl who made the wreath—fate chooses to bring together a young couple, and they take a walk in the forest or around the lake.

In Warsaw, families often go down to the banks of the Wisła and throw candle studded wreaths that float on the water in a myriad of colors and magical light. Thousands of wreaths are thrown in and the beaches come alive with song and dance.

Relli wanted very badly to join the Gilewskis in this celebration, the last Wianki of her life, she kept repeating.

I turned her down once and again, hesitant to let her visit her Polish family alone. Perhaps she still had doubts about the move? Perhaps she wasn't telling me the whole truth? Perhaps she won't want to come back? So many doubts plagued me, but the more I refused the more persistently she asked. She wouldn't let go, and I had difficulty putting my true fear into words.

Finally, worried that any further refusals would make her angry and cause her to become resistant again, I decided to allow this adventure. I gave her candy and gifts for everybody, for Aunt Hela and Uncle Stefan, and most of all for six-year-old Małgosia, their eldest granddaughter, whose father never returned from German captivity. Relli has known this girl from the day she was born, and they have a warm and loving relationship. She thanked me when I suggested we go together to buy Małgosia an item of clothing and a toy.

On the day of the holiday Relli went on her way, happy and content, laden with packages, and I hoped for the best. My hopes were crushed, though I must admit that I contributed to the misunderstanding that led me to a sleepless night. I did not properly assess, nor did I check with her, when the celebrations along the river ended. They took place on the opposite bank from our home, so I had no easy access. To make a long story short, night fell, the hours ticked by, and the girl did not return. There was no one I could call, and wandering the banks of the river among thousands of revelers was pointless. I saw the sky lit with fireworks and the river illuminated with thousands of candles. The sight was beautiful, but my fear exacerbated.

I waited. It was past midnight, and I watched the clock persistently. The girl was gone. I decided there was no point in going to bed since I wouldn't be able to sleep. My anger at myself for allowing her to go made me even more nervous than I already was. At seven in the morning I began to get ready for work. The girl was still gone.

I left a note by the phone, asking her to call me at the office immediately upon her return. The morning went by and the call did not come. I was very nervous and very, very worried. I planned to take a taxi after work and go to the Gilewski home to search for Relli.

Finally, around three in the afternoon, she called. She made the call immediately upon her return, as per my request, and went into a deluge of words, a rapid and cheerful description of the celebration. I couldn't get a word in edgewise, and so I made do with thanking my lucky stars for her return, putting reproach off until that evening.

When I returned home Relli welcomed me with a smile and a hug, continuing to describe her night, as if in direct continuation of our phone call. It turned out that the family had returned home after midnight. There was no way for her to return to Saska Kępa, and since she was very tired, Hela spread some blankets for her on the floor of Uncle Stefan's workshop, where the little reveler slept until the late hours of the morning.

Later that day she went to visit Marysia and Małgosia. Since she knew I was at work, Relli explained, she was in no rush to get back home.

By that point she'd managed to dispel my anger, and I decided to avoid any unnecessary conflict. The deed was done. She had a wonderful time with her family and was grateful to me for letting her attend. She'd innocently extended her absence without being aware of my concerns. How could she have known? The celebration always continues late into the night, and she assumed if I let her go I wouldn't be waiting for her to return early. I realized that my mistake was in not finding out beforehand how late the night would go. I continue to learn, even from my mistakes.

Warsaw, July 10th, 1950

Relli is growing used to her new name, and hardly ever introduces herself as "Lala" anymore. She herself declared that now that she is living with me at the embassy she is in the process of becoming an Israeli girl and must use the name given to her upon her birth by her parents. She looks at their photos a lot, making room for them in her life. She refers to Janina as her adoptive mother or her second mother, and calls Józef "Mr. Abramowicz."

When we ride the embassy car she chats to the driver, Czyżyk, an amiable and humorous Jewish redhead from Warsaw who knows the city well. She tells him, with explicit pride, that she is living with me and will soon go to Israel. It would take a few months, but she is already on her way, as she says.

I am astounded by her ability to adapt. It's as if she's stripped the character of Lala the Polish Girl and is now working hard and fast to enter her new character, Relli. When I take her with me to visit other embassy employees she makes friends with their children regardless of age or gender. She uses Polish, hand gestures and mimicking to play with them, and everyone enjoys themselves, most of all me. Sarah and Abraham Yeshuv of Tel Aviv, whom I've grown close to, have a three-year-old daughter named Rivka, whom everyone calls Kiki. She has curly red hair and is alert and sweet. Kiki is infatuated with Relli and asks that she babysit her. Sometimes Sarah takes the two girls down to the river or the park. Relli teaches Kiki Polish and her newly acquired knowledge is impressive. It relaxes me to know that while I'm at work Relli is in good hands. The Kopyt family, members of Kibbutz Naan, have also opened their home and hearts to us. Relli is friends with their son Assaf, who is about two years younger than her. When we visit, the two of them play checkers, dominoes, card games, and Battleship on graph paper, which Relli taught him. Again, proof that kids have a language of their own.

Back in the days when I was so concerned about dealing with Relli's transition into Judaism, life at the embassy, and preparations for making Aliyah, I never imagined that Israeli children would be my saviors, performing the difficult task at hand with such natural ease, using their kid language.

Adda is Relli's role model. The two girls had become instant friends. Relli is only one year older than Adda, but her stubborn personality and life experience make her much more mature. Adda is pretty, full bodied, tan, and sparkly eyed. She is wise, cheerful, and intelligent. During her time here, she'd managed to learn some Polish. Her vocabulary is sparse and her grammar is problematic, but she and Relli still communicate well. Relli enriches Adda's Polish and Adda teaches Relli some basic

Hebrew and tells her about Israel. They spend hours together. Their relationship, and others, make my life easier, knowing that Relli is in good company while I am at work.

I admire the warmth and affection with which Adda has opened her heart and arms, a kind of private acceptance project. With her natural grace and positivity, with the tender aroma of a happy childhood among a loving family, she projects a kind of invisible, yet strong aura onto Relli. She has taken Relli, who has always been alone, under her wing, sharing all the good in her life. Adda is the first Israeli Jewish girl Relli has met, and she is the perfect role model.

And another thing: I've noticed Relli zealously maintaining her independent personality. I ask myself: does she not also envy Adda? Perhaps both are true.

Warsaw, July 15th, 1950

Today's hair salon event was very dramatic and I'm writing about it without delay so as to convey its full essence and the turmoil that ensued. It's late, Relli has calmed down and fallen asleep, and I'm recounting...

When I returned from work today I found Relli on the sofa, her head buried in a pillow, and stifled weeps escaping into the room. I was alarmed. I sat down beside her and tried to get her to tell me what happened. She raised her head. Her hair was wild, her eyes red, and she pointed wordlessly toward the half-open bathroom door. I went over. She refused to join me. When I opened the door I could barely stifle my scream. It was utter chaos. The sink and bathtub were filled with murky soap water, in which floated string or hairs, it was hard to tell. They were in a variety of colors: yellow, different hues of brown, and even black. There were soapy puddles on the floor and lots of soppy towels strewn about. My floral cape, which always hangs on the door, and which I like to wear around my shoulders when I brush my hair before work so as not to get any on my clothes, was also dumped in one of the puddles, wet, stained, and shameful.

I kept asking, What happened? What happened? And was answered by wails coming from the sofa. I saw that the girl would not speak and decided to be practical. I went to the kitchen to make dinner, knowing that in spite of her thinness, Relli is a voracious eater. The smell of the omelet, the sight of sliced vegetables, and the hot cocoa and fresh bread I brought from the bakery worked their magic. Relli stood up, wiped her face, and joined me for dinner. We'll clean the bathroom after we eat, I said matter-of-factly. Bon appetit!

She seemed especially hungry, as if she hadn't eaten much all day. As she ate she slowly began to describe what had happened that day. After I left for work Adda came over as usual. The two of them went into the bathroom, undid their braids, and took turns brushing each other's hair, using my cape and having a lovely time. Then Relli suggested playing hair salon.

How do you play that? Asked Adda.

We'll bring your dolls over and open a salon.

What do you mean?

It's simple. We can wash the dolls' hair, dry it, and then give them hairdos or even haircuts.

The girls became excited. They went upstairs to the ambassador's apartment and chose about a dozen of the biggest, prettiest dolls from Adda's expansive collection. Eva, Adda's mother, has a sister in France who sends Adda lots of gorgeous dolls dressed in chic Parisian styles. The prettiest one is Nataly. She is almost twenty inches tall, and has long, shimmering brown curls wrapped in a purple velvet ribbon that matches her purple and pink dress.

Rejoicing, the girls brought the dolls back to my apartment and placed them on the sofa to wait for their hair appointments. One by one, the dolls' hair was cleaned with soap and rubbed with egg yolks to soften it. After washing the dolls' hair, the girls took towels out of the closet to dry the washed and sticky hair. But then, horror of horrors, the hair refused to dry. Some of it fell out in clumps, some in strands, some changed colors— bright blond turning faded yellow, gleaming brown becoming an indefinable murky tone, black turning gray. The dolls looked very pathetic indeed with their fabric or plastic scalps exposed, their heads covered in bald spots. Some of them got water in their eyes, which now refused to open or close, as they did before visiting Adda and Relli's hair salon. The sink and bathtub drains clogged with multicolored hair which now floated in the soap water, dyed with the removed hair color. The destruction was overwhelming. Nataly, who received a haircut before the wash, looked sad in her short, tangled hair, glued to her head in thin strands.

The two girls stood, stunned, in the messy bathroom, and began to cry—Adda over the loss of her pretty dolls, and Relli out of guilt for having proposed the idea. Adda got a hold of herself first. Let's go ask my mother for help, she offered.

Relli recoiled with shame and fear, but being the brave and responsible child that she is, said quietly, I'll tell her. It was my fault.

Adda hugged her. We're both to blame!

Thus, hand in hand, they climbed the stairs to the

ambassador's apartment and told Adda's mother what had happened, their story interrupted from time to time by bursts of tears.

Eva, a kindergarten teacher with a sensitive educational attitude, could barely make sense of the story. She decided to come and see with her own eyes. Back in my apartment, she collected the dolls and did her best to calm the girls. Seeing how sincere their regret was, she stifled her anger for the damage caused to the doll collection.

Adda returned home with her mother and the ruined dolls and Relli remained in the apartment, awaiting my return with a mixture of sorrow and fear for the punishment awaiting her. Her biggest fear, however, was that Julek and Eva wouldn't allow her to continue to play with Adda, realizing what a wild child she was, and what crazy ideas she had.

When she finished her story and we finished our dinner, I suggested we clean the bathroom together. I avoided voicing my opinion, myself unsure what the Barzilai family's reaction would be.

After Relli went to sleep, I went up to the ambassador's apartment to discuss the hair salon debacle. I was relieved to find that both Eva and Julek, though they were saddened by the destruction of Adda's doll collection, saw the girls' actions as innocent child play gone awry. They both emphasized how profound the girls' sorrow had been, and said they thought they'd already punished themselves enough.

I'll admit that as an adult with no children of my own, I was in a dilemma, but I took comfort in their forgiving attitude and in the fact that it never occurred to them to separate Adda and Relli. They were well aware of the beautiful friendship between the two and the mutual enrichment they offered each other.

As I sit here, writing, Relli stirred in her sleep and said, Tzipora, one thing's for sure: when I grow up I don't want to work at a hair salon.

Warsaw, August 5th, 1950

The Barzilais returned from their annual vacation the day before yesterday. Julek was on a business trip to Israel, while Eva and the children stayed with her sister in France. Last night they invited us to dinner at their place. Julek wanted to give Relli regards from her aunts and uncles in Israel. I met your father's sisters, Aunt Rita and Aunt Roma, he said. They were very interested to know all about your life in the embassy, and all about how you look and how you're feeling. They had lots of questions, all coming from their love and concern, and I was glad to give them very good answers. They came bearing lots of gifts for you from the entire family. Unfortunately I couldn't bring back the things they wanted me to, but I promised to tell you about them and everything they'd prepared for you. I hope you and Tzipora will forgive me and that you understand the limitations of my work, which prevented me from bringing the gifts.

I looked at Relli and couldn't help but see the disappointment on her face. Neither could Julek. He pulled Relli into a paternal hug and said, I know you're upset, but I do have a surprise for you: a gift from me. I hope you like it. He put his hand in his pocket and fished out a little green box with a small lock. Open it, he told Relli. Go on, open it.

Relli opened the box hesitantly. Her eyes lit up with a smile. Inside the box was a delicate silver chain with a small pendant.

Take it out and we can look at it together, he said.

Relli took out the chain and placed it on the table. The ambassador called Adda over, and the two girls stood on both his sides as little Avner nestled in his lap. Now children, who can tell me the shape of the pendant I brought Relli from Israel?

It's a Hanukiah, cried Avner!

You're almost correct, Julek said with a smile. It looks a lot like a Hanukiah, but it's a menorah with seven lamps, the symbol of the State of Israel.

It's so beautiful, gasped Avner.

Relli looked at the shimmering pendant, charmed. It's so special, she breathed.

Now let's put it around your neck. You'll be wearing the symbol of our country and yours around your neck.

Relli bent down and Julek gently put the necklace around her neck. Adda gave her a hand and led her to the closet. She opened the door to reveal a mirror so that Relli could look at herself and her new necklace.

Relli gazed into her reflection, then turned around and approached the ambassador. With the spontaneity of a child she reached out her arms, embraced his neck, and kissed his cheeks.

Afterwards

This jewel, as well as its original box, is still kept in Relli's home to this day. It would be another forty-four years before, in 1994, by a chance of fate, Relli's relationship with Adda Shalev-Barzilai would be renewed. Relli would then show her the silver pendant given to her by Adda's father in Warsaw in 1950. They would become true friends once more, sharing many interests and reminiscing from time to time about their childhood in Warsaw, so long ago.

Warsaw, August 10th, 1950

Relli had another surprise yesterday. Eva Barzilai also brought her a special gift from Paris. She'd bought a gorgeous piece of silk which was the perfect size for a child's blouse. The silk is printed with red-and-white checkers and very delicate, as fits the giver, Eva, an elegant and beautiful woman. It also suits the receiver, a blond, fair skinned girl. She looks nice in red. Relli's joy knew no end.

Upon her return to my apartment, she took a piece of paper and drew some designs for the blouse she would make from the fabric. Finally, she chose the sketch she liked best and showed it to me. The girl truly has good taste. Not so long ago she was forced to flip her pajama top so she could use it as both a daytime and nighttime shirt, and today she designed a blouse for herself from French silk. Relli has come a long way in quite a short time.

The blouse she drew really is cute. It has puffy and shirred sleeves and laces around the collar, with ruching around the neck and shoulders.

The next day we went to the Joint's tailoring workshop, which employs Warsaw Jews. We ordered the blouse Relli designed. The seamstress complimented the young designer on her sketch and fine taste. I was touched by Eva's gift. It was so kind of her to come up with a thoughtful gift for Relli. I thanked her profusely.

However, life is constantly strewn with both joy and disappointment. Relli's right hand had healed from the nitrogen scars and was covered with new, smooth skin, but one day last week the blisters began to grow again, as if they'd never been burned off. Relli cried with despair, and I had trouble consoling her. I finally shared my decision not to repeat the painful, ineffective medical treatment, and promised that in Israel her aunts and uncles would surely find a better alternative. I couldn't truly comfort her, but at least she was relieved to know we wouldn't be going back to that clinic.

Afterward

Much later, after she arrived in Israel, Relli would write to Tzipora that at some unknown point during her journey on the ship Komemiut from Venice to Haifa her blisters simply disappeared. When she got off in Haifa and shook hands with the relatives who waited there, she was amazed to find not one blister remained. Perhaps the salty air and strong sun of the Mediterranean had cured her. Relli would never suffer the blisters again.

Warsaw, August 15th, 1950

Relli's journey to Israel is approaching. For a while now I've been asking myself how I can send an eleven-year-old girl on such a journey alone. A plan has been forming. I'll join her on the train to Venice. The train makes no stops other than for border control, and the ride lasts four days and four nights.

I'll say goodbye to her in Venice, and she will continue onto the ship along with Miss Basia, whom I met when I handled her case at the embassy. Miss Basia, or Aunt Basia, as Relli calls her, is a childless widow, a Holocaust survivor whose husband and brother died at Trawniki, where Relli's parents and grandfather also found their cruel end. A strange coincidence. Miss Basia lives in Lodz with her sister and brother-in-law, but she's the only one immigrating right now. She seems like an independent, industrious woman, pretty and put together. Her initial meeting with Relli went well and I hope the plan will succeed. In order to deepen their relationship, we've decided that Relli would spend a few days with Aunt Basia in Lodz. We took the train there together with Abraham and Sarah Yeshuv from the embassy staff and their daughter, Kiki, toured the city and the impressive zoo in Helenòwek, where we had our picture taken, which Relli loves. At the end of the day I left her with Aunt Basia and her family.

Relli came home yesterday, pleased with her visit and overcome with her experiences—a first time meeting with a religious Jewish family, and encounters with two Jewish orphans, Holocaust survivors who had been adopted by Jewish families after the war, Monika, who is two years younger than Relli, and Zosia, who is three years older. Relli described these encounters in detail and I feel a need and an obligation to recount them here, in Relli's own words.

Basia's apartment is small. The rooms are connected like train cars, one room leading into the next. The entry hallway leads into the kitchen, and then into the room where Basia's sister and brother-in-law sleep, which also contains the dining table, sideboard, and closet. It is the central room of the apartment, and it's very crowded. It leads into the last, smaller room, where Aunt Basia sleeps. I stayed there with her. In the daytime, when all the doors are open, you can see the entire length of the apartment. Tzipora, I'm describing all this because it has to do with what happened to me there the first morning.

When I woke up Aunt Basia wasn't in bed. She must have woken up early and I didn't even hear her. I woke up to the sound of strange mumbling mixed with singing. I had no idea what I was hearing. I got up and noticed that the door to the adjacent room was slightly open. I went over on tiptoe and peeked in. The mumble grew louder, and I saw something very strange.

In the middle of the room, close to the window, was Aunt Basia's brother-in-law. He wasn't exactly standing. He was swaying. He was the one making those sounds, singing and crying words I didn't understand. I was especially interested in the tablecloth around his shoulders and back. It was white and shiny with black stripes and long tassels.

Why would a grown man wear a tablecloth? He also raised his hands, and his left hand was wrapped in black ribbons that looked like iron cords, and the plug to the iron was around his forehead. I thought he was strange the previous night at dinner, when he mumbled something at the table before we started to eat. He was wearing a round, black head cover, not really a hat, and I didn't know why he was wearing it to dinner. I was too embarrassed to ask. But now, this strange dance with the tablecloth and the iron plug were so incredible that I couldn't help myself. When we were alone on the street I asked Aunt Basia if her brother-in-law was a little crazy.

She was surprised. Why do you say that? She asked. I described what I saw, and Aunt Basia smiled and said, Relli, he was praying. That's how Jewish men pray.

Praying?! What an odd way to pray. Please explain to me, I said, why was he wrapping himself with a tablecloth and putting an iron plug on his forehead and iron cords around his hand?

She laughed and explained that what I'd heard and saw was a mid-week morning prayer, in which men wrap the teffilin, those straps, around themselves. There are also two frontlets, like little houses, and inside are Torah portions written on parchment. One of them is tied to the forehead, and the other to the left hand. The thing he wrapped himself with was a tallit, not a tablecloth, like I'd thought. I listened to her, a little bit scared. I didn't ask her any more, but I'm asking you, Tzipora, do my aunts and uncles in Israel behave like this too? Will they make me do it? And what's a Torah?

I assured Relli that as far as I know her relatives in Israel are not religious, and anyway, only men pray like that. As to the Torah, I told her, this matter requires a longer answer, and we'll put it off until a different time. I have to think about how to explain the gist of it to her. I'll consult with Towa, my colleague. She might be willing to teach Relli the basics. I'll write more about Relli's meetings with the orphaned girls later.

Warsaw, August 22nd, 1950

Relli's excitement about her visit to Lodz did not abate. She continued to describe her meeting with eight-year-old Myszka—baby mouse. Relli was sympathetic and empathetic toward the little girl. I wonder if she isn't also secretly envious. She must be, though she'd never voiced this emotion. Still, I can feel envy, as light as it may be, in her story, never forming into a thick fabric that would overshadow the meeting.

In order to entertain Relli in Lodz, Basia took her to visit some friends who had recently adopted a Jewish orphan from the orphanage in Krakow. The couple, childless, had survived the war and decided to expand their small family. Relli was charmed by their modest yet tasteful apartment, and most of all of Myszka's room: a cute, colorful room with lots of dolls in all shapes and sizes. Myszka is a skinny, dark child who wore a large white ribbon in her hair. She was sitting on the bed among her dolls when Relli was brought into the room. She is a very quiet child, but she responded to Relli's open and talkative nature. She told Relli that the nickname Myszka was given to her at the orphanage after the war. She didn't know her real name, or anything else about herself, like who her family was, where or when she was born, or how she'd survived the war. She remembers a little bit from the orphanage, and of course the recent months, after being legally adopted. Her adoptive parents seemed a little old to her, an eight-year-old girl. She said they were very strict yet very affectionate. From Basia's stories, I learned that these people are in their thirties, but, like many other survivors, aged prematurely, their difficult experiences leaving deep scars in their souls. The two girls found a path to each other's heart. Relli told Myszka about her nearing immigration, her fear of the unknown country and foreign people whom she is meant to be a part of, the strange language written in the wrong direction with all those hard sounds. She was open about her concerns regarding her relatives in Israel: who are they? What kind of people are they? Where and how would she live? Would she miss Poland? The language and literature she loved so much? So many questions concern her, and many have no clear answer. She has no one to discuss these matters with. She has Adda, of course, but she doesn't speak enough Polish and she lives in a different world, a world of safety and love. Sometimes, Relli told Myszka, she speaks to Tzipora, but normally she refrains from revealing her secrets.

Now that she's opened her heart to Myszka and even told me about it upon her return to Warsaw, I felt the urge to write about it. Maybe someday I can give this journal to her?

Relli told Myszka that her main difficulty is in changing her identity—in leaving behind Lala Abramowicz, a proud Polish girl, and beginning to be Relli Głowinski, the Jewish girl she was from the time she was born and until age four. But from four to eleven she'd been somebody else, who had to hide her former identity. She was told it was best if she forgot about it, and never mentioned that she was actually two girls, and now she was told she had to go back to being only one girl. Who should she choose to be? And how could she learn to be someone she hasn't been for seven years? It was as if she had taken a time out from being herself and now she had to go back to it, to get back inside another girl. She tried to explain to Myszka that these changes were shaking her to her very core.

Myszka didn't understand, perhaps due to her young age, or perhaps she was too invested in her own confused world. But she listened carefully, and the mere fact of her listening gave Relli some comfort. Relli explained that Myszka's situation was much better. She now had parents and her own pretty room; she was on her way to live like a normal child in Poland, surrounded by love.

Myszka agreed with this assessment hesitantly. She was too young to comfort Relli with soothing responses. Relli left their meeting in turmoil and showered Basia—and later me—with questions about Myszka's fate and about her own unknown future.

Basia and I had an honest conversation about whether or not this meeting had been a wise idea. Since Basia had only good intentions, I didn't criticize her choice, only noted to myself that Relli's treatment required lots of care. I realize now that her family in Israel will be faced with ongoing difficulty, and so will Relli.

On a positive note, Relli's meeting with Myszka brought me and Relli closer together and exposed me to the inner workings of her soul.

Afterward

It would be another forty-three years before Relli and Myszka met again, in 1993, when Relli participated in a conference in Jerusalem for people who survived the Holocaust as children under a borrowed identity. One woman walked in late to a workshop and looked familiar to Relli. Relli didn't give it much thought, but when it was that woman's turn to introduce herself she spoke quietly and hesitantly: I came here because I've spent my entire life looking for someone who knows me. My name is Monika, but that isn't the name I was given at birth. I don't actually know when I was born and who my parents are. I was found as an eighteen month old, wrapped in a blanket, by the train tracks leading to Auschwitz. The two peasants who found me assumed I was thrown out of a train car. They concealed me in their house, where I grew up in poverty. After the war I was given over to a Jewish orphanage and adopted by a Jewish family. My adoptive parents and I later moved to Israel. They've died, and I'm here first to tell you that I am very angry at my biological mother for saving me and sentencing me to a life without identity. Secondly, I'm hoping to meet someone who used to know me.

The participants all listened with bated breath. They all attempted to defend the lost mother for her bravery in saving the life of a little girl, but Monika persisted in her anger. Relli listened and thought, I know this woman, but where do I know her from?

Then she remembered, and waited impatiently for the end of the session. She went over to Monika and introduced herself, reminding her of their meeting in Lodz in 1950. Monika didn't remember and tried to avoid Relli, but Relli insisted and suddenly, in a flash of memory, said, Wait, your name wasn't Monika then, you had a nickname, an unusual one, I remember, it was Myszka—baby mouse!

The woman turned pale, tears filling her eyes. How did you know that? She asked Relli through a choked throat.

Relli described Myszka's room back in Lodz. The two of them could not get over their excitement at this surprise encounter in Jerusalem, forty-three years later.

At the end of the workshop Relli gave Monika a ride back to her home in Holon. On the way there, Monika told her all about her life. In the years since they occasionally speak on the phone and visit each other. They are connected by the thick threads of human fate, drenched in the tears of those who were children during the Holocaust and survived under false identities.

Warsaw, September 3rd, 1950

In the bustle of preparation for Relli's journey to Israel I forgot to write about the third encounter she had in Lodz.

Aunt Basia has Jewish friends who were charged with the care of a fifteen-year-old girl named Zosia. Basia knew this girl well and once again thought an introduction with Relli would benefit both parties. When they met, Zosia told Relli her unbelievable story. Zosia used to be her name back home. Being four years older than Relli, she remembered her biological parents and relatives well and knew specific biographical details about herself. Like Relli and Myszka, she too had survived the Holocaust under a false identity. Like them, she also lost all of her family. Like Myszka, she was put in a Jewish orphanage. Soon after the end of the war she was adopted by a Jewish couple that had lost its daughter in the terrible war.

Zosia was a pretty child, well-developed, intelligent, and impressive. Her adoptive father was a member of the Communist party and held a senior position in the Polish government after the war. The family's conditions of life had improved, and Zosia entered a warm home with loving parents that enveloped her with kindness and generosity. She enjoyed some truly happy years after the hell she'd been through during German occupation.

At some point Zosia's adoptive parents were sent on a political delegation in Scandinavia. Since the adoption procedures had yet to be completed, Zosia could not get a passport and could not be taken along with them. The adoptive parents left Zosia behind with good friends in Lodz. During their time in Scandinavia, they decided not to return to Poland. The father used his connections and money to find a way to smuggle Zosia through the port city of Szczecin. Unfortunately, the plan had been uncovered and the girl was captured when she was almost out of the country. She underwent exhausting questionings, her interrogators trying to make her reveal information about her parents' desertion. Eventually she was released and told in no unclear terms that she could never leave Poland. She returned to Lodz, to the family of her parents' friends. Somehow she'd gotten in touch with her adoptive parents who had managed, after a long time, to make it to Israel and settle down in Tel Aviv. Zosia gave Relli their address, 10 Ha'avoda Street in Tel

Aviv. She knew she would probably never see them again and that she would remain in Poland on her own.

Relli was shocked by Zosia's story. In a reversal of roles compared to her meeting with Myszka, Zosia explicitly expressed her envy of Relli's new unfolding life. They only met once, but Zosia's impressive figure was painfully etched into Relli's memory.

This story made my heart ache too. I feel incredibly frustrated knowing that none of us at the embassy can help the poor girl.

Relli had an epiphany which she shared with me. She realized that luck had smiled upon her, at least a little bit. In spite of the hardship that had been her lot so far, she would still have a future. This future is unknown and the road is paved with question marks, and yet, she may be happy in that faraway land to which she would depart in less than a month. She said she always tries to believe the best.

You're an optimist, I said, smiling.

What's an optimist?

It's you, I answered, and you didn't even know it. An optimist tends to believe in the good in life, in a good future. God bless you, Relli, for being this way.

Tzipora, are you giving me a compliment?

Of course I am. A big one! Believing the good paves the road for hope. You have the wisdom of finding the positive aspect of your life, and this will always give you strength. I believe in you and in the bright future you see ahead. I know you'll get it, and I feel like I've received a gift by being part of this happy future, in spite of it all.

Relli looked at me, removing her glasses to wipe away the tears, and whispered, Thank you, Tzipora. Thank you for everything.

Afterward

Relli would remember the Tel Aviv address given to her by Zosia. In her first years in Israel she would even remember the family name. As a soldier she would go visit the address. There, she would find the adoptive parents, extinguished, lonely, weathered people, struggling to stay alive as survivor immigrants in the promised land. This would be almost a decade since she met Zosia in Warsaw. The sad couple would tell her that Zosia had graduated from university with terrific scores. She married a non-Jewish man and continues to live in Poland.

With time Relli would forget the family's name. One day in the 1970s she would stop by the address again. The building seemed to have aged. It was neglected, its walls peeling, its stairwell dark. The names on the mailboxes would not spark her memory. Only the name Zosia would remain etched in her mind, along with a large question mark.

Venice, October 10th, 1950

I'm staying in a modest hotel overlooking a canal that laps the hotel's stoop. The moon is hanging in the sky like a giant lamp illuminating the quiet sky. Countless stars are shining, big and small, in the high heavens. I wonder if Relli can see this bewitching sight from her ship, sailing somewhere in the Mediterranean, carrying her and hundreds of other immigrants to Israel.

Venice is an unreal city that seems to float gloriously among the canals, pointing its steeples into the sky. I had a chance to walk around today. I'll stay for two more. And Relli? She will continue across the sea and reach Haifa, my city and port, on Saturday, October 14th.

I continue to write in my journal, which I've been keeping since December of 1949, documenting my life and Relli's. The past ten months have been very special. I feel both satisfied and deflated, as if I'd just completed an inordinately difficult task. I admit that I'd taken on the mission offered to me by Relli's aunts that day back in Tel Aviv without any idea of what I was getting myself into. These have been ten months of non-stop worry, tension, and coping. Coping with Relli, on all of her complexities. This kept me constantly busy for ten months straight.

Relli is resilient, opinionated, and stubborn. She is plagued with a pain and sensitivity that cannot be easily undone, if at all. When I arrived in Warsaw I found a neglected, restrained, distant child. Now I have sent a different girl to Israel, still carrying lots of emotional baggage and accumulated suffering that have left lifelong scars. I hope that the love of her family and life in the developing Israel will allow her, as is her optimistic belief, to turn a new leaf over under the blue skies and warm sun of our land.

In the past ten months I've barely had any time to myself. All of my resources had been recruited to the mission. It was hard, but I succeeded. In silence, I can admit to myself that redeeming Relli and sending her to Israel is the highlight of my life. I was assisted by Julek and Eva, by the Yeshuv, Kopyt, Vardi, Uchmani, Niv and Degani families, and by Towa Klaiff-Rubinsztein, the embassy's legal counsel. The entire staff encouraged me along, each person helping in his or her own way: through a word of advice, an expressed interest, and mostly through support.

Most wonderful of all were the children of embassy employees, of different ages, all Israeli born, and usually shy, who opened their hearts and accepted Relli as one of their own. This must have been a response to her friendliness and desire to fit in from the moment she chose to return to her old name, Relli. But the fact is that the children were the ones to make the move easier on her and me. No intelligent comments from me or the other grownups would have worked as magically as the language of children, innocent and naïve, spoken directly. I've already written much about Adda. I think I'd defined her as having taken on a private immigrant absorption project. I don't think I exaggerated and I stand behind my words today. Adda, with her big, inclusive heart, deserves plenty of credit.

But, I admit again, Relli had a significant part in fitting in with this group of children. It was her idea, for example, to put on a play in which all children would participate. She chose the story of Cinderella, wrote lines, and passed them along among the children, teaching them short, simple statements in Polish. She directed the show and starred in it too, of course.

Adda recruited two Polish sisters from the neighborhood to play the evil stepsisters. The entrance to the villa where we lived was chosen as a venue. It had an impressive arched stairwell leading up to the Barzilai residence. To Relli it was a readymade palace. Adda, who is musical like her father, knows how to play the piano that is permanently positioned in the hall, and accompanied the show with music. In short, the children had a celebration and the parents enjoyed themselves too, not to mention how proud Relli was to have had an idea and act on it.

And I? I beamed at the compliments she and I received. The play was performed a few days before Relli's departure and served as a kind of goodbye get-together. I was surprised when most adult guests brought her parting gifts. It was a very respectable, moving event.

Venice, October 11th, 1950

The last event I'll write about is Relli's goodbye to Warsaw on October 5th, 1950. The immigrant train waited on a side platform of the station from the early hours of the morning. I arrived with a very emotional Relli. The porter carried her large suitcase and my smaller one. Relli carried a doll and a walking cane, a memento from her trip to Zakopane in the Carpathian Mountains. It's a long cane made of light wood and carved with szarlota flowers, white flowers with petals that resemble felt, and which grow in the mountains. The cane didn't fit in the suitcase, but Relli wouldn't give it up. I'll carry it, she said, the entire journey. It's carved with the letters H.A., the initials of her Polish name, Halinka Abramowicz. It's a special keepsake, so that I never forget who I used to be for seven years, she said. There was no point in arguing with her.

The morning was cold, and wet, large, prickly raindrops washed over the platform. But in spite of this the passengers were in no rush to get on the train. The parting was also wet with tears streaming from all eyes. They all knew it was their last day in Warsaw and their parting from Poland. The people who came to see them off knew it too. For friends or relatives that were awaiting approval for a later immigration, emotions were different, but no less intense.

We met Aunt Basia on the platform. To our surprise, at the end of the platform we also found the entire Gilewski family. In spite of the early hour and the bad weather they had made it.

Aunt Hela and Uncle Stefan, their three adult children, Marysia, Krysia, and Tadek. Marysia held the hand of her daughter, little Małgosia, who wept uncontrollably. She'd known Lala since the day she was born, and saw her as her true cousin and protector. Małgosia's mother explained to her that Lala was going to a faraway land and that they wouldn't be able to play together anymore, and for the little girl this was heartbreaking news.

Józef also came to say goodbye. His face was grave and I detected a deep sadness in his eyes. In spite of everything that had transpired between them since the death of his wife, deep inside he must have still loved the child whose life he'd saved and whom he adopted years ago.

Relli, I called, fighting against the hubbub of voices, trying to maintain eye contact with her as she responded to the different calls, Lala, Lala. Everybody wanted to hug and kiss her and she felt the same. Her tears mixed with theirs. I felt a lump in my throat. Józef watched the bustle of emotions from afar and tried to come closer, but she avoided him. Nevertheless, when the announcer called all passengers aboard the train, her Polish manners, imbued within her like a second nature, won out. She shook his hand. A tear ran down his cheek, and I could tell he wanted to hug her. Relli did not respond to his gesture, nor kissed him, nor offered her own cheek to be kissed. She said goodbye for good coldly, politely, distantly.

We boarded the train and sat down by a window. Relli continued to wave goodbye for a long time, to her old family, to the city of Warsaw, and to the Lala Chapter of her life, which was fading away as the train gained speed, rushing off toward the future.

Afterward

Relli would maintain a correspondence with Hela and Stefan until their death at a very old age. In 1975 she would secure the honorific Righteous Among the Nations for Józef and Janina Abramowicz.

Her relationship with Małgosia Szlicht would last to this day. Małgosia would be invited to visit Relli in Israel twice, in 2002 and in 2009.

Relli's parted ways with Józef ended at the train station. She would never see him again.

Chapter Three: Relli

Love at First Sight   200
First Hours   203
Coming Home   206
Hide-and-Seek   210
The First Sabbath   212
The House in Pardess Hannah   214
A Student at the Pardess Hannah Elementary School   218
Fears   223
Understanding   227
A Family of Dreamers   231
At the Swimming Pool   235
Grandma Cipora's Book   240
Possessions   244
The Last Letter   247
What's Your Name?   251
Trawniki   254
Relli Writes to Lala   257
Lala Answers Relli   259

Love at First Sight

On Saturday afternoon, October 14th, 1950, the immigrant ship Komemiut, a freight ship converted to transport immigrants, approached the coast of Israel. Out on the horizon, to the east, the line of land blackened. The setting sun behind us painted the beach and the mountain range red. After sunset, as we drew closer to shore, we spotted lights illuminating on the range, down the slope of the mountain, and on the waterline. Haifa, the city of the Carmel, met us twinkling with thousands of lights from the top of the Carmel to the Lower City, arching through the bay and the Krayot. The lighthouse on top of the mountain turned on its axis, illuminating us from time to time with bright light. Darkness descended, and we sailed closer and closer, enthralled by the wondrous site of Haifa and its neighboring towns all lit up.

When we were very close but still outside the port, the ship slowed down to a stop. It began rocking violently, and after a while a rumor passed between the passengers that we indeed reached our port, but that, since the Sabbath was not yet over, we were not allowed in. We would dock for the night on the other side of the breakwater and only enter the port the next morning. It was hard to sleep that night, both due to excitement and due to the rough rocking of the ship. The waves crashed against the breakwater and then back against the ship. It was a stormy and thrilling October night. I barely slept a wink.

At dawn I went up to the deck and stood near the railing, gazing at the beauty. I was mesmerized by the breathtaking and colorful view of the city as the rising sun colored the awakening views golden. A mountain blooming on top, few brightly painted houses along the ridge, and more crowded structures down the slope as far as the eye could see. At the center of all this beauty a golden structure glimmered in the sun.

I didn't know what I was seeing, but I was captivated by the magnificent beauty of this city that people called Haifa. Many people went up to the deck, some excited and others throwing up over the railing, seasick with the force of crashing waves.

I stood alone, arriving alone, taking in the sights, insatiable. Inside of me awakened an unfamiliar, indecipherable emotion, a secret connection to this special place that was winning my heart at first light. If this is Israel, meant to be my home and homeland from now on, then I could say I liked it a lot.

I, who grew up in dark and gray Warsaw, was arriving in my new, bright, and blossoming country. Only yesterday I was still Lala, a Polish girl living under a false identity, and now I was beginning my return from exile. I'm coming home, coming back to myself, to my roots, my family, and my people—all new and foreign to me. My new country is conquering me, heart and soul, with its views as it enters a new morning, my morning of renewal.

I had no idea at that moment where my aunts and uncle lived and where I would live. At that moment, at that bewitching hour of dawn, I made a decision: whatever happened, as an adult I would live in this city, in Haifa. I let my imagination wander, promising myself that when I grew up I would start a family and do so here, only here, in Haifa. I fell in love with my new homeland, leaving Poland, my place of birth, days and mountains behind.

I fell in love with this city, which stunned me with its natural grace and glory, the richness of its colors and its breathtaking views. It was love at first sight, and it only intensified with the years.

202 | Relli Robinson

Afterward

In the future, when I joined the Israeli Defense Forces, I would ask to serve in Haifa and spend my days of mandatory service in the Engineering Corps in Haifa, and later serve as first sergeant in the navy, also in Haifa. I would fall in love with a Haifa native, David Robinson, my Dudu, whom I would marry. After studying at the Hebrew University of Jerusalem and completing our studies in America, we would return to Haifa to build our home. Michalle, our daughter, would be born in America, and our son, Nattiv, would be born in Haifa.

First Hours

The sun climbed up the horizon. More and more passengers went up to the deck, pushing their way to the railing, watching the city, and wiping away tears of joy. Suddenly, the motor rumbled and a boat approached us from the port. An Israeli flag blew in the cool morning air from their boat's mast, greeting us. The boat approached the ship, words I could not understand were exchanged between the boat's crew and the ship's crew over a loudspeaker. The boat was tied to the side of the ship, a ladder was lowered from the deck of the ship onto the boat, and three men climbed up. The first two were wearing brightly colored uniforms, and I was told they were from the Israeli Coastguard. The third man was tall and skinny, wearing an open-collared baby-blue shirt and khaki shorts. He came up on deck and stepped forward, shading his eyes from the blinding sun as he looked searchingly at the passengers.

I narrowed my eyes, investigating the face of this man, when suddenly my mouth fell open and I choked with excitement. I recognized him, my uncle, Chaim Głowinski, who had visited me in Poland three years before. He was the uncle who wrote on the back of his passport photo, *See you Soon, Your Uncle Chaim.* I jumped out of the crowd, skipping toward him. He spotted me and opened his arms to catch me and lifted me into the air. *Welcome home!* He said in a trembling voice. Uncle Chaim, a practical, purposeful man, did not let go of my hand from that moment on. We went down to the sleeping hall where I'd spent nights throughout the journey beside Aunt Basia. He greeted her and thanked her for accompanying me. As he picked up my suitcase and I picked up my walking cane and doll, Uncle Chaim explained to Aunt Basia that he had a special approval to

take me off the ship and take me to the port in the Coastguard
boat. The ship would soon be entering the port and it might take
several hours until all the immigrants went through the registry
and reception process. *It's going to take lots of patience*, he told
Aunt Basia, preparing her for life in Israel.

Then Chaim quickly led me onto the Coastguard boat, where
the two men who had come up with him were already waiting.
The boat detached from the ship and sailed into the port. We
entered the arrivals hall, where clerks were already waiting at
desks to handle the immigrants arriving on the Komemiut when
it finally docked. Uncle Chaim took care of the process with
speed, received a citizen registration slip on my behalf and led
me confidently to the port gate, through which we walked out
onto Sha'ar Palmer Street.

In just a few moments you'll meet the entire family, he said
with a smile. *They all came with me this morning and are
waiting for you at Café Eden.*

We walked into the café, which was only a few dozen
meters away from the gate, on the corner of Sha'ar Palmer and
Ha'atzma'ut Avenue. I was instantly surrounded by my aunts
and uncles. They all wanted to hug and kiss me, introducing
themselves by name: Aunt Rita, Aunt Roma and Uncle Zalman,
Uncle Paweł and Aunt Anni, and Aunt Moni, Uncle Chaim's
wife. They all spoke to me in Polish, expressing their joy and
excitement. All four aunts wiped their eyes, while the uncles
smiled at me. I was enveloped with warmth, and felt at ease
in spite of the initial strangeness. They immediately offered
me orange juice and chocolate cake. As I ate and drank I
memorized the new names, attaching them to the faces.

That morning, as I woke up early to my new life, I tried
out a new hairdo with a part down the middle, not on the side,
as usual. My Aunt Rita, sitting next to me, glanced at me and

announced, *The first thing we have to do is comb your hair and move that part.* She took my hand, led me to the bathroom, undid my braids skillfully, brushed my hair, and parted it on the left side. Then she braided it, tying the ends with new white ribbons she'd brought with her and fastened a white plastic barrette with colorful flowers over my forehead. She finished quickly, pointed at my reflection and flattered me and herself: *Now you look so cute, with your hair done up right.*

By the time we returned to the group Uncle Chaim had already brought his truck around and loaded my suitcase. We all got on and sat on the benches in back, except for Aunt Moni, who sat in the cabin.

As the ride began, I heard somebody saying, *We're going to the village of Pardess Hannah, to Aunt Rita, Uncle Abraham, and Cousin Nurit's house. We'll have lunch there and you'll stay there. It'll be your home. You'll live with them.*

The truck was on its way, riding down the coast and along a road that twisted among orchards and plantations. Aunt Rita and Aunt Roma sat on both my sides and explained the sights.

I couldn't get enough of the greenery. It was so different than the gray landscape of Warsaw and the blue expanses of the Mediterranean that I'd gotten used to during the journey. *It's such a green land*, I said.

Uncle Zalman turned to me. *Did you know that each color symbolizes something?*

I only know that red symbolizes love, I answered.

Good, said Uncle Zalman. *Now I'm here to tell you that green symbolizes hope. I like to think it's hope for your new life in Israel.*

So do I, I said, then added silently, to myself, I hope so very, very much.

Coming Home

The truck pulled up by a small iron gate on a street of tall palm trees. A sand path led from the gate through an avenue of myrtle bushes. At the end of the path was a small, modest home, surrounded by fruit trees and ornamental trees. The house in Pardess Hannah; the house that would become my home.

Uncle Abraham and Cousin Nurit waited on the stoop; more kisses and hugs. Uncle Abraham also spoke Polish. Nurit and I looked at each other, measuring each other's braids. Hers were longer and thicker, and her hair was parted in the middle, which suited her. Her gray-green eyes sparkled with tears and her hug was warm and enveloping. I curtsied, Polish style, and she smiled awkwardly. She understood Polish but could only speak Hebrew and German. The aunts all went into the kitchen to help Aunt Rita serve lunch. The large, round table in the main room was already set. I suppose Aunt Rita prepared it all before leaving to meet me in Haifa.

The entire family gathered around the table. Uncle Chaim pulled out three bottles of wine from a bag. One light colored one for the men, and two others, deep red and sweet, for the women and us girls. He poured it. Uncle Abraham, the host, stood up and said formally, *Hello Relli, Welcome to Israel, welcome to your family, welcome home. L'chaim!* Everyone clinked glasses and repeated, L'chaim! Aunt Roma translated for me. Interesting, I thought, I guess Uncle Chaim is very well respected in the family if everyone is toasting for him.

To this day I remember the red borscht served in deep bowls, the meatballs with potatoes in flat plates. In a large bowl at the center of the table a pile of shredded and sugared carrots glowed bright orange. I looked at the two plates set before me and began transferring potatoes from the flat plate to the deep bowl of borscht.

Rita, sitting next to me, began to cry.

I glanced at her, surprised, and asked, *Aunt Rita, why are you crying?*

She stroked my hair and said through a choked throat, *You really are your father's daughter. He only ever ate his potatoes in the borscht. When they were served separately he transferred them in, just like you're doing now.*

I've been eating this way since I can remember. I had no idea I got it from my daddy, I answered, touched.

After the delicious meal everybody had tea. Just like in Poland, I thought. We also had some tasty cakes made by Aunt Moni and Aunt Anni.

One thing surprised me and bothered me. Four languages were spoken around the table at once. Everyone spoke Hebrew to Nurit and Polish to me, of course. The aunts and uncles spoke German between them, sprinkled with some Russian that I could understand. I realized Nurit understood German, too. My skin bristled at the sound of German. The hard sounds took me back to dark, distant days. I couldn't figure out how my family here, in Israel, could use that horrible language so freely. I didn't say a thing at first. Only later that night did I ask Aunt Rita about it. She explained they'd all been brought up speaking three languages: Polish, Russian, and German, and learned Hebrew when they moved to Israel. *German is like a mother tongue to us*, she said, *one out of three mother tongues*. She didn't let herself get into a discussion of what the language symbolized for me or reminded me of. I felt she was being insensitive, but I had no choice but to adapt.

After the aunts and uncles from Tel Aviv said goodbye I went to lie down and fell asleep for a while. Other relatives arrived to dinner. Yael, Uncle Abraham's eldest daughter from his first wife, and Zvi, her husband. They were a nice young couple, also from Pardess Hannah. My relationship with Zvi was special from the very beginning. He was a young man, all kindness, funny, beaming light and joy. We had no common language to use at first. He was born in Vienna and spoke no Polish, whereas I couldn't speak Hebrew or German. But our body language, our eyes, and our smiles created a brave connection.

My first day in Israel was full and busy. At night I felt my heart overflow with everybody's warmth and amiability. When I finally went to bed I truly felt as if I'd come home, to my family, and to my land, just as Uncle Abraham had said at lunch.

Afterward

Four languages were always in use in the house in Pardess Hannah: my aunt and I spoke Polish to each other, Rita and Abraham spoke German to each other. My uncle spoke only Hebrew to Nurit and to me, and Nurit and I spoke Hebrew between us. Rita spoke German to Nurit. Sometimes, when the adults didn't want us to understand, they spoke Russian, but I could still pick up the gist of what they were saying. Friends who came to visit wondered how Nurit and I didn't get confused. I suppose it was a little strange to pass the salt around the dinner table in four different languages.

As to German, I picked it up at home. I now understand German and can speak a very basic, very badly accented version of it. With years I also picked up some Yiddish from

Marie, a Romanian immigrant who lived in Pardess Hannah and helped Aunt Rita with household duties. After watching a documentary about Toulouse-Lautrec we nicknamed her Marie-Charlet, after his lover.

A few weeks into my arrival I noticed that each Friday night as we drank wine we all said *L'chaim*. I asked Uncle Abraham why we always toasted Uncle Chaim and never Aunt Moni or the rest of the family. Abraham burst out in laughter and explained the meaning of the word *l'chaim*—to life, and the blessing it implied.

Nevertheless, for the rest of my life, whenever anyone cheers *l'chaim* I feel my heart aching in longing for my special uncle, Chaim Głowinski.

Hide-and-Seek

My second day in Israel. A bright land, captivating in its beauty and freshness. The sky is blue, so different than the pale gray-blue of Warsaw. Here in Pardess Hannah, at my aunt and uncle's yard, everything blooms in shades of green. A pleasant afternoon October sun paints the treetops and bushes a reddish gold. The large guava tree in the middle of the grass, with its bright green fruits, strange in their bumpy pearish shape, smelling pungent and new. The guavas peek from between the dark green leaves with their red veins. Around the tree is a round carpet of ripe, fallen fruit, some pecked at by birds. Their smell pinches my nostrils. All around are citrus trees the likes of which I'd only seen in books or movies before. Now here they are, real, close enough to touch. The orange clementines are like golden bulbs glowing among the dark leaves. My eyes are drawn to a strange tangled hedgerow of thick and meaty elliptical leaves, glimmering like delicate jewels, bright strands of silver sparkling in the sun.

Suddenly, the calm and awe are interrupted. The voice of four or five girls sounds from the front gate. *Nurit, Nurit*, they say. *We've come to meet your cousin, Relli, the one who came from Poland.*

I don't understand the words, but I enjoy the sounds. Hands are offered and a wave of friendship carries me away. They suggest we play hide-and-seek. Even the Polish girl must know that game. I stand among them, already dressed as they are, blue elastic-waist shorts and a short-sleeve shirt. My legs and arms stand out in their paleness in the circle of tan girls, but this does not stop them from accepting me as one of them.

The game begins. One girl leans her forehead against the front door, closes her eyes, and counts to ten. Everybody scatters to their hiding places: some among the trees, some behind the house. I linger for a moment, wondering, Where should I hide? My eyes fall once more on the hedgerow that had caught my attention before, charming me with its shades of green and the silvery strands on the leaves. I run quickly and hop into the bushes, face and hands first. That very moment, dozens, maybe hundreds of tiny, thin thorns—those silver strands that had charmed me—cling to my face, arms, and legs. I let out a cry. The girls pounce out of their hiding places and stand, stunned, watching me stuck in the sabre bushes.

One of them gets a hold of herself and calls my aunt and uncle from inside the house. I stand still in the bushes, tears blinding me, pierced with thorns, and unable to move. The tiniest motion only exacerbates the pain.

Uncle Abraham arrives, looks around, hushes the shouting girls, and attempts to soothe me. He grabs my arms with his strong hands and pulls me back swiftly. With one quick pull he releases me from my thorny prison.

The girls all disperse awkwardly. Abraham spends that entire afternoon and evening gently and patiently removing the tiny thorns from my body with tweezers. A lukewarm shower soothes my skin, and the crying finally stops.

That first game of hide-and-seek in my new homeland, with my *sabre* friends, was a painful acceptance of a prickly hug, which, with time, became an embrace of affection, friendship, and sweetness, just like the flesh of the sabre fruit.

The First Sabbath

I was very busy that first week, becoming acquainted with the house, the yard, and the village. I met Nurit's friends from school and from the neighborhood. I went with my aunt to the center of the village to buy some school supplies and clothes. The days went by quickly and Saturday arrived. I knew nothing of the day's special designation, but it was clear from the morning that it was different than other days.

My uncle, the farmer, woke up early just like every other morning. He fed Tikwah the mule, the chickens, and the dogs—Tiki and Gura—who'd spent the night outside. We girls and Rita, on the other hand, slept in.

Around eight-thirty in the morning magical aromas spread from the kitchen into our nearby room—freshly brewed coffee and freshly baked cake, just sliced generously by my uncle. My uncle made milky coffee for my aunt and milky tea for me and Nurit. He brought us these delicacies in bed. Tea and cake! What a treat, so sweet and delicious, the special pleasures of Saturday morning.

Next, Nurit and I got up and were assigned table setting and breakfast preparation in the "big room." I was charged with chopping vegetables for a salad. My uncle looked over me and teased me that if I kept working so slowly and carefully my future family would starve by the time meals were ready. I was sorry, years later, that my uncle passed away before getting a chance to have a meal at my home. He would have enjoyed himself. He would have been surprised to find that even with my meticulous care, I get everything done on time, managing to feed my family, and even guests.

After a lingering, ceremonious Saturday morning breakfast Nurit and I rushed off to a Scouts' meet. I was very excited about my first encounter with the youth movement and wanted us to leave early. We didn't have time to wash the dishes, and my kind uncle volunteered to do so for us.

These memories of the flavors and aromas of those indulgent Saturday morning hours at the house in Pardess Hannah have stayed with me to this day. It was one of the few special treats of our childhood. We were generally not spoiled children and were not coddled. We helped around the house and farm and did a portion of the grocery shopping. Therefore, we knew how to savor every gesture of indulgence. Uncle Abraham always knew how to impart his kindness in his quiet way, giving us lots of love and, once in a while, a treat.

The House in Pardess Hannah

My uncle Abraham built our house when Pardess Hannah was established in 1929. He used cast iron to make thick walls and covered them with a brown tiled roof, mostly covered with different shades of green climber plants that blossomed in gorgeous colors. The front entrance was actually in the back, facing the farm. The door opened onto a long and narrow hallway. On the left were two doors, one next to the other, also narrow, which led into the bathroom and toilet. The fridge stood at the end of the hallway since it didn't fit in the tiny kitchen. To the right of the fridge was the door to Abraham and Rita's bedroom.

Across from the front door was a door leading into the "big room," as we called it—a kind of living room with dark wooden furniture that my aunt and grandmother brought with them from Danzig in the early 1930s. At the center of the room was a heavy round table with six darkly upholstered high-backed chairs. The table was expandable, and seated twenty people during the Passover Seder. A cumbersome sideboard stood against the wall. Its top part had glass doors that revealed European porcelain treasures—from Germany, Czechoslovakia, France, and even Poland. A big and faded sofa formed a seating corner by the window.

The "big room" was the center of the house. We sat here in the evenings to listen to the radio and play Monopoly and Rummy. On Friday nights, Saturdays, and on holidays we had our meals in there. A door opened from the "big room" into my aunt and uncle's bedroom, and another led into the "little room," which had access to the kitchen and to a small porch that led out onto a path. The path connected the house to the front gate and the main street, which was then called Shemoneh-meot Street and is now called Ha'nadiv Avenue. The name Shemoneh-meot, which means eight-hundred, was given to the street upon the founding of the village and signified the price of lots paid by the village founders to the Palestine Jewish Colonization Association. This is the avenue that, to this day, connects Pardess Hannah to its neighboring village of Binyamina.

The "little room" was Nurit's and mine and also served as a weekday dining room. Nurit's bed was by the window, and my folding bed, its top part made of a wooden shelf—was perpendicular to it. Across from my bed was a small closet that the two of us shared. Next to it was a bookcase that stretched almost as high as the ceiling. At the center of the table was an elongated elliptical table with four chairs. This was our weekday dining table, which we also used to do our homework. At night the table was pushed aside near the bookcase and stacked with the chairs, so that the folding bed could be turned around and opened up. We set our beds in an L shape so that our heads were close together. Each night before we fell asleep we had long heart-to-hearts, sharing our secrets. Nurit, who was six months younger than I was, had heard stories of Cousin Relli, who would one day live with her in her home, since she was very little. Aunt Rita had nurtured this hope all these years. When I finally did arrive, Nurit accepted me as her sister. She was kind enough to share everything with me: her room, her clothes, her books, her toys, her friends from school, the neighborhood, and Scouts. Most of all, she shared her parents' love and her own.

On weekday mornings I had to wake up first, fold my bed away, return the table to the center of the room and set the chairs around it. Only then could the rest of the family gather for breakfast. Nurit could allow herself to linger a little longer in bed, but she too had to be up and have her bed made before breakfast was served.

Abraham was the first of us to wake up for his morning farming duties. Then he prepared breakfast while Aunt Rita made us sandwiches to take to school. When I could already smell the omelet frying I knew I had to hurry out of bed to prepare the room in time.

The house was very small and had not been renovated or expanded in many years. I quickly learned that it served as the center for our extended family. This is where everybody got together for the Passover Seder, which was led by Abraham, and for which Rita cooked all the traditional delicacies. It's hard today to imagine how she'd managed to prepare such a feast on two burners, in the austere days of the 1950s.

For years to come, on holidays and school vacations the house and farm attracted all cousins, near and far. It was the center of life for the Robinson and Głowinski families. This is where we all came to spend our vacations, to rejoice and mourn together.

Afterward

I loved the house in Pardess Hannah, the warm and supportive family that lived in it, and the warmth that enveloped us together. I would continue to return to this home from the Kfar Hayarok agricultural boarding school, the army, the university in Jerusalem, and even from America. The house would remain a cornerstone of my life, drawing me back to it until the death of Aunt Rita in 1998. It would remain in my memory, carrying a longing toward childhood and youth, the experiences we shared there. That small house contained so much love, happiness, and laughter. It charged me with enough energy for an entire lifetime. It would always live on in my heart as my childhood home.

Cousin Nurit and I grew up as sisters and we continue to maintain our strong bond. I received the sister I never had, my own age, filled with kindness and tenderness, understanding and endless generosity.

A Student at the Pardess Hannah Elementary School

Sunday, October 22nd, 1950, was my first day at the elementary school in the village. That morning Nurit and I left the house, hand in hand, walking down Shemoneh-meot Street, at the end of which, across from the central bus station, was the school. It was a white two-story building with wide open balconies. Adjacent to it was a large field with such contraptions as basketball hoops, dodgeball nets, and more. The field was surrounded by a pine thicket through which one could take a shortcut to the center of the village. Farther away there was a soccer field, the school dining hall, and a vegetable garden tended by students.

The bright buildings, the elevated balconies, the trees, and the sand won me over immediately. The memory of the Communist school in Warsaw, that abhorrent gray building with its paved yard flashed through my memory for a moment and was pushed away, never to upset me again.

There were already some students in our classroom. The principal had decided to enter me into the sixth grade, where children my age, born in 1939, were enrolled. Though I'd skipped first grade in Poland, the handling of my immigration and my move to the embassy building caused me never to complete the sixth grade. Now that I was enrolled in the sixth grade once more, time had caught up with me and everything was as it should be.

The girls from our class and the other sixth grade class surrounded us immediately, each of them in turn introducing herself by name. They'd all heard that Nurit would be arriving with her cousin from Poland, and some of them had already met me at Scouts the previous day.

I made an effort to remember all the strange names, giving the girls my hand and curtsying. In my excitement I didn't notice them stifling their laughter at this gesture.

Then an exceptionally pretty girl with big bright eyes, braids, and fair curls around her forehead stepped forward. She gave me her hand, smiled wide, and said, *I'm Noga*. I looked at her, unable to understand her name. She repeated it slowly and loudly, enunciating each syllable: *No-ga*. Rather than curtsy again, I burst into uncontrollable laughter. I didn't know how to explain to everyone that I'd never heard anyone named "foot," which is what Noga meant in Polish.

They all stared at me, confused. The school secretary, who spoke Polish and happened to walk by came over to see what all the fuss was about. She explained to the other girls why I was laughing and translated for me the beautiful Hebrew meaning of the word Noga—a glowing light.

The bell rang and the homeroom teacher, Shlomit Miller, walked in. She put her arm around my shoulder and officially introduced me to the classroom by the name chosen for me by the principal—Erella.

The first class was an English class. Since I'd already studied English in Warsaw, I was able to fit in. I raised my hand and answered the teacher's questions correctly. From the corner of my eye I could see Nurit, who was sitting beside me, taking pride in my success.

As I scanned over the other kids I couldn't help but marvel at their tan skin and their liberated behavior. The atmosphere was complete different than what I'd known in Poland. One phenomenon in particular amazed me: many of the girls in my class, including Nurit, sucked their thumbs. Each of them did so a little differently. One sucked her thumb while stroking her own cheeks with the other fingers. One twisted her hair around the fingers of the other hand. Another rubbed her nose with the fingers of the hand that was in her mouth. Yet another used her other fingers to pull on her earlobe. The more I looked, the less I could believe it. Where was I? With time, I got used to the sight of my friends sucking their thumbs, mostly during classes. They claimed it helped them focus. Not only had I never seen school girls in Poland sucking their thumbs, but I'd never even been aware of the fact that kids did that. I'd never sucked my thumb, not as a toddler, and certainly not as a school girl.

After English class Mr. Ben-Abraham showed up. He was the other sixth grade's homeroom teacher and taught both classes math, geometry, and art. He was also very welcoming. I followed the class closely, understanding everything on the blackboard, since I'd already learned it in Poland. But I couldn't participate, nor speak out loud, since I didn't know any Hebrew, not even the names of numbers. It was a very frustrating experience.

I kept quiet during Hebrew class and Bible class as well, sitting there like a deaf-mute, unable to perceive anything being said and incapable of speaking a word. It was truly embarrassing.

The last class was a celebration: art class. I'd always been a good artist, able to draw in accurate detail. I'm told I'd inherited this talent from my mother. Mr. Ben-Abraham noticed my abilities and encouraged me with a smile and compliments.

Though I was silent in the classroom, I was not shy during recess. I took part in all the games, determined to fit in with the other children. It was easy to learn the game Tiki Bel-bel-bel: two groups stood in facing lines on both ends of the field. A representative of one group ran over to the other, slapping one of the many up-facing palms. He then had to hurry back to his own group while calling out *Tiki bel-bel-bel-bel-bel* until he got back, never stopping for breath. At the same time, the kid from the other team whose palm was slapped had to chase the first kid, also calling out the gibberish statement. If the runner managed to make it back to his or her team in time, the chaser was taken hostage. If the runner was caught, he or she was taken hostage by the other team. The rules were simple and I was a fast runner. I spent the first recess watching the game, and by the second I was already playing.

At the end of the school day, Nurit and I walked home with other girls who lived on our street.

My heart was filled with my love of learning. I knew I had a bumpy road ahead, and decided that I would work hard and excel in order to find my place and belong.

Afterward

At the end of the first trimester most of my grades were marked "not ready yet." By the end of the second trimester I got an excellent mark in agriculture for my initiative, as toolshed attendant, to clean up the shed, sort out the tools, and take inventory. Our wonderful, venerated agriculture teacher, Mr. Ben-Yaakov, or Zallo, as he was called in the village, appreciated my ingenuity and industriousness and implemented the idea with all other attendants.

My "not ready yet"s gradually dwindled, and by the end of the school year I was in the top of my class. By the time I completed eighth grade I received a scholarship for high school, an honor granted only to 8,000 out of 25,000 students from all over the country. I was very proud, and so was my family.

And Noga? By way of converging fates she married a schoolmate of mine from Hakfar Hayarok High School, my good friend Ehud from Be'er Tuvia, and so my friendship with her, the girl I met on my first day of school in Israel, and with Ehud, continues to this day, sixty years later.

Fears

Fears... I try to recall: when have I ever been afraid, and from what? I've never thought of myself as a fearful person, but as an alarmed one. I become alarmed when someone surprises me by jumping out from behind a door and yelling, *Boo!* I become alarmed when I hear my name called after thinking I was alone. Sudden noises make me jump. I turn pale and my heart begins racing and beating loudly. It takes my breath away. I react in extreme ways to being spooked.

But I am certainly not a fearful person. Since I can remember I was never afraid when many other children were. I never had a fear of strangers, never worried about entering unfamiliar spaces, had no fear of the dark, and wasn't even scared of needles. Whenever we had to receive vaccinations in school I always raised my hand, volunteering to go first. I would offer my arm bravely, close my eyes, and look away. I would receive the injection with childish bravery, enduring the prick and the sting without a word. Then I would declare, *It didn't even hurt!* I wasn't afraid of doctors, not even from the dentist. The dentist I had back in Poland operated the drill by stepping on a pedal. There were no electric drills and certainly no anesthesia, but I simply wasn't afraid.

In moments of honesty, I admit to myself that I was never afraid even in very trying moments. I wasn't afraid of leaving Poland for the unknown; a journey of discovery and acquaintance with the real me, my biological family, my people, my culture, my new country. I was curious, but not afraid. Later on, in Scouts, when we had night walks through dark orchards or sandy dunes, and when tests of bravery had us sneaking into a watermelon bed to steal the fruit not far from the guard post, I had no fear. When someone had to stand guard by the tent camp I had no problem performing the task.

Later still, as a teenager and an adult, and to this day, I've felt that fear is a luxury that perhaps I could never afford. The circumstances of my life had trained me to be independent, and I've always trusted my resourcefulness. I never let myself be afraid. I consciously knew that I mustn't, so I didn't

Still, even I suffered of anxiety for a long period of time. It invaded my thoughts and dreams, causing me many sleepless night. It was a deep, private anxiety that I refused to share with anyone. It took years before it left me and no longer shook my confidence, which was the worst part. This anxiety first plagued me soon after coming to Israel. I received a warm welcome from my family and enjoyed a supportive and loving environment. I learned Hebrew meticulously and was soon able to communicate with friends, excel at school, and be an active member of the Scouts. I was involved and felt appreciated.

Then what was it that had frightened me so much? I noticed that after Nurit and I came home from school and had lunch, while we rested, read, or did our homework, Aunt Rita never took an afternoon nap. Around two p.m., after the news, she sat next to the radio in the "big room," listening intently. Nurit and I were ordered not to interrupt. She was like an addict.

Why is this so important? I asked.

Oh, Nurit said, *it's just the radio show she always listens to.*

I know it's a radio show, but what is this show that's got her so worked up?

It's called The Search Bureau for Missing Relatives.

And?

It's a show where an announcer reads the names of people who live in Israel and are searching for their relatives with

whom they'd lost touch during the Holocaust. Or sometimes they read the names of survivors looking for their families. They're all looking for a glimmer of hope. Mommy has been listening to it for years, since the show began airing. She keeps waiting to find other survivors from the big family they had in Lodz and Warsaw.

I see, I said. *Thank you.*

And that's when I became afraid. A subtle cold snaked up my body, gripping my heart. At first it was only a light concern, but with each passing day it grew deeper and more intense. At night I dreamed about it and during the day I pictured very real images.

What if one day she heard on the radio that the Głowinski family, her brother Michał, her sister-in-law, Franka, and their daughter, Relli, had survived? They spent the war in hiding and were now searching for their family in Israel. Other times, I imagined a knock at the door, we would open it and find three people standing outside: man, woman, and child. They would identify themselves and everyone would become choked up. I would be the only one standing aside, staring at that girl who calls herself Relli. If she was Relli, then who was I?

The more I considered my thoughts and dreams, the more I was able to convince myself that my imagination was running away with me. Still, I couldn't get rid of that secret anxiety that had taken over my heart and mind. Perhaps I wasn't really me? The proof was indisputable: pictures, certificates, physical resemblance, and personality traits straight out of the genetic family tree. It was clear as day—I was Relli Głowinski. Nevertheless, fear gnawed at me, shaking my confidence. The more I was afraid, the more I hid it, stifling it so that it didn't dare crawl out. I couldn't share this anxiety with anyone. If they knew I was afraid, they might become suspicious too, investigating the issue, and who knew what they might find out.

On the other hand, it was clear that I was me, I was Relli, and that my fear was pointless, taking over with cunning and gripping my soul. It haunted me, and I fought it off, stifling it, trying to make it disappear. Eventually, my inner logic and my ability to talk myself out of anxiety reached the desirable conclusion. I was able to kill my fear, banishing it from my being.

Most importantly, I got my confidence back, believing in who I truly was—Relli Głowinski, daughter of Michał and Franka. I'd overcome my anxiety, burying it deep, forgetting all about it.

Afterward

It would be years before I even considered this long-lost anxiety, having forgotten all about it. Then, one day, Nava Gibori, the instructor of my Life Documentation class, would suggest some writing prompts that included the subject of fear.

Fear? I would ask out loud, surprised. The subject would seem so foreign.

Then, later, in what I like to call *a conversation with Relli*, I would remember that I too was once afraid, very afraid, for very long, back in 1950. This would be the first time I would write about those fears that lay dormant among my other secrets for sixty years.

Understanding

Listen to me, Relli, and try to concentrate, Uncle Zalman repeats in his tender, loving voice, filled with endless patience. *Please, concentrate.*

I'm listening, I'm concentrating, I say impatiently. I count to ten silently to stop myself from raising my voice.

Pay attention: two trains leave two stations that are a hundred kilometers apart, one riding at a speed of sixty kilometers per hour, the other at a speed of forty kilometers per hour. Let's try and calculate together, when will they cross each other's paths? What do you think? How can we solve this?

Uncle Zalman, we've already solved a similar problem and I told you I understand.

I'm glad you understand. Now please explain it to me.

Oh, come on, Uncle Zalman. If I say I understand then I understand and I don't need to explain it.

But Uncle Zalman took time to check my textbooks and notebooks as well as Nurit's, and to linger over the math and geometry material. He patiently repeated the irritating formulas of geometry and algebra, never losing hope in my ability to understand, yearning for me to be able to explain. My kind uncle, never raising his voice, smiling and stroking my hair. *A person can truly comprehend something only when explaining it to another. Think about it, Relli, and remember it always.*

Uncle Zalman, Aunt Roma's husband, never had the pleasure of being a father. He gave his abundant, soothing, confident love to his nieces and nephews. Years later he was like a grandfather to my children. He liked to make up special nicknames for us. He called me Rellooniu even when I was forty years old. He liked to call Michalle, my daughter, Michalki, while my son,

Nattiv, received the name Nattiva'le. He called Nurit Nur'le well into her middle age.

Uncle Zalman came from a special breed of men. Born in Lithuania, he came to Israel as a teenager on his own. His mother died giving birth to him and he'd been raised by his grandmother and aunt. The rest of his family stayed behind in Lithuania and were all murdered in the Holocaust. After the war, he Hebraized his name, changing Wiershubski into Ben-Shaul.

In Israel, Zalman joined the pioneers who paved roads in the south. He paved the road to Beersheba, as well as roads in the Gaza Strip. That's where he met my uncle Chaim, who had preceded his family, coming to Israel on his own in 1920, when he was only eighteen years old. Zalman and Chaim became close friends. Family folklore has it that as young men they were so skinny that they had to share one narrow bed just to keep warm through the cold desert nights.

When the rest of Chaim's family joined him in Israel, Zalman met Chaim's younger sister, Roma. The two married, and the good friends became brothers-in-law. Roma and Zalman moved to Paris together to attend the university. He studied engineering, and she studied journalism. She never graduated, but her studies improved her command of French. She was also an active member of the Esperanto Club. Upon their return to Israel, Zalman found a job at the new construction company Solel Boneh, and remained with the company for many years. Before his retirement he worked at the Construction Control department of the Ministry of Defense. He was a modest and honest man who loved man and country. The best expression of his love and devotion was his relationship with us, the family children. He was always happy to play, tell us stories of national history, and teach us pioneer songs. To this day I recall the lyrics of a song he loved: *Tel Aviv, oh, Tel Aviv, a sandy city by the beach; soon you will be world renowned and out of reach...*

On vacations in Tel Aviv he took Nurit and I to his work, showing us a new bridge he'd planned or a blueprint for a new road. Most of all, he liked to help us with our algebra and geometry homework.

Aunt Roma and Uncle Zalman were frequent visitors to Pardess Hannah. They would arrive on Fridays, spend the night in the "big room," and return to Tel Aviv on Saturday night. They didn't have a car, and would arrive by the shared cab going from Tel Aviv to Haifa down the only road that connected the two cities and passed through Pardess Hannah, riding down Shemoneh-meot Street, right by our house. On Saturday night we would walk them to the central bus station, where they caught the first bus to leave after the Sabbath. They always arrived bearing gifts, new clothes, books, and fine quality candy. Aunt Roma always brought me the Polish made Krówka toffee candy, which were my favorite back in Warsaw.

My dear uncle taught me how to solve math problems, but more than that, he taught me that understanding meant internalizing and explaining. His uncompromising approach was that only when I've internalized the material enough to explain it could I claim to have understood it.

The components of the issue you are dealing with, he said, *become building blocks for your understanding. The process of inner construction, of internalizing, ripens into an ability to explain, and the ability to explain is the secret of understanding,* he repeated once and again.

Afterward

Throughout my life, in any subject I met, I would strive to understand, challenge myself to internalize, and allow the internalized to become comprehended. If I've understood something well enough for it to touch me and become a part of me, I knew I could explain it to myself and to others. I could know that I truly understood.

The principles taught to me by Uncle Zalman would remain with me always. His unwritten will would stay with me: only the ability to explain signifies internalization, and in turn, understanding.

A Family of Dreamers

Dreams are hereditary in our family, Aunt Rita used to say. She could recount the dreams that her grandmother, my great-grandmother, had—dreams that had later come true in her own family. I listened to Rita's stories with a forgiving smile, thinking it was nothing more than family folklore.

But there were two dreams, one dreamed by Grandma Cipora, my father's mother, and the other by Aunt Rita, which could not be written off as folklore. They were bound to my fate and my parents' and left no doubt as to the fact that women in my family had prophetic dreams. How remarkable!

Grandma Cipora was a mother of five. She had a very strong relationship with her eldest, Michał, my father. At the end of the 1920s, when my father left Lodz and started his business in Danzig, Grandma, Aunt Rita, and Uncle Paweł followed him there. The four of them lived together in perfect harmony. In 1925 Grandma and Aunt Rita moved to Palestine. They lived in Tel Aviv and returned to Danzig a year later. In the beginning of the 1930s they came to Palestine again and built their home here. First they lived together in Tel Aviv, and after Aunt Rita married Uncle Abraham Robinson and moved with him to Pardess Hannah, Grandma followed her to the village, renting a room from the neighbors across the yard, allowing both her daughter and herself some privacy. Paweł and Anni got married and immigrated to Palestine in the mid-1930s.

Grandma and Daddy shared deep love and unique closeness. They corresponded frequently and regularly, keeping each other up to date on their happenings and sharing their lives from afar. Daddy always supported Grandma financially, taking care of her wellbeing. He visited Palestine in 1937 to announce his intention to marry his beloved, Franka Fersztendik, whom he'd met after his family left Poland. Franka was born in Warsaw, had lost her mother at a young age, and grew up with her father, Dawid, and her younger brother Ben, or Beniek.

My parents were married on May 1st, 1938. I was born on March 11th, 1939. Grandma Cipora never met my mother, but they wrote each other plenty of emotional letters. My mother, who didn't have a mother of her own, treated Cipora as her adoptive mother, and Grandma saw Franka as an additional daughter of her own. Mommy often sent Grandma family photos, especially after I was born. She shared every significant development of my childhood.

When the war broke the letters dwindled. Later, when my family was trapped inside the ghetto, they stopped altogether. In the meantime Uncle Chaim joined the British army and was taken hostage by the Germans in Greece in April 1941 along with other volunteers from the Land of Israel. They were imprisoned in British POW camps in Germany. He and Grandma were able to correspond regularly, if rarely. Grandma was consumed by worry for her two sons and her eldest son's family. Her health faded and anxiety depleted her.

In early November 1943 Grandma Cipora met Aunt Rita with a gray face and tearful eyes. In a crushed voice she said, *I dreamed that Michał died. I know it's true. He said goodbye to me. I know he's gone. I have no reason to live.*

No matter how much Aunt Rita and the other relatives argued that no news meant good news, Grandma wouldn't budge. She refused to listen. *I dreamed it*, she said, *I know. My Michał is gone*, she repeated persistently. Ever since that morning she barely ate until finally she stopped altogether. Her health deteriorated and in the spring of 1944, she died. The family later found out that on November 3rd, 1943, my parents had been murdered in the Trawniki camp, chillingly close to the date when she'd had her dream.

Aunt Rita kept recounting this dream to me, attesting to Grandma's ability to foretell reality from a distance, with no proof of its veracity.

Rita, like her mother, dreamed prophetically. She described one such dream to me upon my arrival in Pardess Hannah.

After my grandmother died Rita grieved for her mother, whom she loved so much, and whom she'd always lived close to. Secretly, she also grieved for her beloved brother and soulmate, my father. She believed Grandma's dream, though outwardly she tried to convince her mother otherwise.

One day, Rita told me, she dreamed that a knock came on her bedroom door. The door opened slightly and my mother walked in, carrying me in her arms. Rita asked Mommy to sit down, but Mommy said she was in a hurry. *I only came to give you Relli. You have to take care of her.* As she spoke, she handed me over to Rita.

Rita took me in her arms and asked, trying to keep my mother from leaving, *But where's Michał? Where's Michał?*

Mommy answered, *I have to run off to meet him. You'll take care of our daughter. You'll take care of Relli.*

Rita woke up from the dream with a gasp. Ever since that day, she claimed to the entire family that she knew Relli would be saved and would make it to Israel one day. Her husband, her sister, her brother, and the rest of the family responded forgivingly. For years there'd been no news from the burning Europe.

But when the war was over Rita's dream became a reality. Uncle Chaim returned from German captivity and Aunt Rita was honorably discharged from the British army, which she'd joined as well after Grandma died. A few months after the world quietened down, the surprising news of my survival was revealed. Aunt Rita rejoiced with the rest of the family, but claimed that she wasn't surprised. *I always knew you were alive*, she said. *I knew you'd survive, you'd come to Israel, and that my home would be yours. I'd dreamed it! It took time for everyone to see I was right*, she said, smiling lovingly.

And I? I too have dreams, but my dreams are not an articulation of events taking place faraway, as Grandma's were. I also don't dream of a future that would come true one day, like Aunt Rita.

My dreams are about the reality of the past, of my childhood. My dreams are bad. As a child, a teenager, and an adult, I never stop dreaming about the evil in my life. When I'm awake I live in the light, steering my life toward the good. But at night I am in the dark, devoid of any compass. I have no control.

At the Swimming Pool

The sunlight danced upon the blue water. Sounds of laughter and the bustle of youth surrounded everyone in the beautiful swimming pool at Hakfar Hayarok Agricultural High School. It was 1954. The new, modern school building glimmered in the sun. The classrooms by the entrance and the dorm rooms were grouped together in bright, captivating structures. The dining hall was on the hill in the center, overlooking the entire grounds, covered in manicured lawns and blooming flowers. Beyond the grounds were farm structures and fields.

The swimming pool was the best part. In those years, when the country was still young, such a pretty swimming pool was a source of awe and a destination for incomparable fun. The pool area was fenced in and surrounded by a lawn. Trees shaded it here and there, enticing in their canopies. The pool was large and L-shaped, appropriate in its size and depth for advanced swimmers and non-swimmers alike: wide steps for a gradual entry to the bottom of the L, shallow water slowly deepening through the corner of the L and up its other leg, until reaching the deepest point and the diving board at the top of the L. The diving board was very high and pretty, intended for strong swimmers to practice their dives.

On summer days many of the school's students spent their free time here, before or after performing their farming duties. The pool was the place to see others and to be seen, a place to expend the bubbly energy of youth and to have a ball.

As a Pisces, I've always been drawn to water. I liked to dip in the sea and the pool, though I'd never received swimming lessons like my classmates, who had learned on the beaches of Tel Aviv or in pools at their home villages. I didn't know how to swim, but I had no fear of the water. On the contrary—I loved it. At the entrance to the pool area, across the lawn, were swimming props for novices like me: special wooden boards, rounded out at one end and cut straight in the other, which one could grab with their hands, the round end slicing through the water as the swimmer paddled his or her feet.

One day in the early afternoon I went to the pool with my classmate, Dina. Dina, a native of Tel Aviv, was an experienced and accomplished swimmer. When we arrived at the pool she suggested we swim together into the deep end. She promised to stay at my side while I paddled with the help of the board. I agreed gladly. I grabbed a board from the lawn, and we walked down the steps and waded together through the shallow water as it gradually deepened. I was tall and could walk in the water for a long time, but Dina, who was shorter, quickly switched to a beautiful, well-styled breast stroke. I watched her with admiration, regretting the fact that I'd never had the opportunity to learn how to swim. Maybe one day, I comforted myself, stretching my arms out and pushing the board away from my body, finding my balance and beginning to paddle, mimicking Dina's motions.

When we reached the corner of the pool the water was truly deep and I couldn't stand in it even if I wanted to. Dina asked if I wanted to continue and I said yes, accepting the challenge, and found myself in the depths of the pool, several meters above the bottom.

We advanced toward the diving board and paused to watch our friends jump off. Our classmates were lined up on the board: first was Racheli Kaufman (who would later become known as renowned ceramic artist Rachel Cadmor). She was doing a handstand, her legs flush against each other, stretched up, her feet pointing into the sky. She looked so proud and erect as she bent down her legs slowly into an arch and performed a perfect summersault into the water. Everyone applauded.

Next up was Mosh (Moshe Yanover, who would later change his last name to Niv). He spread his arms upwards and to the sides in a forty-five degree angle, like an eagle spreading his wings. He seemed to glide through the air as he jumped off the board, bringing his hands together in midair, stretching like a taut arrow, and disappearing into the water. The vision was breathtaking in its beauty.

After him was Danny Wagner, a blond, handsome boy who was a central figure in our class. Danny was smart, witty, an accomplished athlete and dancer, a talented flautist, beloved by all the girls and well-liked by all the boys. He was graceful and bursting with youth. I wanted to linger some more and watch Danny jump off the board. His diving style, like Racheli and Mosh's, was famous.

But Dina kept pushing me: *Relli, let's swim to the very edge of the pool!* I advanced at her side, trying to catch up and simultaneously keep my cool; a little anxious to be in such deep water. I grasped the board strongly, speeding up my leg work when suddenly, without any warning, I felt the board slipping from my grasp, my fingers sliding down the slippery, wet wood, and… and… the board was gone!

I didn't know what happened. All I could hear was Dina's laughter. I later found out that when we were right at the deepest point she decided, as a joke, to swiftly, cruelly, and stupidly pull the board out from under me. What was she thinking? What did she expect?

Without any kind of support, I sunk right to the bottom of the pool. I didn't dive like a well-versed swimmer, holding my breath and opening my eyes. I did nothing of the sort and made no movement in an attempt to float myself up. I went down like a rock, into the depths. The sudden shock left me without a thought in my mind; without any kind of survival instinct. All I did was hug myself, as if in defense, my body folding into the fetal position. This is how I arrived at the blue floor of the pool. I realized then that I was drowning. Simply drowning. I felt the floor below me, while a voice inside me whispered, *I've drowned…*

At that moment I felt a pair of strong arms taking hold of my shoulders and pulling me up. It was Danny, Danny Wagner who I'd seen on the diving board, preparing for a stunning dive. When he saw what was happening—Dina pulling the board from under me and me disappearing into the water, he jumped off the diving board, no longer concerned with style, slicing through the air at once, breaking the water with his fists, diving toward me as fast as he could, and arriving before I could inhale any water. He pulled me up to the surface and out of the pool, pulling me out toward life.

Afterward

A bond of friendship was formed between Danny and me that day, and it has lasted well into the eighth decade of our lives. During mandatory military service, Danny would serve as a command car driver and would be involved in a bad car accident on his way to Kibbutz Yotvata, near Eilat, which he helped found as part of his service in the Nahal. The accident would leave Danny's legs paralyzed.

Later, he would go on to marry Nurit. They would have two boys, Yuval and Uri. Yuval would serve as a helicopter pilot in the air force and would also be involved in an accident that would paralyze him. Both of them would go on to live a fully active life, facing challenges from their positions in wheelchairs. They are both brave, determined men who never let themselves off the hook.

Yuval would start a family and become a father of three. He would continue to serve in the air force in spite of his disability and would become a lieutenant colonel at headquarters. At the same time, he would conceive of the non-profit organization Access Israel, which enables the social integration of people with disabilities and their families with honor, equal rights, and maximal independence. Yuval has been the head of the organization since its founding in 1999.

Nurit, Danny's wife, would become a leading figure in Israeli nursing services.

The Wagners are a warm, close-knit family. Their home is always open to our family of friends, alumni of the second class of Hakfar Hayarok. Throughout the years, we have assembled there every year to celebrate Independence Day together.

Danny Wagner would excel in life—both in his work in the banking industry, and in his family. I will always remember how close I came to losing my life, and how I owe it all to Danny, who was at the right place at the right time, and did the right thing.

And Dina? That is not her real name. The girl would transfer out of Hakfar Hayarok after the first year and we would never see each other again.

Grandma Cipora's Book

In my hand I am holding Grandma Cipora's book of poetry. It's a thick book, its hard cover dark green and faded at spots. Her name is printed diagonally across the cover in black lettering: *C. Głowinska*, as was customary to write wives' names in Polish. This spelling tells me that the book had been purchased after her marriage to Grandpa, Hanoch Głowinski. Did she pick it out herself or did someone give it to her as a gift? There's no way of knowing. There is no dedication or date. The book is made of high quality paper and is lined with thin blue lines for handwriting. The pages had acquired brown spots with the years. About half its pages are filled with handwriting on both sides, usually in black ink, but others are written in blue or purple.

This is Grandma's book. With her clear, round handwriting she copied down poems and ballads, mostly by Polish poets such as Juliusz Słowacki, Kornel Ujejski, *Maria* Konopnicka, Helena Bojarska, and others. There are also some by German writers, which were copied down in German, a language that Grandma spoke fluently. They are mostly long, over ten pages at least. Upon careful reading, I could only find two dates attesting to the time the poems were copied. The first is December 12th, 1891, and the other is February 6th, 1907. I got chills when I found them. It had been so many years.

Grandma Cipora wasn't the only one who wrote in the book. Aunt Roma told me that Grandma taught her children to copy beautiful literature they'd read into the book. Sometimes, when Grandma was on vacation and her five children stayed at home with a nanny and relatives, they had a ritual in which my father picked pieces for the other siblings to copy for their mother.

Thus, upon Grandma's return, she had a surprise waiting for her: poems copied into her special book by her two daughters and three sons. Indeed, the poems are copied down in different handwriting. The name of the copier does not appear, only the name of the poet. When reading it, there is no way of knowing who copied each poem. In a few spots, Grandma added her initials, C.G. in tiny lettering, but these instances are rare.

What a shame. I would have loved to know who'd copied which piece and who liked each piece. I'm mostly curious to know which pieces my father copied. The handwriting evolves with years, and thus his handwriting from the final letter I have in my possession, from January 1941, looks nothing like his handwriting as a boy in the early twentieth century.

The book came into my possession in 1996, after Aunt Roma died. She kept it safe through the years since Grandma's death in 1944. Aunt Roma was considered the artistic one in our family. She read a lot, spoke different languages, was knowledgeable in art history, and wrote poems for the children of the family on special occasions before I arrived in Israel. Aunt Roma and Uncle Zalman's apartment in Tel Aviv contained an impressive collection of art books which today enriches my own library. My first visit to the Tel Aviv Art Museum, which was on Rothschild Avenue at the time, was made with Aunt Roma. She took me to see an exhibition by Marc Chagall. We later went to see other exhibitions. She taught me the pleasures of museum visits, explained the empathy felt by viewers when they emotionally connect to a piece of art. Aunt Roma was also a theatre lover and took me more than once to see a play with her and Uncle Zalman at the Habima Theatre near their home. She also taught me the importance of reading books in English. *Only by reading fine literature will you be able to learn the language, she always said.*

I knew she was right. That was how I'd learned Hebrew, too. At first I read Hebrew translations of my favorite Polish books. But English? Reading English for fun? *Romka*, I said, using her nickname, *that's going too far!* But with the famous Głowinski persistence, she talked me into it. The first book in English she bought me was *Gone With the Wind*, which I'd read in Hebrew and loved. *You already know the plot and love the characters*, she said, *so what's the problem? Make an effort and read it again in English.*

Aunt Roma was right. I began to read in English and the foreign, difficult language became more familiar.

Occasionally when I visited Aunt Roma showed me Grandma's book. She always said, *You still read Polish and one day this special book will be yours. You might even read it and use it as something to remember us by.*

I was a curious teenager. I didn't truly understand what she'd meant nor the value of the book. I used to only skim through it, but in recent years I've been reading it carefully once a year, on Yom Kippur. I use this day to take a moment with my family—Grandma, Daddy, my aunts and uncles, all long gone. They'd left me this wonderful keepsake from their home in Lodz. The book is like a window through which I can look at a distant world that began back in the nineteenth century. She and her children lived without televisions and DVDs, without cell phones or computers, probably without even a radio. Their stimulations were so different than ours. Was their world any poorer for it? I believe it was emotionally deeper and more enriched.

I picture them sitting by the light of the gas lamp and copying down poems with a fountain pen, careful not to let the ink drip, immersing themselves in the poem and working hard to copy it flawlessly. Most of the poems in the book are romantic, dealing with the love between a man and a woman, within a family, and among humankind. There are also poems of the love of man for God, such as Kornel Ujejski's poem about the man living in the desert. There are melancholic poems of longing, and others depicting traditional Jewish life. I was surprised to find a ballad by *Maria* Konopnicka called *W Piwnicznej izbie*, loosely translated as *In the Cellar*, which I'd learned back in fifth grade in Poland. As was the custom then, I had to memorize it, and I remember the first verses to this day.

Grandma Cipora's book of poems and ballads is an asset of familial and cultural heritage, and I cherish it. It is an object with a being of its own, which has been alive for over a hundred and twenty years. It contains an entire world of emotions and human experiences, moving in its uniqueness.

Possessions

My beloved aunt Rita died on Saturday morning, October 17th, 1998, when she was ninety-eight years old. My mythological aunt, as I like to call her, was clearheaded and sharp to her very last day. She was an opinionated, determined woman of great will power, uncompromising and, to be honest, stubborn. Sometimes, when I tried to convince her of something and was able to strike a chord, she would answer, *I've lived this long and come this far only thanks to my stubbornness.* She was right, I thought. Perhaps not only dreams are hereditary in my family. Persistence is too.

Her death, though foreseen, saddened me to no end. I felt myself becoming orphaned a third time. We waited with the funeral until Nurit, her only daughter, arrived from Canada. She stayed two days after the end of the shiva, in which we began to dismantle the house in Pardess Hannah.

Upon Nurit's return to Canada, the responsibility of continuing to empty the house fell to me. It was a complicated, emotionally taxing job, saying goodbye to my aunt's personal effects, and was physically challenging as well.

Those days, I still worked at the University of Haifa and was only free on Fridays. For two months I drove to Pardess Hannah every Friday morning and only returned to Haifa before the Sabbath began. Two people helped me in my task. One was Dudu, my ex-husband, whose father, Professor Nathan Robinson, was Abraham's brother, and to whom Rita was also a beloved aunt. The other was my son Nattiv, who came from Tel Aviv. They took turns each Friday and both helped me a great deal. When we began the mission I determined that nothing would be thrown out before being looked over, and that all written materials were to be read before a decision was made. This process slowed us down, but it was important and proved itself beyond anything I could expect. My aunt had lived in the house for over sixty years. She was a hoarder who never threw anything out, even if it was cracked, broken, torn, moldy, or was no longer of any use. Each possession must have had its own right of existence in her eyes by mere fact of having belonged to her or another family member at one time.

The closets were filled with all sorts of items: clothing items purchased in Danzig in the 1920 and 1930s—crumbling leather belts, wallets, and bags whose original shape and color was barely recognizable, alongside wide brimmed straw hats from old-time Tel Aviv. There were also pin heeled sandals that she must not have worn ever since moving to the village and becoming a farmer. Silk and lace items hung alongside work outfits. There were also cotton clothes and colorful knits. Everything was crowded together and a pungent smell of mold and old age emanated from the closets that hadn't been aired in years. At the end of her life, Rita's body betrayed her. Her eyesight faded and her legs could barely carry her. As an old woman, a proud Polish woman to the very end, she never admitted to her limitations and refused to receive any help.

The old sideboard from Danzig still stood in the "big room," formidable in its dark glory. On the top shelf, in the glass vitrine, were beautiful porcelain miniatures shaped as animals, dancers, and other characters, alongside refined vases decorated with silver and gold. On the exterior shelf was a picture frame containing Rita's decorations from her service in Egypt as part of the British army, and from the Haganah organization in Israel. Alongside them were the dusty trophies she'd won playing Bridge in and around the village. On the bottom part, closed behind carved wooden doors, were piles of dishes, from the serving set of Grandma's days, its golden ornamentation faded, to chipped plastic plates and cups and glasses of all colors, designs, and sizes. The linen closet was stuffed with cotton, linen, and silk tablecloths that used to be white and were now yellow, gray, or black, crumbling lace tablecloths and doilies, and old starched cotton bedding alongside contemporary no-iron sheets. Touching these made me very emotional. My childhood days returned to me with intensity, as if it were only yesterday that we'd sat together around the Seder table, covered with the large linen tablecloth, back when it was still white and glowing. I walked around the empty rooms. We'd donated all usable pieces of furniture. The rooms seemed to echo with the voices of relatives; the ones I'd loved so much and that were no longer alive. I miss them so much.

More and more memories submerged my eyes with tears. We moved methodically from room to room, exposed through my aunt's collected possessions to her long and rich life, which had spread over three continents: Europe, Asia, and Africa. I kept thinking of the idea of possessions telling a story. A person's possessions, which accompany her through life, the things she buys or receives, keeps and cherishes, the ones that outlive her, they all tell the story of the person to whom they belonged.

I often yearn for a possession, if only a small one, a simple one, that belonged to my parents; something that their adult hands touched when they were already my parents. I want so badly to have something of theirs. All I have is their pictures, and I am grateful for those, but the yearning for an object that belonged to my mother or father, or both, this yearning has no end, and will never be fulfilled.

The Last Letter

The kitchen was the final assignment, left for the last Friday. The work was especially hard. Food products that had been hoarded without my aunt's noticing clung to each other and to the oilcloths on the shelves. Nattiv and I worked hard, me standing on a ladder, he standing below, holding a thick garbage bag into which I threw the items after checking each one to make sure it was no longer needed.

The kitchen cabinet stretched all the way up to the ceiling. I remember when Uncle Zalman planned and built it. Now the style is to build narrow kitchen cabinets that contain about three shelves, but back in the 1950s, my uncle designed the kitchen so that each shelf had its own door. The doors were wide and low, and the shelves wide and deep. Fifty years later the doors could barely be opened. The hinges were rusty, the effort great.

Exhausted but glad to find us nearing the end of our mission I said to Nattiv, *That's it, there's only one final door in the right corner, where the ceiling meets the wall.*

But the door wouldn't open. Nattiv handed me a hammer and chisel and I ended up ripping the door off its crumbling hinges. The smell of mouse excrement hit my nostrils, and I found piles of old newspapers, all torn apart, which must have been eaten up by mice. I worked wearing thick plastic gloves, gathering everything I could and throwing it into the bag, still worried that something valuable might be hidden there.

Then I felt something hard. I pushed the newspapers aside and found a red cardboard box, the kind that used to contain chocolates. It was designed as a drawer that pulled out from the narrow end of the box. I held onto the rectangular box, which was about ten by fifteen centimeters in size, and barely one-and-a-half centimeters tall. It was seemingly empty and light. I was about to toss it into the garbage bag when my hand paused in midair.

What's wrong, Mom? Nattiv asked.

I said, *I just remembered that I'd promised not to throw anything out without checking first.* As I answered, I pulled out the inner drawer of the box and found a letter inside. I pulled it out gently. The thin piece of paper had yellowed with the years but remained intact. The date January 28th, 1941 appeared on the top left corner, and the letter was addressed to someone named Sewek. *Dear Sewek.*

Strange, I said to Nattiv. *There was never a Sewek in our family. Who could it be?* I opened the folded letter and was shocked to find my father's signature at the bottom of the first page. The next page was written in different handwriting and signed by my mother. The letter also included two pictures of me as a baby. The same date was on the backs of the pictures.

Mom, what's wrong? You're so pale! Please come down from the ladder, my son urged me.

Nattiv, Nattiv, I said, unable to hold back my shaking and my tears. *The last item we've found in Aunt Rita's house is a letter from your grandparents, my parents. It must be the last one they sent before entering the ghetto. It's addressed to somebody named Sewek.* I stepped off the ladder and into my son's embrace. I put the letter and the pictures in my purse. It was getting dark and there was no electricity in the house, since it had been disconnected upon my aunt's death. *Let's go, Nattiv, let's each go home. I'll read the letter when I get to Haifa and tell you what it says, I promise.* I was secretly afraid to read it before driving all the way to Haifa.

I took to the road with great excitement and took out the letter again immediately upon my return home. I read it over and over, unable to stop crying. I gathered from its contents that it had been sent to my parents' friends, Sewek and Dorka, who had escaped from Poland to Lithuania and planned to continue to Palestine. Mommy and Daddy wrote to them in Vilna, a letter that would be passed on to the family in Palestine.

I recalled that Aunt Anni, widow of my youngest uncle, Paweł, had a friend named Dorka who had recently returned from years in Canada and now lived in Tel Aviv again. I called my aunt to confirm this information and set a meeting with Dorka. A few days later I drove to Tel Aviv with the letter. Dorka was very happy to see me. She remembered my mother well and told me I resembled her. My mother was a tall woman who stood out in her elegant clothing and straight posture. It was the first time in my life that anyone who'd known my mother mentioned a resemblance. Dorka complimented my posture and said she'd had chills when I walked into her home. I was beside myself. It was as if Mommy, whom I remember only from pictures, had suddenly come to life. The knowledge that I was reminiscent of her empowered me.

Dorka described the circumstances of the letter, how she and her late husband Sewek carried it to Palestine through Lithuania, Russia, and Turkey. They made their difficult and fretful journey during the years of World War II. While bombs exploded all around, they'd managed to make it safely to Tel Aviv. Upon their arrival they gave the letter and the pictures to my uncle Paweł, who delivered them to his mother, Grandma Cipora, who lived next door to my aunt in Pardess Hannah. I suppose Aunt Rita had kept the letter since then, though she'd never mentioned it to me and must have forgotten where she'd hidden it.

Thus, in its mysterious ways, fate brought me the last letter my parents ever sent. This was their final call for help from occupied Warsaw, just before they were locked up in the ghetto. In their despair they wrote from the universe that was collapsing all around them to their family in the free world, in Palestine, asking for help. This final letter, containing pictures of me less than two years of age, fell into my hands fifty-seven years after it was written.

The ways of destiny are unknown and the passage of possessions and their meanings in our lives is wondrous. This is the only possession I have from my parents—something they'd touched with their own hands. Now, all these years later, I, their daughter, am holding it in mine. I read my parents' last letter, lingering again and again on the words which cry out in black ink from the yellowing paper.

My father writes, … *I hope that the family doesn't forget us, because in my state I cannot find a way out or provide my own council, though I still haven't lost my energy… Sewek, please tell my family they must make every effort to procure travel documents for us! I'm attaching pictures of my little miss, Relli. See my pride and joy.*

Please kiss my family for me.

Yours,

Michał.

And my mother adds, *I don't think I'm exaggerating when I say that our daughter is a very mature, gentle, and special girl… Please kiss Mother and the entire family for us. Please have them try to get us papers so we can enter another country. Any country in the world will do!*

Yours,

Franka.

What's Your Name?

The poet Zelda wrote, *Each of us has a name given by God and given by our parents.*[1] When I was born my parents called me Relli. The *R* and the *L* came from my maternal grandmother's name, Rachel Luci, and the I was meant to resemble the Hebrew word *sheli*—mine. My father, who spoke Hebrew, said, My daughter, *ha'bat sheli*—Relli. This was my name until I was three years and ten months old.

When I was taken in by my rescuers, Janina and Jòzef, they were unable to call me Relli. The sound would seem too foreign to Polish people and would awaken suspicion in that hostile environment. They chose to call me Lala, which meant doll in Polish, probably because of my blue eyes and blond curls.

At the end of the war, when I was enrolled in school, the question of my name came up again. Lala was a nickname, and so a Polish name of my choosing was required. I picked Halinka, and became Halinka Abramowicz. But at home and among my friends I was still Lala.

In 1950, when the process of my return to Judaism and my Aliyah to Israel began, my name became an issue once more. I'd always known my real name was Relli and I'd seen it written on the backs of photos in my mother's handwriting, but the name had a strange ring to my ears. As a Polish girl, I was used to women's names ending with an *A*. I therefore agreed to be called Rella. I liked the double *L*. As per my request, the name Rella was registered in my travel and immigration documents. The clerk at the Haifa Port merely copied what he'd seen, literally translating the double *L* into Hebrew, making my name in Hebrew Relala.

---

[1]Translated by Marcia Lee Falk.

When I arrived at my aunt and uncle's house in Pardess Hannah I was immediately addressed as Relli. They did not ask my preference. They knew my name from my parents since the day I was born and had no doubt as to what to call me. I had to get used to it without putting up a fight. I accepted my fate—from now on, I was Relli.

When Aunt Rita enrolled me in the village school, the principal, Abraham Rosen, a renowned educator and a patriot, believed, like many others, that new immigrants should have Hebrew names. He said, *Mrs. Robinson, what's going on here? You finally managed to get the girl out of there and into Israel, and now you let her walk around with this name, Relli? She must have a Hebrew name.*

Rita explained the origin of my name, but he wasn't convinced and determined, *Let her choose, either Rachel or Leah.* My aunt returned home with Mr. Rosen's suggestions. I did not like the name Leah and was unable to pronounce the name Rachel. I objected, which is something I'm good at.

Aunt Rita returned to the school to share the conundrum with the principal. He considered the matter again and suggested that my name be Erella or Ariella, and my nickname would be Relli. Without a choice I picked Erella, which is how the teachers and other village people called me. Among my family and the other children I was Relli.

When I finished eighth grade the family decided to enroll me into the agricultural high school Hakfar Hayarok. I was not involved in this decision, and though I wanted to go to high school in Hadera with Nurit and our classmates, I was forced to accept this verdict and move into the boarding school. In retrospect, I can say that my aunts and uncles had made an excellent choice. The four years I lived and studied at Hakfar

Hayarok were some of the most formative, most enriching years of my life. Agricultural schools were some of the leading high schools in the country back then, and my school was new and modern. I was part of the second class of students to graduate. We enjoyed a rich social life, interesting farm work, and a high level of learning. We were divided according to learning abilities, and I was entered into a class in which all students had finished eighth grade with honors and received a Ministry of Education fellowship. The friends I made at that school have been my extended family my entire life.

The duality of my name continued. My friends called me Relli while the teachers called me Erella. When my enlistment order arrived in the eleventh grade my friends had a big laugh when they discovered the name that appeared on the envelope: Relala. This was my name in all military documents, and I always had to explain that it was a mistake, and that my name was Relli.

Afterward

Eventually, as a student at the Hebrew University of Jerusalem and before leaving for America to marry my fiancé, Dudu, and continue my studies there, I would pay the Ministry of Interior Affairs five lira and would finally, at age twenty-three, officially return to my original name, Relli, the one given to me by God and given to me by my parents; the one I'd parted with when I was three years and ten months old.

Thus, in the course of twenty years I would have seven first names: Relli, Lala, Halinka, Rella, Relala, Erella, and Relli again. I was forced to replace my personal, my national and my religious identity two-and-a-half times: first from a Jewish girl to a Polish girl, then back to Jewish, and finally Jewish-Israeli.

Trawniki
November 3rd 1943 – November 3rd, 2006

I had a dream—
If I had graves
I would paint them floral
If I had gravestones
I would gloss them with tears
If I had a place
To give a greeting of peace
The absence is huge
My life is choked

Invisible fate
Had brought me there
To Trawniki
A Polish town
Where a labor camp
Became a valley of death
This day, sixty-three years ago
Ten thousand prisoners
Were shot, burned, buried alive

With the Haifa Municipality Delegation
I've come to the land
That had absorbed my parents' blood
From a gray sky
And white snow
A ray of light
Broke through a cloud
A large circle of teenagers
Glowing beads falling from their eyes
To my right are Ziv and Rona
Carrying pictures of my parents
My son says the Kaddish *prayer*

Doron reads Psalms
I gather my strength to speak
Michalle sings softly
Filled with sounds
Loraine, Daniel, and Rona,
In their caressing velvet voices
Nattiv ends with El Male Rachamim

We brought stones from Israel
Stones from Nattiv and my daughter-in-law Kinneret,
Delivered from the blue coast of the Sea of Galilee
Stones from my garden
Remembrance candles
Orit gathered wild flowers from the cold hill

Hope
Rose in a broken whisper
Carrying the pain of horror
Misunderstanding, yearning,
A resurgence from a far-off land
And I—
Fog in my eyes
Shaken up
Clinging to my son
Dozens of boys and girls
Come together in an arch of embrace
I've received the honor of holding a memorial service
For the first time in sixty-three years
In a black plot of land
By an old train station
Words of song and prayer
We brought the warmth of youth with us
The love of daughter, grandchildren, and great-grandchildren
I have won

The tremble of shock
The burn of longing
For graves that would never be
For the flowers that would never be placed upon them
For gravestones that would never be glossed with tears
For the absence in their death
And for life
The life they ordered me to live
The memory of their love
Has paved my life with hope for kindness in the world

Relli Robinson
Testimonial, Haifa Municipality Delegation
Poland, November 1st-8th, 2006

Relli with her son Nattiv at the Memorial Service at Trawniki,Poland ,
Nov. 3rd 2006

Relli Writes to Lala

Lala my dear,

By writing to you I double our affinity. I wish to point to our mutuality. In spite of this, I write to ask that you, my borrowed identity, step away and back inside. I ask you to leave me be.

There are no words to describe my devotion, appreciation, and love for you. You were able to hide me deep inside you. You were able to pretend and stifle my longing. You were able to make me disappear. You, Lala, knew how to be amiable, adaptable, polite. You were brave, wise, introspective. You conquered your fears and your secrets. A survivor. It's thanks to you, Lala, that we've survived. You hid me inside of you and together we became you.

When the storm was over, when we were discovered, you wouldn't let me emerge. We were only six years old. You were stronger than I was and determined that we would remain Lala. Your surroundings supported you and I sunk deeper still.

At age eleven you suddenly cracked. Without preparation we met a beautiful and tan girl, overflowing with love and warmth, spreading the rays of the Israeli sun. She was open and honest, and with inexplicable suddenness I burst out of you. Adda took my hand, not yours, and I, Relli, slowly overtook you, Lala.

We said goodbye to Poland, crossing Europe and the Mediterranean. The ship docked in Haifa, and I said goodbye to you and walked onto my land with my head held high. I was the one who then stifled you inside me. When I grew up I thought I'd said goodbye to you for good. I was wrong.

I recently returned from a trip to Poland, where, without my intention, you burst out of me, as if it hadn't been more than fifty years. In Poland we answered both names at once. To those who came with us from Israel we were Relli, but to our old acquaintances from Warsaw we were Lala. Strange how natural it felt.

We walked hand in hand to meet the dead. At my parents' memorial service we trembled with love, pain, yearning, and tears. At your parents' grave our tears fell with love, immeasurable gratitude, and admiration for who they were and what they'd done. On both occasions, Nattiv hugged and comforted us. He doesn't even know you. He only knows me, Relli, his mother.

This conflict is the reason I am writing to you today. Please Lala, return to hide yourself within me. Disappear. Let me go. From the day I returned to Poland I cannot get away from you. You emerge, you react, you interfere with my thoughts and feelings. You want to exist again. But I cannot let you, my dear Lala. You are deep inside me, like the burning lava at the heart of the earth. This lava must be contained within membranes that keep it from bursting out and shaking the planet's course.

I beg you Lala, say goodbye, go back to your hiding place of over fifty years and continue to live deep inside of me. I promise to remember you and perhaps, from time to time, to imbue you with real being. But please, stop shaking my own being. I am Relli and wish to continue my known life as Relli. You, my hidden beloved, will be a secret in the folds of my consciousness. You, Lala, are my borrowed identity. You were, you are, and you always will be the most significant person in my life.

Yours,
Relli
December, 2006

Lala Answers Relli

My beloved Relli,

I've read your letter several times. Thank you for being so honest and open about what is going on inside of you.

I was glad you went to Poland, though I knew the experience would shake you up. I admired your courage and self-control in the emotional situations we experienced there. In Poland we both exist simultaneously, as you mentioned in your letter. It happened naturally.

There in Warsaw you began your existence as Relli. There, too, you were forced, under the cruel circumstances of war, to accept me without preparation. It all happened with such uncompromising decisiveness. The surroundings forced you to stop being you and start being me.

You were so young when my identity was forced upon you. I, Lala, did my best, as you said. As your borrowed identity, I enveloped you so deep inside me that no one even suspected you existed. Though your existence was often at risk, it never failed the challenge. We survived.

And we'd grown used to living in secret. When the storm died down we were six. We didn't want to be Relli again. I admit I was the one who prevented you from emerging. I made the decision for both of us together with everyone around. It was decided we would continue to live as Lala. You are right about that.

You are also right when you describe our meeting with Adda. She was a Jewish girl from Israel, the first we'd ever met, and you pounced wildly from within your hiding place. You wanted to connect to the inner truth of who you really were. You gave Adda your hand and introduced yourself as

Relli. The decision was made—you began the long road back to being Relli. I fought against you at first. We were confused. But you called the shots and you made the right choice, the choice of the life that had always been meant for you, a life as Relli, the life taken from you through bloody years of death and loss.

The road was long, emotionally and physically. We crossed Poland, Czechoslovakia, Austria, and Italy by train. We sailed through the Mediterranean Sea. The further we advanced, the farther away you moved from me. By the time the ship had docked in Haifa, you'd decided to say goodbye.

You, Relli, stepped confidently off the ship on Sunday morning, unto your new land, determined to fight your personal battle and fit in. You were met with a land of sunshine, glowing with familial love, but unwelcoming to new immigrants from "over there," who arrived after the Holocaust. I, Lala, sunk deep into you. I silently watched as you struggled to become Relli, to meet yourself in childhood photos, to know your family, to learn the language and the behavior codes of children and adults. To become a part. Secretly, I admired how you handled these many challenges.

This letter you wrote me, the first one in so many years, has touched my heart. I was glad to have been with you on our trip to Poland, to have the two of us as one.

But now we are back in your country and we are you once more. I cover myself in your love and sink back down. I know you always remember me and carry me inside of you, in a hiding place, cordoned off and inaccessible. That is the only way you can live as Relli.

Cheers to you, Relli, your identity is your own.
Yours,
Lala,
Your borrowed identity of fifty-six years ago
December, 2006

Chapter Four:
My Family in Words and Images

My Mother

My mother, Franka Głowinski, née Fersztendik, was born in Warsaw on July 13th, 1906. Her father, Dawid Fersztendik, was a wealthy trader. Her mother, Rachel Luci Rozenfarb, was a homemaker. I am named after her. Grandma Rachel was a beautiful and impressive woman who died when my mother was a teenager.

When she was born my mother was called Frajda Małka. With the years she'd taken on the name Franka, and the name Frajda Małka only appeared in official papers. I like that. I too have learned a thing or two about living with more than one first name.

My mother grew up in Warsaw with her father and her brother, two years younger than her. He was called Beniek, perhaps a nickname for Ben or Benjamin. There's no way of knowing. The two of them were very close and devoted to their father. Unfortunately all traces of my only uncle on that side of the family were lost during the war, and all my efforts to track him down and discover his fate had failed. Logic has it that, had he survived, he would have sought out the Głowinski family in Israel.

My grandfather, Dawid, was locked along with my parents in the ghetto and was transferred with them to Trawniki, where they all died on November 3rd, 1943. It seems none of the

Fersztendik family had survived. It is a rare last name, and in 1973 when the entire State of Israel fit into one phone book, I searched for it, encouraged by my children, and found only seven families by that name. I wrote to them all and received replies that all led me to a dead-end. My mother's family had been eradicated in the Holocaust.

Any factual or personal information I have about my mother is limited. Her beauty stands out in all her pictures, from youthful high school images through her photos from Paris, where it seems she studied art. She was a tall woman, famous for her careful appearance. The images attest to her good taste and fashion sense. In a photo from my parents' wedding day on May 1st, 1938, she is glowing, surrounded by her and her mother's friends, as she wrote in her fine handwriting on the back of the picture. In a photo from the hospital when I was a week old, the one at the beginning of this book, she is elegant: hair combed, face made-up, nails manicured. She is wearing fine bed clothes—the classic image of a Warsaw lady.

When I was born Franka devoted herself completely to motherhood. My aunt Anni, who visited Poland in the summer of 1939 said that every day my mother rode the suburban train for thirty minutes in order to buy fruit and make juice for me. She made sure to dress me in fine clothing and take my picture. Mother often wrote to Grandma Cipora in Israel, sending pictures and sharing their lives in Warsaw. But this happiness was short-lived.

When the war broke, my parents' world went into upheaval. They found themselves in a whirlpool of tragedy, unable to control what was happening before their shocked eyes.

The older I got, the more I learned to admire my parents for the fateful decision they'd made to give me a chance to survive, smuggling me out of the ghetto and leaving me, their most precious only daughter, with the Abramowicz family. This bravery must have been accompanied with fear and uncertainty regarding my ability to survive on the Aryan side. Still, they took the risk and by doing so gave me my life.

The years in the ghetto weakened my mother's health and nerves. She was offered a chance to try her luck on the Aryan side as well, though in a separate hiding place, under the custody of Józef Abramowicz. She turned down the offer and the chance. She was decisive in her decision to remain with her husband and father, sharing her fate with theirs.

She and my father hoped I'd be lucky. They trusted my personality, my upbringing, and the values they'd imparted on me. They'd raised me as a confident, open, curious and sociable girl. They taught me to speak good, rich Polish, taught me the love of books. Within the hell of the ghetto they'd inconceivably succeeded in raising me in an island of sanity, love, and culture. They sent me into the unknown with faith not only in luck and the Abramowicz family, but in me. Luck and the Abramowicz family proved themselves. Thanks to the resilience my beloved parents had imparted to me, so did I.

As a mother of two and a grandmother of six, I am often at awe at how my parents managed, through the dark years of my early childhood, to equip me with life skills that stayed with me through all my hardships.

I never heard much about my mother from Janina or Józef. I suppose that during the war they preferred to make me forget my personal past. When the war was over they were decent enough to show me my family photos, but they never discussed my parents with me. I knew no personal information about my parents until I came to Israel. My family here was also limited in its ability to bring me closer to my mother. They'd never met her. They knew her only from pictures and letters, with the exception of Aunt Anni, who'd visited Poland when I was a baby. Unfortunately, the events of the time forced her to cut her visit short, and she'd only met my mother a few times. What little I do know about my mother comes mostly from Aunt Anni, who is almost a hundred years old. Her friend Dorka, who'd delivered my parents' last letter, describes my mother in a similar fashion.

Another source was Pan Aleksander Malec, who was my parents' neighbor in the ghetto. I met him in Israel in 1975. But his stories of the ghetto were so sad. His Franka wasn't the tall and beautiful Franka, a cultured, well-educated woman of grace and good conversation, the one whom Anni and Dorka had met. The Franka that Aleksander had known spent two awful years in the ghetto and was transferred from there to a labor camp and to death.

My Holocaust mother.

Who was my mother as a free person? I'll never know. My longing for her comes from the fountain of absence that had accompanied me through childhood, youth, and into adult and elderly life. Her images adorn my home and her passport photo is always in my wallet. I carry her with me everywhere, in my heart, which misses her always.

My Father

My father, Michał Głowinski, was born on January 15th, 1899, in Lodz. His mother Cipora Lipszyc, daughter of Rachel and Mordechai, was also born in Lodz. His father, Hanoch Głowinski, son of Avner, came to Lodz from the town of Konin. He owned a sawmill.

My father was the eldest of five children who were born close together: Rita in 1900, Chaim in 1902, Roma in 1904, and Paweł in 1905. Their father, Hanoch, died unexpectedly of a heart attack at the end of 1905. My father took responsibility for his younger siblings, helping his mother as best he could. He shared with them what he'd learned in school, the secrets of the Hebrew language and basic information about the Land of Israel. He was the first Zionist in the family, according to Aunt Roma. *He was the one who imbued us with awareness toward Zionism*, she said.

But fate has a strange sense of humor, and my father ended up the only member of his nuclear family to remain in Poland. In the early 1920s he served in the Polish army. After he was honorably discharged, he decided to become a businessman. He found his way in the Lodz textile industry and a few years later moved to Danzig and started a textile and carpeting wholesale and importing business. His mother, Rita, and Paweł moved to Danzig with him. Chaim went to Israel in 1920 and Roma followed him there.

While father made a name for himself in Danzig, Rita and Grandma decided to move to Israel. Paweł soon followed. My father's business grew and he opened new offices in Berlin and Warsaw. Throughout the years he supported his mother and the rest of his family financially. It was a close-knit family, and they maintained a strong connection with each other and with each other's new families. Most of all, the siblings all took devoted care of their widowed mother.

After my parents met and decided to get married, my father visited Palestine in order to declare his intentions. This visit also had another purpose, as Aunt Rita had revealed to me. Chaim, Paweł, and Roma were already married, and Rita was still living with their mother. Father asked Rita to focus on her own life and start a family. He made her promise, conditioning his own marriage on hers. He promised to continue to support their mother, but insisted that Rita make a life for herself. She promised. When she met Abraham she shared her decision to marry him with my father. My parents were married in May 1938 and Rita and Abraham were married in October 1938. Rita always remembered her older brother's concern for her. *Your father*, she often told me, *was the best friend I ever had.*

Upon Hitler's election and the German takeover of Danzig, which had been an independent city, my father was forced to liquidate his business for meager compensation. My parents moved to Warsaw, where they lived on 49 Plac Żelaznej Bramy.

When the war broke life changed irrevocably. The world my parents had known was upturned. They tried to escape through Danzig and Gdynia but failed. They were forced to return to Warsaw, and were trapped in the ghetto in 1941 along with my grandfather.

In the ghetto, Father was employed in the Schultz sewing factory. In 1943, the factories and their employees were all transferred to Trawniki. Before leaving the ghetto my parents were able to smuggle me out. They gave me and what little possessions they still had to my saviors.

Father, who grew up speaking three languages—Polish, Russians, and German—and who spent several years in Danzig, was immersed in German culture. Like many others, he was unable to fathom what was happening around him and couldn't believe that the Germans he'd known most of his adult life were capable of such atrocities. He recruited all of his resources to protect his small family from the burning chaos. He'd been ambivalent about leaving me behind, afraid to say goodbye to his only daughter and concerned about my unknown fate and what the distance between us would do to me, such a young girl. But my hero father stood by my mother and together they decided to give me a chance to survive. From the depths of love and despair they raked out their gift to me, the hidden message of their decision: *You can do it!* They believed in me.

After saying goodbye to his little girl, Father continued to care for my mother and her father. With his optimistic and congenial nature, he always hoped for the best. He wanted to believe they could survive and always had hope, as Józef had written to my family in Israel. His naïve and human hope for life; the hope of such an honest, strong, loving man, was shattered.

My aunts and uncles spoke of my father often. My aunts both described how handsome and impressive he was: tall, broad shouldered, with fair hair and blue eyes. Like my mother, his photos show him dressed well, with matching tie and handkerchief, a true Polish gentleman. My uncles spoke of his love of sports, which is also documented in many photos of him, skiing and rowing a kayak. All siblings spoke much of how he cared for them since they were little children. Their eldest brother was a father figure. He shared everything with them generously, organizing games and helping with their homework. As they grew older, they knew he was their stronghold, their defense, the keeper of their secrets, who listened and advised them in their times of need.

Naturally, there were disagreements between them, some fights, maybe even some physical brawls. *But,* they always said, *any fight we had was only between us four younger siblings. Your father was always a role model to us. He was a leader, authoritative and responsible. We loved him, respected him, and did as he said.*

Janina Abramowicz with Lala
Warsaw, 1945

Józef Abramowicz

Helena (Aunt Hela) and Stefan Gilewski

My grandparents, Dawid and Rachel Luci Fersztendik, my mother Franka
and her brother Beniek, Warsaw, 1910

Grandma Cipora

I never had the chance to meet my Grandma Cipora, my father's mother. I heard a lot about her from my aunts and uncles and from my cousins, Nurit and Ruth, who knew her as little girls. Their stories bring her to life and when I conjure her in my memory I sometimes feel as if we'd met. She knew of my birth, and had worried for me and my parents throughout the war, when Poland was cut off from the rest of the world. In November 1943, around the time of my parents' murder, she woke up one morning and said she knew her eldest son was gone. That day she fell ill, gradually deteriorating, and died several months later of heartbreak and physical and emotional depletion.

Grandma died before I came to Israel, and thus, like my parents, is only known to me from pictures and stories. Still, I miss her, think about her, and often wonder what kind of relationship we could have had.

Grandma was born in Lodz in 1871. Her parents, Chaya Rachel, daughter of Rabbi Zecharya, and Mordechai Shmuel, son of Rabbi Moshe Hacohen Lipszyc, were wealthy and observant. Grandma was the youngest of many siblings. When she was born most of them were already married and she had nieces and nephews her own age. Almost the entire family was murdered in the Holocaust.

As a young woman she married Hanoch Głowinski. For ten years she was unable to conceive. At the end of the nineteenth century she traveled to Vienna and was treated by a famous specialist. Upon her return to Poland she finally conceived and had five children in six years. Grandpa Hanoch came from Konin and ran a sawmill in a suburb of Lodz. He died suddenly of a heart attack at the end of 1905, when he was only thirty-five years old. Cipora, a young widow, raised her five children on her own. My father was only seven when his father died. Paweł was only one.

Upon her death the pampered and elegant lady whose home was filled with servants and caretakers became an independent woman running her husband's business on her own. She gathered her strength, changed her habits, and devoted herself to maintaining her family and raising her five children. When people raised their eyebrows at the sight of her riding a carriage to the sawmill every day she replied that she had a responsibility for her children. A young, religious, Jewish widow running a business was a rare vision in those days.

World War I and the Russian Revolution delivered a hard blow to Polish economy and Grandma lost all her wealth. Her parents, who had supported her, passed away. However, as the youngest of many siblings she was embraced with much love. Her home was open to her many nieces and nephews who came to stay and celebrate holidays and special occasions with her and her children.

In the 1960s, when I was in school in America, I met some of my father's second cousins. They were in their late seventies, but could still remember fondly their aunt Cipora, in whose home they often spent time when they were young.

In 1998, after Rita's death, Nurit and I found Grandma's photo collection. It included dozens of photos of young people, all with warm dedications: *To the one and only Aunt Cipora,* or *To beloved Aunt Cipora,* and more.

She also knew how to open her heart to those less fortunate. She took it upon herself to raise two of her more distant nieces who had lost their parents. I have five children, she said. Two more would only make our household merrier.

Grandma never married again, declaring that she preferred to raise her children alone than force them to accept a stepfather. She stayed beside her children her entire life.

In the early 1920s she moved with my father, Aunt Rita, and Uncle Paweł from Lodz to Danzig, while Chaim and Roma moved to Palestine. In 1925 she moved there too along with Rita. Grandma had trouble feeling at home in the little Tel Aviv of those days, bathed in sunlight and covered in golden sand. She returned to Danzig shortly thereafter, but then went back to Palestine in the early 1930s with Rita, who had become a zealous Zionist and insisted that they live in the Land of Israel. The family all lived together in Tel Aviv, other than my father, who remained in Danzig. When Rita married Abraham and moved to Pardess Hannah, Grandma moved with them and rented a room in the house next door.

Grandma was a religious woman who followed all decrees and wore beautiful wigs. She brought her terrific Danzig wardrobe with her to Palestine. Nurit and I liked to open the foldout sofa in the "big room," inside which were stored Grandma's clothes, and use the blouses, scarves, lacy dresses, and jackets as inspiration for drama class and Purim costumes.

Like her children, Grandma was raised in three languages: Polish, Russian, and German. She was well-versed in these languages' history and literature. She could only read the Hebrew of the prayer book. Grandma was a socialite, curious and critical, opinionated, insistent upon European upbringing, and passionate about respect for others, simultaneously demanding respect for herself from her children and other young family members.

She had a heightened sense of aesthetics; an elegant woman dressed in fine taste. She collected silver and porcelain trinkets from Europe. She taught Nurit German. Nurit often described the collections Grandma let her play with in her rented room: perfume bottles and fine lace handkerchiefs embroidered in pastel.

Grandma liked to read, especially the poetry which she copied into her private book. She was a fan of European royalty history and was an expert on regal lineages. She was also masterful in embroidery and crocheting. She made tapestries, tablecloths, and other beautiful creations. Her colorful handiwork, over a hundred years old, as well as her collections, now decorate my home and remind me of her.

Grandma Cipora is buried in the old part of the Nahalat Yitzhak cemetery in Tel Aviv. When her grave was cleaned and redesigned in the 1980s, an inscription was added per my request: *In memory of her son and daughter-in-law, Michał and Franka Głowinski (née Fersztendik), who were murdered in the Holocaust.*

Aunt Rita

As a girl and young woman Rita was bubbly; a person who loved life, adventures, and work. In spite of her urban past in Lodz, Danzig, and Tel Aviv, she gladly joined her husband Abraham on his farm when they married in October 1938. Before she'd met him, she dreamed of joining a kibbutz. She'd even been accepted to Kibbutz Bet Alpha, but her responsibility for her mother and her siblings' objections thwarted her plans.

When she arrived in Pardess Hannah she invested her energies and creative resources into turning their modest home into a warm and inviting place where the Głowinski and Robinson families could meet. She took pride in her hosting skills.

After her mother died in 1944 Rita joined the British army, leaving Abraham in charge of Nurit, then only four-and-a-half. Abraham supported her decision, knowing this was her way of coping with her mother's death and her concern for her two brothers—one in Poland and the other as a POW in German captivity.

In order to be accepted into the army, Rita had her own date of birth forged, from 1900 to 1905. She served in Egypt and had the exceptional and coincidental honor of being among the welcome party for soldiers released from German captivity, including her brother Chaim. During the War of Independence she served in the Haganah.

After Abraham died in 1964 Rita continued to work in the orchard for many years, nurturing her multiple friendships. Her command of Polish, Russian, German, Hebrew, and a bit of English and Yiddish, helped her find a common language with many people of different origins. Rita loved people. Her social involvement found its expression in decades of volunteer work at the hospital in Hadera. Until her late 80s, through the heat of summer and the cold of winter, she took two buses each way, never missing her weekly volunteer shift.

At home she was a generous hostess, captivating her guests with her wonderful sense of humor, which survived till the end of her life, when her body was already betraying her. She bore the hardships of fate and ill health with head held high, keeping her difficulties to herself while smiling at the world, dismissing all concerns with a joke. Rita was an independent thinker, uncompromising and persistent, who stressed the principles of integrity and fairness. She carefully preserved her "Polish honor" and her self-sustaining nature.

She lived alone in her home until the age of ninety-eight, and spent the last six months of her life in a nursing home, which she regretted dearly, refusing to acknowledge that she was no longer able to take care of herself.

Aunt Rita is remembered by everyone who knew her as an exemplar of wisdom, courage, determination, respect, and the love of humankind.

She was like a mother to me. She often repeated the dream she'd had about my rescue from the awful war. She explained the similarity in our personalities as one that always exists between nieces and aunts. I've never been able to find support for this theory, but our resemblance is indisputable. She acted as loving grandmother to my children.

Rita often demonstrated the gift of clairvoyance. In the early 1950s there were no phones in people's homes and no immediate way of planning visits. Once every few Saturdays she would smile mysteriously in the morning and tell us, *We'll be having guests over today.*

How do you know? We asked.

Trust me, she said, adding no more. She was never wrong. A few hours later we would gape at the sight of Uncle Chaim's truck pulling up at the gate. He usually came with Aunt Moni, Uncle Paweł, and Aunt Anni. The four of them lived close to each other in Tel Aviv and came to Pardess Hannah together. Aunt Moni and Aunt Anni were excellent bakers, and the cakes they brought with them were cause for a celebration. Rita would laugh, hug her relatives, and turn to us. *What did I tell you?* She'd ask. *I knew they would come today.* There was no way to explaining it. She was simply always right.

Rita was an expert in Polish cuisine. Her gefiltefish would melt in our mouths. Her *p'tcha* and her pickled herring were also great, not to mention her *kapuśniak*—cabbage soup—and her borscht.

With time, she nicknamed me Reluchna. My children, who remember her fondly, often mimic this. In response, I called her Rituchna.

Rita's and Abraham's only child, Nurit, has been living in Canada for many years, and so I was the one to stay at Rita's side in her final years, taking care of her as best I could. I loved Rita. Her image is in my heart and mind always. It saddens me to think that she won't be able to read these lines, a commemoration of her among our many shared beloveds.

Aunt Rita is buried in the founders' plot of the Pardess Hannah cemetery, alongside her husband, Abraham.

Uncle Abraham

My uncle, Abraham Robinson, was born in Suwałki, an area of Lithuania that was often transferred between the rules of Russia, Lithuania, and Poland. He is the fourth of the seven Robinson siblings born to David and Bluma, néc London. David was a descendant of Rabbi Yom Tov Lipman, son of Rabbi Nathan Heller, who was famous for his commentary on the Talmud. Rabbi Lipman was born in 1576, and the Robison family tree commemorates all generations that followed. David was an observant man and a scholar. He spoke Russian, Polish, German, and Hebrew. After completing his basic religious studies he continued to study at home, and later received a governmental teaching diploma. He was a teacher and later a principal at the Suwałki high school. His wife, Bluma, daughter of Shmuel London, the famous Talmud scholar, was a talented musician who also came from a well-educated family. Her older brother, Ephraim Abba London, also known as Yefim Semionovicz London, was a doctor and medical researcher, an expert on physiology. He was associated with the Russian czar, and was very close with his sister and brother-in-law, helping to raise their seven boys, Jacob, Aaron, Isaac, Abraham, Nehemia, Nathan, and Pinhas, who were born after the death of their eldest brother, Avigdor, who died as an infant.

David was unable to provide for his large family with his modest teacher's salary, and so Uncle London supported them, influencing the education of the boys. He was the one who convinced David and Bluma, who were religious people, to send their children to a secular high school and to university. Thus, all the Robinsons studied in universities in Poland, Germany, and Czechoslovakia, receiving doctoral degrees in medicine, law, economics, and sciences, as their oldest brother Jacob and his wife Klara helped pay for their tuition. The youngest, Pinhas, was sent to Israel to study at the Herzliya Hebrew Gymnasium and later as part of the first class at the Hebrew University Medical School. All of them received a Zionist education and were members of Ha'halutz movement.

Uncle Abraham studied agronomy in Germany, believing this would train him to be able to contribute to the development of the Land of Israel. Before he graduated, Abraham answered the excited call of Zionist leader Yosef Sprinzak, who came to Berlin to urge Jewish students to make Aliyah, claiming that the land required working hands, not academics. Uncle Abraham returned to Suwałki, married his sweetheart, and brought her to Palestine with him in 1921.

At first they settled in Ein Hai, which was later called Kfar Malal, and is today Hod Hasharon. Later on they moved to Kibbutz Gan Shmuel. But Abraham's wife had trouble adjusting to life on a commune, and so the couple left the kibbutz and moved to Pardess Hannah, which was founded in 1929. In the meantime, their daughter Yael was born. Abraham's wife was unable to survive the hardships of life in the new land. She became ill and was hospitalized for years until her death.

Abraham persisted in his agricultural work and in raising Yael. It was years before he met Rita, after which he received divorce papers signed by a hundred rabbis, as was customary at the time, and married Rita.

Rita joined him in Pardess Hannah. She received Yael with open arms and did her best to compensate the child for the absence of a mother. Nurit was born on November 11th, 1939. Yael later married Zvi Fisher, who had made Aliyah with a youth movement from Vienna, where he'd lost his entire family in the Holocaust. The young couple joined Kibbutz Beit Oren.

In 1944, after Cipora died, when Rita decided to join the British army, it was agreed that Nurit would be sent to stay with her half-sister Yael and her brother-in-law Zvi in Beit Oren. Little Nurit took this exile very badly. She stopped eating. Today what she did would be called a hunger strike. Nothing helped, and she wouldn't eat a bite of food until Abraham was forced to take her home. Once she was back in her home, her familiar kindergarten, and the care of her loving father, the girl recovered, though she continued to yearn for her mother.

As a father, Uncle Abraham showered his daughters with love. When I moved into the house in Pardess Hannah he opened his heart and home to me as well. He was an active participant in our schooling, explaining Bible passages before the famous Cassuto commentary could be found in every home. Uncle Abraham explained the historical processes we learned about at school. He made sure we spoke proper Hebrew and clarified the rules of grammar. His proficiency in English was also very helpful to us, as he patiently translated difficult reading material and helped us prepare for weekly dictations and exams.

Abraham was a man of the letter, who liked to read fine literature and history. He was immersed in both past and present and was like a walking encyclopedia, preceding Google by decades. He had a knack for details, names, and dates, and always spoke calmly and interestingly.

I remember that when I joined the army after studying at the agricultural school I had no idea who the Beatles were. When I came home for leave Uncle Abraham was the one to school me on this hip issue.

He was a fascinating conversationalist and could be consulted on any matter. I loved his patient listening and admired his sage advice, always presented calmly as a wide blanket of knowledge, combining an interest in me and whatever was on my mind. As a child, he was the one Nurit and I came to with different requests and he was our advocate with Rita, who was a more strict, European (not to say Polish) disciplinarian. When we had to ask permission to participate in some event, trip, or overnight activity, or to come home late at night, we would first ask Uncle Abraham. Though he always said we had to ask Rita too, we knew if we had him by our side, he'd be able to talk her into it in his quiet style.

He was always happy to help us out. For example, when we were required to wait at the train station early in the morning for a national Scouts trip, he woke up earlier than usual to tend to the animals before giving us a ride in his mule-drawn wagon. When I was a soldier and later a university student, he also rose early to take me to the train station so that I didn't have to walk.

Abraham was a very restrained man. He did not express his love physically, with a hug or a caress, but rather with a warm look and actions of confident love. He served as my anchor of stability and trust.

Before I left for America in 1962 he called me in for a private conversation, secretly sharing with me the arrangements he'd made for the time after his death and his concern for Rita, trusting me to ensure her wellbeing after he was gone. Neither of us knew his prophecy would come true.

We corresponded regularly during my years abroad, long and personal letters. In those days, the phone was only used for emergencies. Uncle Abraham wrote to me at length about everything and I shared my adventures with him, seeking his council from afar.

Abraham was a humble, hardworking, honest man. He didn't find his place among the wheelers and dealers that appeared in the village establishments and unions. He continued to work hard his entire life, teaching us the love of the country in the most ideal sense of the concept, as he'd known it in his years in the youth movement in Lithuania and as a pioneer who built this country and made its soil bloom.

He died suddenly of cardiac arrest at the age of sixty-eight. He is buried in the Pardess Hannah cemetery, in the village he'd founded and whose land he loved.

Nurit, Pardess Hannah, 1951

Nurit with her husband, Eli Kochav, Canada, 1999

Uncle Chaim and Aunt Moni

In his eighty-four years on this planet, my uncle lived a life filled of doing for his family, his friends, his country, and his people. In 1920, when he was eighteen years old, he ran away from his Lodz home and arrived alone in Palestine. He began his pioneer work by paving roads around Rosh Pina as part of the "valley group," with whom he'd also paved the Afula-Nazareth road and later on roads in Beersheba and the Gaza Strip. In 1925 he moved to Tel Aviv and became one of the city's first road pavers as part of the Office of Contracting, which later became the Solel Boneh Company, where he worked until his retirement, spending decades as the head of the roadworks department. In little Tel Aviv Chaim was one of the founders of the Ha'poel union, as well as Ezra Rishona, the first aid medic organization. He'd always been riveted by sports, and joined the Ha'poel Israel motorcycle team on a 1931 European tour.

Moni (Bronisława) Lipszyc came as a swimmer from Vienna to participate in the first Maccabiah—the Jewish Olympics. She stayed in Palestine and married Chaim in 1935. Their daughter Ruthy was born in 1937. Chaim, a family man, encouraged his mother and siblings to join him in the Land of Israel. He was one of the first volunteers to join the British army. After being taken captive in Greece in 1941 he was transferred to a POW camp in Germany. Upon the end of the war he returned to Palestine and joined the Haganah. When the State of Israel was founded he became one of its sporting developers. The list of organizations, establishments, and associations he'd helped erect and lead is long and impressive. The most outstanding are the Soccer Association, the Sporting Association, the Basketball Union, and the Israeli Olympics Committee, in which Chaim served as honorary secretary from its establishment in 1952 and until his death in 1986. His life's work was the Sportoto, which many liked to nickname his baby. He was chairman of the Sportoto from the organization's foundation until the day he died.

It is also worth mentioning that Chaim was one of the minds behind the stadium in Yad Eliyahu, which was built in order to put the city of Tel Aviv on the international sports map. He was also one of the founders of the Wingate Institute, and a dormitory was named after him in honor of his seventy-fifth birthday. He headed many Israeli Olympic delegations and was among the Israeli representatives at the Asian Sports Federation. Mr. Israeli Sports, as he was nicknamed, made many friends in international sports establishments all over the world, who helped build up the status of Israeli sports and supported his fight to prevent the mixing of sports and politics.

In 1977 he received the honorary title Beloved of Tel Aviv.

Alongside his work and widespread contribution, he always found the time to invest in his family, both nuclear and extended. He was attentive to others' distress and cared for everyone, especially the children. To me he was like an illuminated signpost leading me with love and confidence through the many intersections of my life, beginning with his first visit to Poland in 1947, and later on in his typical way, bringing me onto the coast with his own hands by taking me off the immigrant ship that was still docking on the other side of the breakwater at the Haifa Port. He was the one who tracked down the agricultural high school, one of the best in the country, for me to attend. At first I resisted leaving my home in Pardess Hannah, but in retrospect his choice had been superior. I was educated in a high quality environment, worked joyfully, blossomed socially, and excelled at school. The friends I made at Hakfar Hayarok High School became my extended family for the rest of my life, over fifty years so far. They liked to call uncle Chaim the Great Głowinski.

Chaim and Moni's rooftop apartment on the corner of Frishman and Dizengoff Streets in Tel Aviv was a magical spot where Nurit and I spent summer vacations and holidays. They always took the time to host us generously, taking us on trips in Chaim's truck and on movie and theatre outings. Aunt Moni took us shopping on Dizengoff Street and bought us the best clothes. We village girls took it all in, indulging in the pleasures of the city.

Aunt Moni was a classic German homemaker, my only non-Polish aunt, though she'd learned Polish from her parents, who'd moved to Vienna, where Moni grew up, the youngest of the Lipszyc children. Everything she cooked or baked tasted incredible and melted in your mouth. She was also a fine knitter. Like my other aunts, Moni was also a lady of fine taste, and generous, always giving useful and beautiful gifts.

On his trips abroad, Chaim never forgot to buy gifts for the family children, and later on for my children. When Nurit and I celebrated our Bat Mitzvahs in the backyard with all the kids from our class, Chaim and Uncle Zalman organized games and activities.

Throughout my life and my entire family's, Chaim and Moni were always there, helping out, taking care. Nothing was too difficult for them. They were always available to lend an ear and find the time and energy to be with us in joy and need. Chaim was the head of the Głowinski tribe. Along with Moni, who was always by his side, be it in his public activism or in his family life, he was our rock and our source of steady faith.

The name Chaim fit him perfectly. He loved life and had the pleasure of enjoying it fully. He was a humanitarian, a friend, a hardworking, honest man, who found his way into everybody's heart. Since he died I continue to miss him with all my heart; Chaim Głowinski, my father's brother, my uncle Chaim.

Afterward

Chaim died at age eighty-four and was buried in the Nahalat Yitzhak cemetery in Tel Aviv, in the Beloveds of Tel Aviv plot. Moni, may she live long and prosper, now lives in an assisted living facility, maintaining her clarity of mind and memory.

Uncle Zalman and Aunt Roma Ben-Shaul

Uncle Paweł and Aunt Anni

Paweł was the youngest of the Głowinski children. When, in the early 1920s, my father decided to build his business in Danzig, he took Grandma Cipora, Aunt Rita, and Uncle Paweł with him. Chaim and Roma were already in Palestine.

Uncle Paweł, a tall and handsome young man, fit naturally into the social life of young Jews in Danzig. He worked with my father, and spent his free time with Zionist movements around the town, planning his Aliyah, until Chaim finally sent him the immigration certificate, an approval to make Aliyah, issued by the British Mandate government.

In Danzig Paweł met the Silberman sisters, Anni and Żeni, two beautiful young women born in Saint Petersburg, who moved to Danzig with their parents in their teens and went to high school and later to commerce college. They were also interested in making Aliyah. Paweł and Anni fell in love and quickly married so that Anni could join him in Palestine using his certificate. Żeni followed them later. After the two sisters were already in Palestine, the Silbermans moved to Lodz, their mother's hometown. They were murdered in the Holocaust with the rest of their family.

In Tel Aviv, Paweł joined his brother Chaim as a road paver. Later on he worked in bread distribution and then as one of the first drivers of the Dan Public Transportation Cooperative. With time he left this job and devoted himself to his true passion—car machinery and spare parts. He spent most of his life selling spare car parts. Paweł and Anni had their only son in 1944.

When I arrived in Israel their family lived on Reines Street in Tel Aviv, in a tiny two-room apartment that was elegantly furnished. Anni, who was fluent in six languages, worked as a translator. She was a good cook and a gifted baker, making gorgeous and delicious cakes and cookies. I often visited them on vacations and holidays, either alone or with Nurit. Like my other aunts and uncles, Paweł and Anni opened their hearts and home to me.

Paweł and I developed a relationship of mutual admiration. From a young age I enjoyed discussing different topics with him and getting his advice. As a teenager, a soldier, and a student, I liked to ask for his opinion. He would look at me with his wise eyes, smile lovingly, and say, *Relli, it flatters me to hear that you want my opinion, but I know in the end you'll do what you think is best. Like the rest of the Głowinski family, you're stubborn and independent. Still, I like to hear you put your problems into words and voice them to me. The mere process of putting ideas into words brings you closer to a well thought-out decision, and it makes no difference if I make the decision or if you do. The important thing is, you see me as someone who is always there to listen to you, just as your father used to listen to me.*

Uncle Paweł was a very sociable man. He and Anni liked to have their many friends over for card games and to go out and enjoy Tel Aviv life.

To everyone's great sorrow, Paweł's health deteriorated at a relatively young age. He died before he turned seventy. I came to see him at the hospital the day before he died and I can still remember his words of wisdom and frustration, spoken softly to me from the depths of his despair. He took my hand and said sadly, *Relli, I know I'm going to die and nothing can change that. Remember, we must do our best to understand what is happening around us and to accept reality when we cannot change it. I'm sad to say goodbye to this life, and even sadder to know there's nothing I can do to stop it.*

I stroked his emaciated hand, looking at his pale face and sunken eyes, hoping he could not see my tears. It was a Saturday afternoon and I'd received the gift of a personal parting. He died the next day.

Aunt Anni, a beautiful, graceful, elegant woman with a sense of humor and rolling laughter, was loved by everybody. Like my other aunts, she liked to pamper me and Nurit and, later on, my own children, lavishing us with expensive and refined gifts bought in the best stores in Israel and Europe. She gave us the best clothes and jewelry.

Her kindness was famous in our family. In 1985, when she was in her seventies, she arrived at my Haifa home with a suitcase. My son was convalescing after a complicated surgery, and Anni announced plainly, *I've come to help you so you can go back to work.* She stayed for almost two weeks, cooking, baking, hosting Nattiv's many friends who filled the house in all hours of the day and night. In addition, she made sure to keep him up to date on English, having been clever enough to bring a game of scrabble to play with him, enriching his vocabulary.

Anni's life story and her stroke of luck can fill an entire book on their own. In the summer of 1939, Anni traveled from Palestine to visit her family in Poland. She arrived in mid-August and was received happily. She met my parents and me when I was six months old. Within just a few days a telegram arrived from Tel Aviv from Paweł, who demanded that she return immediately. Everyone was surprised. Her father and uncle advised her to stay with them, where she felt happy. Anni was concerned with the content and tone of the telegram and had trouble making up her mind. Finally, my father advised her to listen to her husband.

She decided to look into the possibility of leaving Poland earlier than planned. My father accompanied her to a travel agency where she was offered two options: she could either fly out of Warsaw on September 5th or leave by train to Constanța in Romania on August 31st, continuing from there by ship to Palestine. Anni, only twenty-eight years old at the time, considered both options and with inexplicable intuition decided that since she'd already made up her mind to leave sooner than planned she would take the train rather than wait another five days for a flight. This decision cast her dice, choosing life.

The entire family came to see her off at the train station, including my parents and myself. Anni told me many times that my mother handed me over for a goodbye kiss and then asked in a trembling voice, *Why don't you take Relli with you?* The two of them exchanged tearful glances. Aunt Anni boarded the train and I stayed with my mother, who must have had a flash of the future, foretelling the hell that would commence the very next day, September 1st, 1939, and for years to come.

Aunt Anni arrived in Constanța and was able to procure, through her personal charms and her good fortune, what she claimed was the last ticket available for a ship leaving for Palestine that night. It was a deck seat, and she spent the entire journey on a deck chair. While she was in Constanța she learned that the war had started.

She couldn't know then that of all the people who came to see her off at the station, the only one to survive would be the baby.

Afterward

After Paweł's death, Anni continued to live independently, working for a living at Koor Industries until her retirement. She held a senior position, utilizing her command of six languages. Today Anni is almost a hundred years old. She lives in a nursing home, protesting her stolen liberty. Anni's sister, Żeni, whom we liked to call Beautiful Żeńka, was adopted by me as an additional aunt, and I was adopted by her as a niece. Żeni married Lonia Gorodetsky and the two started a family in Jerusalem. For years, she ran the Jerusalem offices of the Shiloah Insurance firm.

Like her sister, Żeni lost her husband at a relatively young age. She continued to lead a striving career and social life, a remarkable woman, admired and beloved. She too lives in an old age home in Jerusalem these days, her health and vitality slowly fading.

I have a very close relationship with Żeni and Lonia's two sons, Gabi and Raffi, who are a few years younger than I am. Ever since we first met, years ago, we've defined ourselves as cousins, and our familial bond has lasted to this day. I always enjoy hearing them refer to me their "beloved cousin"— especially since, technically, we are not cousins at all.

Tzipora Neshem

Tzipora Neshem, daughter of Mordechai Dusznicki, was born in Lithuania in 1905. She grew up in her father's estate, Dusznica, near the town of Suwałki. At school, she met the Robinson children, as well as the Kierniańskis, the family of my mother-in-law Rachel (Hela) Kierniański, who lived in the Moskowczyzna Estate, also near Suwałki. Tzipora's life became entangled with both these families'.

She was a member of the Zionist youth movements in Suwałki. After high school, she continued to commerce and bookkeeping college. In the early 1930s she immigrated to Palestine, where she decided to Hebraize her last name. The name Dusznicki comes from the Polish word *dusza*, which means soul, or in Hebrew, *neshama*, and so she chose the name Neshem. To her friends and family she was known as Feiga'le (Yiddish for "bird," which in Hebrew is "*tzipor*.") The children of her relatives and many friends nicknamed her Tzipa.

Tzipora was a short woman with dark eyes and hair. She was energetic, industrious, and focused. Upon her arrival in Palestine she found a job with Tnuva Exports in Tel Aviv, making use of her studies. When the state was established she moved to Haifa and found work with the newly formed Ministry of Defense, caring for the wellbeing of discharged soldiers, mostly in matters of housing. From there, she was transferred to the Ministry of Foreign Affairs, where, at the end of 1949, she was elected for a two-year assignment at the newly formed Israeli embassy in Warsaw. She was charged with handling survivors who applied for immigration documents.

Tzipora lived independently her entire life, never marrying. She was a very amiable person, who had dozens of friends all over the country. Her parents and her sister's family were all murdered in the Holocaust. Two other sisters survived in Russia, but she was unable to regularly correspond with them because of Iron Curtain limitations of the 1950s and '60s. She hoped to be able to reach them from her position in Poland, but her attempts were unsuccessful. It wasn't until the late 1970s that she was able to get in touch with a niece who was married to a Russian man, had started a family and veered away from her Jewish roots. This correspondence did not last long. Tzipora's two eldest sisters died somewhere in Russia. She mourned the loss of her nuclear family and kept in touch with her cousins and their children, who lived in Israel.

Upon her return from Poland she bought a small apartment in Haifa for key money, as was customary at the time, on Moriah Avenue, on the Carmel Mountain. Her one-room apartment overlooking a green valley and the sea was always open to visitors. She loved to host and cook delicious meals for her guests. Her soups and eggplant salads were famous.

In Haifa she found a job with Bank Ha'poalim, receiving promotions until finally she was appointed manager of the Carmel Center branch on Mahanaim Street. After leaving the bank she found work with the Carmel Institute for Developing Countries, which was affiliated with the Ministry of Foreign Affairs.

Tzipora was an active, hardworking, and devoted woman. She was always direct, saying what was on her mind, never hypocritical. She was known as a discreet person who was always prepared to lend a hand either outwardly or in private, according to circumstances. She always spoke the truth. She was a culture aficionado, a lover of music and theatre, an avid reader who loved to travel.

Tzipora loved children and the many children of her friends and relatives loved her. She remembered everybody's birthdays and made sure to surprise them with gifts.

She has declared that the epitome of her many achievements was her campaign for my redemption, my return to Judaism, and my immigration to be with my family in Israel. Our relationship deepened with the years, changing forms through my childhood, youth, military service, and adulthood as a young wife and mother in Haifa. She was very close with my children.

As a childhood friend of my father-in-law, Professor Nathan Robinson, and my mother-in-law, Rachel Kierniański, Tzipora saw it as fate that I, the little girl she helped come from Poland to Israel, later became Relli Robinson, daughter-in-law of her close friends.

My relationship with Tzipora was long lasting; a true connection of love and friendship.

Afterward

Tzipora Neshem died in 1986 after prolonged suffering following a stroke. In her nobility, she donated her body to science. Several months after her death she was buried at the Sha'ar Tamar cemetery in Haifa.

Pan Aleksander—Mister Aleksander

Do you remember the names of any other people the Abramowicz family rescued? Dr. Bauminger asks me as he takes my testimony for the Yad Vashem file on Janina and Jòzef Abramowicz, opened in order to honor them as Righteous Among the Nations.

This isn't going according to my plan. He asks questions and I give detailed answers, since his questions require detail. However, Dr. Bauminger, the head of the commission, takes down my answers in shorthand.

I glance at his notes from the other side of the desk and become impatient. *Excuse me*, I interrupt him, *but isn't there a questionnaire or some other method for me to give my testimony? It doesn't seem right to have you editing my words.*

Dr. Bauminger looks up at me, surprised. *This is how I always work*, he says drily. *There is no questionnaire.*

Then perhaps I can prepare my testimony myself, in my own words, and mail it to you?

If you think you're able to do that, go ahead, he says, insulted.

I pay little mind to his feelings. I only care about giving an accurate testimony, a direct one, from my heart and in my words. *Yes, please give me the address and a deadline by which I should send you the testimony.*

Dr. Bauminger isn't pleased, but he accepts my offer.

Dr. Bauminger, I stop him when he's already in the process of collecting his things and closing the cardboard folder he'd opened when we began talking. *You asked me before if I remember any other names.*

Yes, I did, he says. *Do you?*

Yes. I remember two identical twins in their twenties, or perhaps their teens, it's hard to say, I was so young. Their last name was Danziger and the only difference between them was that one of them had a mole above her knee. Whenever they came over I asked them to lift their dresses so I could tell them apart. Their mother was called Halina Danziger. Unfortunately I can't remember the twins' names. I never saw them again after the war, neither in Poland nor in Israel. I don't know what became of them.

But I can remember another man. I only remember him as Pan Aleksander, Mr. Aleksander. I never knew his last name. I remember him well. He was a tall, handsome man, a nice man who was very kind to me during the war. He was hidden in Józef's workshop and often visited us at the apartment on 6 Krochmalna Street.

Unfortunately I never saw him again after the war, either. His relationship with the Abramowicz family must have ended. I asked about him occasionally but never received an answer. I was very sorry not to have him in my life anymore. I liked Pan Aleksander and felt that he liked me too.

Dr. Bauminger listens with true interest and reopens the cardboard folder. *I have a testimony here from Stockholm, signed by an A. Malec,* he says. *Do you think that might be the man you're referring to?*

I don't know. Perhaps the A is for Aleksander? Would you please read it to me?

Of course, he says and starts reading.

I listen intently, tense and excited, and feel tears slowly rising in my eyes and rolling down my cheeks. The testimony was indeed given by Pan Aleksander, the man I knew in Warsaw during the war and who I'd last seen in 1943, more than thirty years prior to my interview with Dr. Bauminger. The event he described in his testimony is very familiar to me. I'd heard about it several times from Józef and Janina.

In his testimony, Pan Aleksander describes how, after Józef smuggled him out of the ghetto, he began working at Józef's workshop. He worked at the back storage and hid there, inside a nook in the wall behind a metal closet, in times of danger. He spent most nights there, too. One afternoon, as he was doing his job, Józef burst into the storage. *Aleksander,* he said, *get in the nook. I'll help you. I spotted a Gestapo jeep pulling up at the factory gate. Don't worry, I'll deal with them, just get in the nook,* Józef said calmly.

After pushing the metal closet to block off Pan Aleksander's hiding place, Józef made himself some tea and walked out of the storage with the cup in his hand, as if that had been his reason for a trip to the storage. He walked confidently back into the workshop floor, where the gestapos were now assembled. Józef approached them lightly and asked politely, *How can I help you?*

We've received a tip about a Jewish man hiding somewhere around here. Here's a picture. Have you seen him?

Józef looked at the picture and cried, *I can't believe it! I just can't believe it! This man walked in here this morning and asked for work. I offered him some money to clean up the yard. He worked quickly and only recently finished. I paid him and he left just minutes before you arrived. I saw the direction he was going. If you wish, I can go with you and help track him down.*

Józef left instructions for his workers and hurried out and into the Gestapo jeep. He rode along with them through the neighborhood for a long time, but of course they could not find Pan Aleksander, who was hiding safely in Józef's storage.

The Gestapo soldiers were impressed with Józef's willingness to help them search for the fugitive. They thanked him with a bottle of liquor and returned him to the factory as he promised to report to them if the man ever returned.

After waiting a reasonable amount of time, Józef went back into the storage to free Pan Aleksander from his hiding spot. Together, they drank the liquor the Gestapos had given him.

After dark, Józef took Pan Aleksander to spend the night in his little apartment on 6 Krochmalna Street, with his wife, Janina, and with Lala, the Jewish girl hiding in his home.

In his testimony, Pan Aleksander commended Józef's resourcefulness, courage, cool, and readiness to put his own life at risk just to save him.

When Dr. Bauminger finishes reading the testimony he notices I've been crying. *I see that this testimony has moved you.*

I'm crying because that is indeed the same man, I explain. *It's Pan Aleksander. I've known this story for years. Please give me his address in Sweden.*

That night when I returned home, I wrote a letter in Polish and sent it to Sweden via express mail the next day. Within days I received a reply. It was the same man I'd remembered from age four, the man I always felt connected to, though I couldn't explain why.

In his response, Pan Aleksander expressed his joy at receiving my letter. He told me that as a Communist who was an active underground member and later, after the war, a member of the Communist Party, he remained in Poland after the war and only left for Sweden in the days of Gomułka in 1968. From his letter I learned that he had family in Israel and was about to visit them in a few weeks. He promised to meet me during his visit and said he had a lot to tell me, because he was the one who introduced my parents to the Abramowicz family. This was a startling discovery for me.

A few weeks later, as promised, Pan Aleksander came to Israel and we met in Tel Aviv, where his family lived. Together we went to Chaim and Moni's house, where my entire family assembled, and where we all heard for the first time how I'd found myself with the Abramowicz family, as well as the destiny of Pan Aleksander's family.

Aleksander Malec, his wife and their daughter, who was about a year older than me, lived in the same building as my parents in the ghetto. He was an active member of the Polish Communist Party, which is how he'd known Janina and Józef even before the war. With time an arrangement was made through the leftist Polish underground, the Armia Ludowa, in which both men were members, that Józef would smuggle the Malec family out of the ghetto. According to the plan, Pan Alcksander would be hired by Józef's small metal workshop, while his little girl would be hidden in the Abramowicz home and his wife hidden elsewhere. As they prepared to carry out the plan the Malecs were contacted by a Polish woman who used to work as their daughter's nanny before the war. This former employee offered to hide both Mrs. Malec and her daughter at her home while Aleksander hid in Józef's workshop. The Malecs were very glad at this offer from a woman they knew well. This solution made it possible for mother and daughter to stay together, and so they decided to accept. Pan Aleksander suggested to introduce my parents to the Abramowicz family so that they may use the proposed hiding spot for me and my mother.

Józef would enter the ghetto through secret passages known only to him. Among other things, he smuggled weapons to members of the Jewish underground who were also fellow Communists. My parents met him on one such visit. They were torn about his offer. My mother did not want to be apart from her husband and father, and the thought of not even being with me, but rather in a separate hiding spot, tipped the scale. She decided not to leave the ghetto. She knew her fate and theirs had been sealed and chose to stay with them, advancing together toward death. My parents decided to hand me alone to the Abramowicz family and attempt, through this fateful separation, to save my life.

Pan Aleksander and his family were smuggled out of the ghetto by Józef, and so was I. The Malecs separated—mother and daughter to the home of their Polish nanny, and Aleksander to Józef's workshop. I was taken to 6 Krochmalna Street.

A few weeks in someone informed on the Polish nanny. The two women and the little girl were caught and killed in the basements of the Gestapo. Pan Aleksander survived.

From his hiding place, Pan Aleksander maintained a relationship with me. He often visited me at the apartment, telling me stories, playing games, and occasionally, when he was able to afford it, bringing me candy. I still remember large chocolate truffles wrapped in silver paper.

He'd lost his wife and only daughter and must have seen me as a connection to his past. He'd heard from Józef about my parents' and grandfather's death.

I loved Pan Aleksander as a child and remembered him fondly for years after the war, though I had no idea that what made our relationship so meaningful was the fact that he was the only person I'd known from the ghetto, my final home with my parents and grandfather. In that sense, he was a tangible connection to a world I'd lost for good. But of course, I only learned this decades later, in 1975, thirty years after the war ended.

After the war, he married a woman who'd also lost her husband and two children. Together they had a son and immigrated to Sweden in 1968.

I invited Pan Aleksander to visit me in Haifa. He came, met my children, and spent hours talking to us and looking over photo albums.

But the surprises did not end there. While he was in my home he asked to call a friend of his from high school. When I asked for her name, it turned that this friend and her husband, Rachel and Israel Adiv, were close friends of Tzipora Neshem's. Not only did they live in my neighborhood, but I'd known them for years and have often visited their home.

Who would have thought they'd also be friends with Pan Aleksander? The man I'd known in my days of hiding, and even before then, in the Warsaw Ghetto. The man who'd played such a central role in my survival and who had disappeared from my life in the fall of 1943, when Janina and I left Warsaw to live on the cherry farm near Lublin.

Fate is a mysterious thing. The unbelievable stories of the Holocaust and their wondrous discoveries would continue for years to come. That awful war is not yet over; its echoes continue to reverberate through our scarred world.

Afterward

After that visit to Israel in 1975, Pan Aleksander contracted a severe kidney disease and died in Sweden. His wife wrote me a short letter about it, after which my connection to the Malec family was broken. I do not know what came of them. I feel blessed to have had the chance to meet Pan Aleksander as an adult and hear the details of my rescue, which neither I nor my Israeli family had known.

Józef and Janina never told me about Aleksander's part in my survival, while all the while he had been the author, the initiator, and the enabler of my escape from the ghetto into the Abramowicz home.

Pan Aleksander's image is etched in my memory as a human compass, directing my fate from the Valley of Death to a path of hope and survival.

And what about my testimony for Yad Vashem?

Over twenty years later, when my son Nattiv visited the archives of Yad Vashem, found the file, and read through the remarks of the commission, discussing the possibility of granting Józef and Janina Abramowicz the honorific of Righteous Among the Nations, he was mesmerized by the opening words of the commission's chairman, Dr. Bauminger: *This is the most intelligent testimony in the history of this commission, and that is thanks to its author. She is now the deputy director of the pre-academic department at the University of Haifa.*

Relli in the Garden of the Righteous at Yad Vashem

A Letter from Józef Abramowicz

Preface

This letter was sent to me in response to a letter of forgiveness I sent Józef in the spring of 1984, after finding out from Helena and Stefan Gilewski that Józef was suffering of advanced Parkinson's disease and that it looked like his end was near.

In my letter I thanked him for saving my life and caring for my parents. I also praised his heroism, the risks he'd taken, and his uncompromising humaneness in helping Jews and saving the lives of many besides me, such as Aleksander Malec and Mrs. Danziger and her twin daughters. These are the names I remember, but there were surely others.

Nevertheless, I made it clear in my letter that I left Warsaw in 1950 hurt and insulted by his abandonment of me after Janina's death, and that I did not forgive the way he betrayed her memory, not bothering for years to come to erect a headstone on her grave.

As a grown woman and mother I was able to offer my forgiveness. I could not and cannot forget the terrible time after Janina's death, which he made worse by his behavior to me, but I sent him my gratitude, my admiration, and my moral indebtedness. His unique personality and actions in the darkness of the cruel war will forever illuminate my memory of him in the temple of exceptional human beings in my heart and in the memories of my children and grandchildren.

Józef replied immediately. He was no longer able to write himself due to the Parkinson's, and so his second wife wrote the letter for him.

Less than a month after receiving his letter I journeyed to Poland for the first time in thirty-four years. I joined a delegation of the United Kibbutz Movement—one of the first youth groups to go on a memorial trip to Poland. Ten days before I set foot on Warsaw soil once more, Jòzef Abramowicz died, holding the letter of forgiveness I'd sent him a few weeks before his tortured death in his trembling hand.

An excerpt from Jòzef's letter of May 14th, 1984

Warsaw, May 14th, 1984

My beloved daughter, the one I always long for and dream about. Lala, you are mine and only mine, for you have no other parents. I am still alive and your children are my grandchildren. I wish so badly that I could see you, if only for a moment, but that is but a dream. Receiving news from you has also been my dream for years, but now, I hold your letter in my hands.

It's hard for me to imagine you as a grown woman and mother. Please send me a picture of you and my grandchildren, to make my heart and eyes happy.

To me you'll always be my little girl. How I wish I could hold you and kiss you, but that would be impossible unless you come see this sick old man who's never forgotten about you; the man who's always been waiting for news from you and has now received a miracle.

I read and reread your letter and hope and pray for it to speak to me in your voice.

A toast given by Małgosia Szlicht on Relli's seventieth birthday celebration in Haifa, March 13th, 2009

Hello everybody,

I'd like to welcome everybody on this festive occasion of Relli's birthday. I'm the one person here who's known her the longest. Please forgive me, but I'd like to remind us of her early history. If only for a moment, I'd like to bring up the 1940s in Europe.

A deep darkness descended over the continent. People lost their faith, their hope, and their lives. On one of those sad days, a girl of three years and ten months entered our family. You must have all met girls that age. This one had blond curls and blue eyes. She was sweet and smart. In my family they called her Lala, Polish for "doll." She brought us lots of hope. Children always represent hope. I've heard this family story so many times.

But sometimes life can be cruel, even to little children. One day, when Relli was ten, her adoptive Polish mother, my great-aunt, Janina Abramowicz, died suddenly. I always think of Relli as a girl to whom fate was usually cruel. She was only ten years old when she lost a second mother. It isn't fair. Children deserve parents and a home.

This is an example of a personal story that begins badly and ends well. Luckily, this little girl finally found her place in this world, in Israel, under the bluest skies on earth, in the lap of her father's family.

I've been following Relli's life for years, and I'm convinced that in spite of all the hardships she took advantage of all the opportunities that life and people have generously offered her.

I am grateful for the fact that our relationship has lasted. To me, Relli is the older sister I never had. I like to be pampered by her from time to time and invited on visits to Israel. I take comfort in her good advice whenever life pulls me to the edge.

Relli, I am in awe of your life. I watch, happy, as your children and grandchildren grow. Be happy and healthy, and live as long as you can!

I'd like to thank everybody for your time and attention. Shalom.

Małgosia Szlicht, Haifa, March 13th, 2009

Relli with Malgosia Szlicht, Carmel Beach, Haifa, Israel, 2002

Relli, 28.01.1941   Lala, 1943
pictures sent by her parents in "The Last Letter"

Relli in the Israeli Navy

Relli graduating from UCLA, California, 1965

Relli, Administrative Director of Faculty of Social Welfare and Health
Sciences, University of Haifa, Israel, 1995

Light and Ashes and the Power of the Self: An Epilogue by Ariel Hirschfeld

Memory, as we know, is more than just groping at the archives of consciousness, and even when clean of embellishments and blurriness, it is made of more than merely facts. Memory is a ray of light illuminating a person's depths, which meets another ray of light, from that person's past. The meeting of these rays is a site of becoming, of reconstruction, creation and assembly of visions whose being can be a formative event in a person's life, a kind of self-birth.

Raking Light from Ashes is certainly one such event in the life of Relli Robinson, and its great power as a creation of a living place is transmitted to its readers. Her life story, the rescue of little Relli from Nazi persecution in Warsaw, is presented not as a story of war, but as a story of peace within war. The greatness of Jòzef and Janina Abramowicz, the Polish couple who adopted four-year-old Relli while her parents were sent from the Warsaw ghetto to a labor camp and then to their deaths, was in the fact that they succeeded, through exceptional intelligence and resourcefulness, to build a bubble of peace and love around the child who had been torn from her parents, a bubble in which she could continue to grow.

What stands out more than anything else in this book is the clear presence of a self, evolving and nurtured through those horrific years. Something in that ray of light which the adult Relli shines at her tragic and sordid past clearly emanates from the kindness and wisdom that this Polish couple bestowed upon her. Relli's story is therefore not enveloped in the familiar aura of trauma and carries none of the stagnation which keeps the horrors of the past alive in the present. Robinson writes out of the peace that had formed within her precisely during the worst days of her life and the life of the Jewish People. This does not mean that the war and the atrocities of the Nazis did not touch her life then and now, but they did not do so in the manner one would expect.

Robinson has preserved a clear note of childhood within her. It is neither a childish voice, nor a reconstruction of childhood, but a tangible remnant of a living childhood, a vital essence beating even within the later, more complex experiences of her life. It is the selfness that protects her everywhere, always. Therefore, when she describes the child's play in Wiśniówka in the midst of war, she does not interpret it through the prism of adulthood and historical irony. Something in those moments of the past remains alive and vibrating in the present, and the sixty years that have gone by since turn from a roadblock into a lens increasing clarity of reflection.

Relli Robinson is not in the business of interpreting her life. The burning of pain and terror are presented without preparation or explanation. Similarly, her wonder at the beauty, kindness, generosity, and outstanding cleverness of some of the people around her do not receive embellishment or exaggeration. Only the gaze directed at them attests to their existence; the gaze of a child who cannot be wrong about such things, a child who, in spite of life in the ghetto and being torn apart from her parents, has not lost her faith in people and the world.

With impressive literary prowess, Robinson has created a riveting multi-voice construction, part fiction, part journal, and part archive, which breaks through the life of the individual to convey a wide array of Jewish fate in the twentieth century. The clear literary style often creates powerful symbolism, constructing a second layer over the words: the simultaneously subtle and shocking analogy between the game of Doctor in the Polish farm (not far from a death camp) and the horrific medical experiments of Dr. Mengele, or the piercing parallels between the bad burn Lala suffers from the chimney in the village and the smell of the burning village upon the Germans' escape and the knowledge of her parents' bodies burning in the camp. The analogies between this small-scale history and the large, human history are not a cerebral, pre-planned structure, but part of the story's profound and mysterious life. Something of the post-Holocaust Jewish memory construct has seeped into this awareness, and without changing reality has emphasized in the life of the individual the reflection of collective fate. Or perhaps this should be viewed another way: something in the identity of little Relli led her to experience on a small scale the echoes of the tragedies surrounding her. But the power of these analogies is not in their tragic nature, but in their duplicity: the children's game of Doctor is normal, and the burn is a domestic accident and has nothing to do with annihilation. It is the domesticity and childishness of it that allow it to thunder ominously in the background.

In Israeli culture the concept of "Polishness" has become synonymous with overinvolved parenting and expressions of hypocrisy and phoniness. As all stigmas go, it is nothing more than ignorance. *Raking Light from Ashes* deals with the deep elements of bourgeois Polish culture, which is the foundation of the Israeli concept of Polishness. Here, like in the stories of Ida Fink, this culture appears in its true and unmarred form, in full power and value—from its characteristic items of clothing and furniture to its behavioral and conversational codes. Here its gentle, grave, committed, and practical nature shines through, the sturdy base for its refined culture. Though of course this should not be taken as reference to the entire Polish population, Relli Robinson's life story depends upon that noble face of the Polish world.

The ray of light cast by a person toward their past is also twofold: the power to see and the quality of inner light do not come from the present, but from early childhood. Robinson illuminates her past with a light that originates in her past. In the days when the world burned down around her, turning into ashes, this bustling light was born within her, through which she is able to view these days of fire and ashes in a light of clarity like no other.

Prof. Ariel Hirschfeld is the Head of the Department of Hebrew Literature at the Hebrew University in Jerusalem. He is the author of several books, a literature critic and a scholar of Hebrew literature, music and arts.

Made in the USA
Middletown, DE
09 March 2024

51131161R00181